Literary Places

Literary Places
A Guided Pilgrimage
New York and New England

JOHN DEEDY

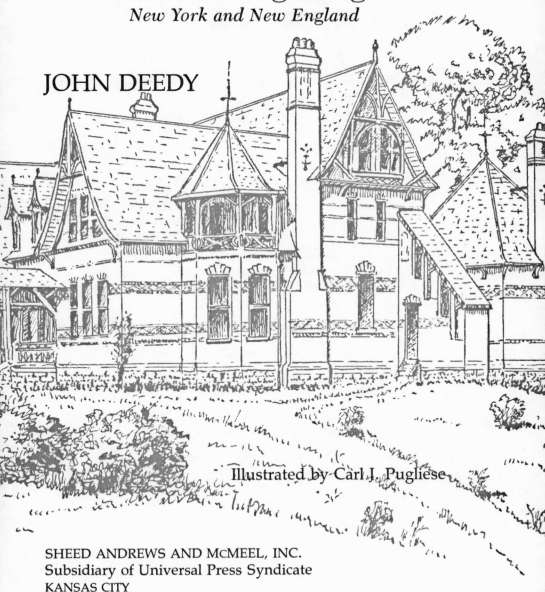

Illustrated by Carl J. Pugliese

SHEED ANDREWS AND McMEEL, INC.
Subsidiary of Universal Press Syndicate
KANSAS CITY

Acknowledgments

The chapters on Thomas Paine, James Fenimore Cooper, Bronson Alcott/Fruitlands, Herman Melville, and Harriet Beecher Stowe were published in substantially the same form as here in the *New York Times*. Copyright © 1972/1973 and 1976. Reprinted with permission.

The chapter on Teilhard de Chardin first appeared in *The Critic*. Copyright © 1975 by The Thomas More Association. Reprinted with permission.

The chapters on Washington Irving and Horace Greeley appeared in *Westchester* magazine.

First Edition

Literary Places: A Guided Pilgrimage Copyright © 1978 by John Deedy.

Library of Congress Cataloging in Publication Data
Deedy, John G
   Literary places: a guided pilgrimage, New York and New England.

   Bibliography: p.
   Includes index.
   1. Literary landmarks—New York (State). 2. Literary landmarks—New England. 3. Authors, American—19th century—Biography. 4. New York (State)—Description and travel. 5. New England—Description and travel. I. Title.
PS144.N4D4   917.4′04′4   78-17775
ISBN 0-8362-7102-5
ISBN 0-8362-7101-7 pbk.

FOR

Ernest LaBranche
R.I.P.

who stoked the sparks of interest

Contents

PART TWO
NEW ENGLAND

Preface

My book is no more than its title. Quite simply, I have set out to provide a guide, with biography and some critique, to people and places in the state of New York and the New England states where persons might commune with the spirits of those who helped create an American literature, or, in the cases of some, a literature that America shares by the reading. Almost inevitably, therefore, the emphasis is on American writers of the nineteenth century, although there are briefer sketches on some twentieth-century figures. Included also is a chapter on the celebrated French paleontologist and philosopher, Teilhard de Chardin, whose last years were spent in New York City and who is buried in Poughkeepsie, as well as sketches on Robert Louis Stevenson and Rudyard Kipling, both of whom had American "periods." My purpose has been to seek out writers whose contribution to literature and the world of books has been distinctive to the point that some "shrine," if you will, is connected with their memory: a home, an inn, a stretch of landscape, a burial ground even. My subjects range from a pamphleteer, in the person of Thomas Paine; to an editor and journalist, in Horace Greeley; to satirists and novelists, including Washington Irving and James Fenimore Cooper, two who helped break the literary chains that bound American readers to European fare—in sum, those who had a hand in moving literature in America on a course of its own.

It is difficult to imagine now, but before Irving and Cooper there was no such thing as an American literature. The land had been settled almost two hundred years before; the nation was a half-century old—but avid readers like Cooper and his wife still were required to exist for their books pretty much from sailing ship to sailing ship. The books came from England and were written, by and large, by Britons. The idea of an American literature was as visionary to the average American of the day as it was preposterous to the sophisticated Briton. Cooper, we know, chafed under the condition, and set out purposefully to change things. His first book resulted from a challenge to demonstrate that he could do what it was presumed only Britons could do ably, or superiorly. That first novel, *Precaution*, was not distinguished, but Cooper had made his point, if only to himself. He wrote more. Others wrote. And soon an old art form had taken on a new dimension, in a new land. No longer, as William Ellery Channing would say, would the thoughts of foreigners pour perpetually and almost exclusively into American minds. America would have a literature as self-formed as its government.

In writing this book, I have not tried to rank writers according to any hierarchy of importance. Nor should significance be attached to the respective lengths of the chapters or sketches, beyond, perhaps, some whimsical interest or bias of my own. Edgar Allan Poe, for instance, is handled but briefly in the "shirttail" section of Part I, not because I regard him as less worthy than some who receive much longer treatment here, but because I consider him less identified with the New York–New England area than with Maryland and Virginia. If this book becomes the first of a series encompassing the whole country, as it may, then Poe will be discussed much more extensively in the geographically appropriate subsequent volume.

Similarly, this book consciously bypasses some people who have a body of literature to their name, but whose place in history is other than literary—people such as Theodore Roosevelt and Franklin Delano Roosevelt. Theodore Roosevelt's birthplace and boyhood home is at 28 East Twentieth Street in New York City; his Sagamore Hill home on Cove Neck Road, Oyster Bay, Long Island, is a fascinating visiting place. So, too, is Franklin Delano Roosevelt's birthplace and home at Hyde Park, up the Hudson Valley. However, the primary identification of both men is as presidents of the United States, and therefore I chose to omit them from my book. I do this somewhat sheepishly, I must admit, as I know I will receive criticism from those who place one or the other, or both, in a literary-statesman tradition. My rationale also accounts for the omission of John Adams and descendants, of Quincy, Massachusetts; John Jay, first chief justice of the United States Supreme Court, whose home in Katonah, New York, is a state-owned historic site; and a few more. Very probably I have overlooked some who should be included in the book, and for that this early apology.

I might say that a few homes with very extensive literary associations are not covered in my book because they are not available to the public for viewing, at least on the inside. One such would be Elmwood, the birthplace and home in Cambridge of James Russell Lowell, poet, essayist, scholar, and diplomat. Elmwood is now the official residence of the presidents of Harvard University. (To be sure, the house in Brattleboro, Vermont, where Kipling once resided is not open to the public either. I have included it in the book because I could not resist passing on the information that Kipling, the epitome of imperial England, lived in Vermont and grappled with the thought of becoming an American citizen.)

Those who follow the leads of this book should be prepared to find visiting places as varied as the literary personalities themselves. Some visiting places are kept as reverentially as a religious shrine. Sunnyside, for instance—the home of Washington Irving on the banks of the Hudson River at Tarrytown—has the mood of the Vatican on the banks of the Po. Sounds are muted, and guides in period costumes flit about like robed nuns, or monks involved in some sacred rite. On the other hand, there is the Walt Whitman birthplace at Huntington, Long Island: well kept, neat as a pin—but noisy, informal, and hemmed in by creeping, commercial America. Just yards away, traffic thunders by on a four-lane road. The air smells of carbon monoxide and the business of quick-food chains. Walt Whitman would be a stranger today on Long Island. Yet there is the birthplace in Haverhill, Massachusetts, of John Greenleaf Whittier. The area remains so marvelously pastoral that one could almost look for Whittier to come strolling over a field or up the road on his way back from Lake Kenoza.

In most visiting places (though not Whitman's), there is a formal lecture tour. Some of the lectures are not only informative, but border on the intellectually brilliant (I think back to my visit to the Emily Dickinson homestead in Amherst). Some lectures get high marks for honesty and accuracy in the face of a difficult biographical history—Poe's, for instance. Some are competent; some, horribly idolatrous (be wary at Sunnyside and at the Mark Twain Memorial in Hartford). And a few are so protective of an image or personality as to distort the individual's life and meaning, at least in part. I have in mind my visit to Craigie House in Cambridge, the home of Henry Wadsworth Longfellow. I waited, waited, waited for the guide (from the National Park Service) to reach the room where Mrs. Longfellow had the terrible accident while sealing locks of her children's hair with hot wax. It was an accident by fire that claimed her life and seared her husband's soul, dramatically affecting his life. But suddenly the tour was ending, and it was obvious that our little group was going to be told nothing about the accident. So I inquired. "Oh, I was hoping no one would ask," the guide remarked. "I don't like to talk about it. It upsets me so."

This book is born of many miles traveled and almost two years of writing during evenings, weekends, and vacations from *Commonweal*. I am grateful for the idea to Philip Nobile, a colleague of a number of years in a number of connections, who suggested that I expand into a book some literary travel pieces that I had been selling to the Travel section of the Sunday *New York Times*. At the time, Phil was an editorial consultant to Sheed and Ward, now Sheed Andrews and McMeel, publishers. I am grateful also to Paul P. Appel, friend and himself a publisher, for his incessant criticism of my focuses and the rate of speed at which I was working. I am grateful to Anne Robertson, a colleague at *Commonweal*, who lent a hand with the typing—two, in fact. And I am grateful to my good wife, Mary, who patiently accompanied me on most of my trips to literary visiting places and who kept the house quiet when I was at the typewriter. The last was probably the toughest job of all.

Most particularly, I am indebted to Carl J. Pugliese for the drawings that illustrate this book. Carl is a fine pen-and-ink artist, a superb sculptor in bronze—and a longtime friend. This is our first professional collaboration. He is an unusually agreeable person to work with, and I feel his illustrations distinguish this book in the same way that Western and Civil War illustrations of his have distinguished several books on those subjects.

One final word: My visits occurred over two years' time, and, since inflation seems to be a respecter of no one and nothing, it may be that the admission prices I describe as modest may now seem slightly less so than at the time of my visits. Even at much higher prices, however, these charges remain a distinct bargain.

PART ONE

NEW YORK

Chapter One

THOMAS PAINE

New Rochelle Would Drink With You Now

Thomas Paine might be mollified were he to return today to New Rochelle, the Westchester community in New York State that was the home of his twilight years. A small lake bears his name; an avenue, too. The Post Office is dispensing Thomas Paine stamps. His cottage has been designated a historic landmark by the Department of the Interior. A hulking stone museum enshrines his modest possessions: writing set, pocket watch, candle snuffers, gloves, and a leather wallet—as flat as when Paine carried it in his pocket.

Nearby, Paine would find a fine Tuckahoe-marble monument featuring quotations from his writings; nearby, too, a marker indicating where his bodily remains should be but aren't—because of the zaniness of a Paine zealot who dug up Paine's bones on the notion they would be more reverenced in England. They weren't. They only became hopelessly lost.

Tom Paine would approve of the various memorials to him in New Rochelle, but his large—and accurate—sense of self-worth would tell him that these were nothing more than what he deserved, and perhaps a whole lot less. The feeling wouldn't be far wrong. For it was Tom Paine, no one else, who in 1776 put it all together ideologically for the Colonies, with a tract that sold 120,000 copies in three months' time and brought to full flame the sparks of independence. That tract, of course, was *Common Sense*. Likewise, it was Tom Paine who kept the ideology of independence together with his *Crisis* papers, essays that appeared at crucial points during the Revolutionary War and had the effect on the national psyche of amphetamines, particularly the first *Crisis*: "These are the times that try men's souls: The summer soldier and the sunshine patriot will, in this crisis, shrink from the service of his country. . . ."

John Adams said that "without the pen of Paine the sword of

The State of New York did better by Tom Paine than the new national
government. It turned over to him a confiscated Tory farm cottage in New
Rochelle. Paine died in New York City, but was brought here for burial. The
granite memorial marks the spot.

Washington would have been wielded in vain." He was probably right—though for all of that, Paine received more abuse than thanks, more recriminations than honors. His was the hero's role, but not the hero's lot. He was the least celebrated of the country's fathers, and the least appreciated.

For all sorts of reasons it should have been otherwise. Tom Paine was on the cutting edge not only of the independence issue but of historic human issues—in England and France, where his common sense led him on behalf of the common man (and woman), and always in America, where his pen worked incessantly against slavery, for a system of free public education, for equality and justice for women. Most of Paine's issues had to wait their times, the woman's rights issue until these days. But when the times came, they arrived—by chance or not—along lines first proposed by Paine.

Yet Americans never really dug Tom Paine, particularly Americans of his own day. Once the war was over, the revolution established, it was a time to settle down, to plant, to build, to grow rich. In such a season it was perhaps inevitable that anyone would be viewed as an agitator, a trouble-seeker, who argued that the work now was to extend the principles of democracy and equality to less free peoples elsewhere. So it turned out to be with Paine. His contemporaries could not fathom the impulses which took Paine to England in 1787 and to France five years later. In England, after the appearance of *Rights of Man*, with its "seditious" sentiments about royalty and the House of Lords, he was declared a traitor and outlawed. In France, during the Reign of Terror, he was picked up by the Committee of Surety for opposing capital punishment for Louis XVI and held for ten months, a lock and key away from the guillotine. Americans figured Paine had bargained for trouble in going abroad and were not surprised that he had found it not only in France but even in his native England. (Paine was born at Thetford, England, in 1737, son of a corsetmaker, and after working as a sailor, teacher, and exciseman came to America at the age of thirty-seven to begin a new career as editor of the *Pennsylvania Magazine*.)

Ostensibly, American objections to Paine were purely intellectual and political. But large hunks of meanness and pettiness were also involved. Paine offended by being notoriously indifferent of dress (he was a pre-hippie, in a way) and somewhat illiberal in the use of soap and water—serious faults in a society hung up on cleanliness and Godliness. In addition, Paine "boozed." Happily for history, he was a creative drinker, but that didn't square him with folks still carrying a heavy load of Puritan baggage. He warmed to writing tasks on brandy (rum and water would do if brandy wasn't handy), and after a third glass the thoughts were said to flow smoothly and need a minimum of editing. The problem was that the writing and the drinking were not necessarily coterminous. Stories survive of Paine's being rescued from a tavern, his beard showing a two weeks' growth and his body giving off a "most disagreeable odor." The drink gave Paine a W. C. Fields proboscis, but apparently did not disturb his longevity. He died at 72 from the effects of a paralytic ailment and an earlier attack of apoplexy.

The real bias against Tom Paine, however, stemmed from two developments of his mature years. First was the appearance of *The Age of Reason*, Paine's book debunking the Bible and organized religion. That "filthy little atheist," wrote Theodore Roosevelt of Paine on the basis of that book, missing the point along with so many others before and since that Tom Paine was not an atheist but a Deist. "I believe in one God, and no more," said Paine on the very first page of *Age of Reason*, "and I hope for happiness beyond this life." But *Age of Reason* wasn't read to find an understanding of Paine or his thesis of a God of reason and nature. It was read to prop negative preconceptions, and that it did aplenty.

Together with *Age of Reason* came Paine's demythologizing of George Washington, the ultimate offense in an America sowing the seeds of a civil religion with Washington as the godhead. Paine bristled that Washington, for reasons of international policy Paine found questionable, had abandoned him during his time of danger in a French prison and was prepared to see him go to the guillotine. This Paine branded a "crime of the heart" and was unforgiving. He accused Washington of being "treacherous in private friendship" and "a hypocrite in public life," and added that "the world will be puzzled to decide whether you are an apostate or an impostor; whether you have abandoned good principles, or whether you ever had any." The accusations jolted Americans and cost Paine the remnants of the goodwill existing toward him among the rank and file.

Paine's catalogue of criticism appeared in a series of letters, the most scathing of which was a long open letter of July 30, 1796. In it Paine rounded the bases. Washington had "no share" in the political part of the Revolution; his generalship was lackluster, decidedly inferior to that of Horatio Gates and Nathanael Greene; his presidential administration was "deceitful, if not perfidious"; he was vain of character and "chameleon-colored." About the only thing Paine skipped was Washington's slave-holding—somewhat surprising in light of Paine's deep feelings on slavery. Paine had running room there. In 1760 Washington paid taxes on 49 slaves, in 1765 on 78, in 1770 on 87, in 1775 on 135; by 1786 his colony had grown to 216 slaves and by 1799 to 317. George was vulnerable but Tom missed the opening. (Also, Paine did not delve into the wondrous matter of Washington's military expense account, leaving that to Marvin Kitman, a revisionist of our own time, who wrote a book about it, *George Washington's Expense Account*, New York, 1970.)

Apologists for Paine attribute his attack on Washington to the pressures of his imprisonment and a lingering mental debilitation. That rationale may overlook the fact, however, that Paine was not hasty in leveling his charges. They were eighteen months in the formulation and followed advice by friends to think twice. Furthermore, Paine had thirteen years of life in which he could have retracted. He never did.

Some of Paine's criticism of Washington is decidedly tendentious, like the suggestion that after the Revolution, Washington "rested at home to partake its advantages." On the other hand, Paine had his legitimate grievance. He was a friend of Washington, a comrade in arms, and was one of the real architects of American freedom. He deserved a thought. Yet he received from Washington "no word of kindness nor of inquiry" during an imprisonment and convalescence that extended almost three years. Washington's failure to respond to Paine's plight is a puzzle even to many apologists for Washington.

Tom Paine found America hostile territory when he returned from France in 1802. Government officials snubbed him, parsons sniped from pulpits, old friends looked the other way, and ordinary folks were rude. Paine even had trouble, shortly after his arrival, in getting a seat on a stagecoach; the driver said he'd "be damn'd" before he'd make room for an "infidel."

Tom Paine settled in New Rochelle on a 400-acre farm confiscated in 1783 from a Tory loyalist and conveyed to Paine by the state of New York "for services he had rendered the country during the Revolutionary struggle for independence." (The state of New York, as it turned out, was considerably more generous to Paine than was the federal government, which dealt niggardly with him.)

In New Rochelle, Paine found no respite from prejudice. When a close friend from his Paris period, Madame Marguerite Brazier Bonneville, moved in as housekeeper with her three sons, tongues wagged that she was Paine's mistress and the children Paine's illegitimate offspring. (Paine married twice, but was living a bachelor's life even before he emigrated from England to America. His first wife died; he separated from the second.) The Bonneville rumors carried to New York City and were eventually published by a Jeffersonian newspaper. Paine sued for libel, and won. The publisher, James Cheetham, received a nominal fine—and a commendation for having written in the cause of religion.

There was more trouble for Paine. On Christmas Eve in 1805 a disgruntled odd-jobs man fired a shot through the window of Paine's cottage, narrowly missing him. A few months later, when Paine arrived to vote at a town meeting, voting rights were denied him on grounds that he was not an American citizen. The electors contended that by taking a seat in the French National Convention in the 1790s, Paine had forfeited the citizenship that Congress had extended all soldiers of the Revolution. This was a contention that dogged Paine and that he countered with the argument that a foreigner (in this case himself) "might be a member of a convention for framing a constitution" without affecting his right of citizenship in his own country, "but not a member of a government after a constitution is formed." Paine's distinction did not satisfy the electors of New Rochelle. Nor did it elicit much support from those to whom Paine protested, up to the vice-president of the United States, George Clinton.

The voting incident appears to have given the proud, sensitive Paine his fill of New Rochelle, for he departed shortly afterward for Greenwich Village, where, health failing, he shuttled between rooming houses on Partition (Fulton), Broome, Herring (Bleecker), and Grove Streets. It was at 59 Grove on June 8, 1809, that Tom Paine died his lonesome death.

There was no welling up of sympathy. Only one New York newspaper—*The Post*—recorded his death, and it in a single paragraph that left *Common Sense* unmentioned and concluded on the gratuitous note: " . . . he had lived long, done some good, and much harm." The Quakers, whom Paine esteemed as Deists, refused his body burial space, so the coffin was loaded on a wagon and taken back to the farm in New Rochelle. Accompanying the remains were Madame Bonneville, two of her sons, Paine's friend Willett Hicks, and two blacks whose chore it was to load and unload the coffin and dig the grave.

At graveside there were no dignitaries, no representative of government to **say** a kind or thankful word. The grave was dug on "an open and disregarded bit of land," where North Avenue runs today. Madame Bonneville, sensing the tragedy of the occasion, positioned herself at the east end of the grave and directed son Benjamin to "stand you there, at the other end, as a witness for grateful America." As the earth thundered on the coffin, she exclaimed: "Oh! Mr. Paine! My son stands here as testimony of the gratitude of America, and I, for France."

There was precious little gratitude among others. More reflective of the common attitude was a quatrain that speedily made the rounds:

> Poor Tom Paine! here he lies,
> Nobody laughs and nobody cries;
> Where he's gone and how he fares,
> Nobody knows and nobody cares.

Buried on his farm, Tom Paine was still not at rest. A final, supreme indignity remained to be visited on him by the British political essayist and journalist, William Cobbett. Cobbett, a Paine detractor turned Paine disciple, brooded that so great a man should lie in so anonymous a place among so undeserving a people. He got it into his head that Paine's remains would be more honored in England, and on an October night in 1819 he and a couple of associates opened the grave, removed the coffin, placed it in a box wagon, and whipped the horses toward New York. An alarm was sounded, and after some delay Sheriff James Seacord, Jr., took off on a Mack Sennett chase. He rode first to Harlem Bridge, where he was told no wagon and coffin had crossed that morning. Then he headed for King's Bridge and learned, yes indeed, wagon and coffin had crossed. Curiously, Seacord abandoned the pursuit at that point and apparently pressed the case no further.

Cobbett shipped Paine's bones to England in a common merchandise crate and predicted to all and sundry that their effect would be apocalyptic. "I shall gather together the people of Liverpool and Manchester in one assembly with those of London," Cobbett boasted, "and those bones will effect the reformation of England in Church and State." It was a nutty dream, capping a nutty and outrageous escapade, and it turned to nightmare.

The bones did not stir England. Cobbett became a laughingstock, the butt of caricaturists and of grim jokes. The money he expected to flow in for a shrine to Paine did not materialize. Cobbett died in 1835 and willed the bones to his son. The son went into bankruptcy, and his property, bones and all, was seized. By way of anticlimactic insult, the Lord Chancellor refused to credit Paine's bones as an asset. The bones passed to a day laborer, then a furniture dealer, then oblivion. They've been lost a century and more.*

Back in New Rochelle, meanwhile, weeds and a widening road-

---

*In 1976, there was a flurry of excitement that Tom Paine's *final* resting place might have been found, when a marble obelisk memorializing Paine was dug up in Tivoli, New York, one hundred miles north of New Rochelle. Had Paine's remains somehow found their way back to the United States, and did this obelisk mark the site of their reburial? They hadn't and it didn't. The obelisk turned out to be the expression of a Paine admirer who wanted his own gravestone to be "something a little better"—and, presumably, different. So, on the side of the obelisk opposite that on which his own name and dates would one day appear ("John. G. Lasher, born March 5, 1797, died March 19, 1877, aged eighty years four days"), he placed the name, dates, and age of Tom Paine. The obelisk was buried by a subsequent owner of the property, who feared his wife would recoil at living next to a gravesite. It stayed underground and forgotten until dug up by a backhoe operator opening up a drainage ditch.

way vied for the Paine gravesite, and both appeared to be winning before the founding in 1884 of the Thomas Paine National Historical Association. The association was not able to turn back the road, which kept widening until today vehicles would be running over Paine's feet if the body were where it was originally placed. But the association was able to bring organization to the commemoration of Tom Paine and, with the help of the Huguenot and Historical Association of New Rochelle, to see to the preservation of objects connected with Paine's living and dying: the iron stove presented Paine by Benjamin Franklin; chairs from Bayeau's tavern, where Paine exercised his elbows; two death masks, including a particularly gruesome one allegedly made by Cobbett after the exhumation; many Paine letters; the remaining fragment of his headstone (with age incorrectly given). These and other items are housed in Paine's cottage, which passed from private hands to private trust only in 1908, and in the Paine Memorial Building, the museum, dating from 1925.

Considering the long years of indifference, New Rochelle's recovery of its Tom Paine history is impressive. It is a recovery in which many people share, but for which only a relative handful can claim credit. How small a handful can perhaps be best gauged from the number of members of the Thomas Paine Historical Association and the Huguenot and Historical Association of New Rochelle: 175 and 250, respectively. On dues of three dollars a year, a small annuity fund, and large zeal, the two groups (lately merged into the Huguenot-Thomas Paine Association of New Rochelle) have rescued a history that threatened to be reduced to Paine's printed works. Not that that would be insignificant; in history as in life, Paine's writings will always be the most important thing about him. But it is nice to have some material mementos as well. . . . Tom would raise his glass to that.

If You Travel . . .

. . .seeking Tom Paine's corner of New Rochelle, pick up North Avenue from Exit 8 of the New England Throughway (Interstate 95), or the Boston Post Road, and proceed north approximately two miles from the downtown part of the city.

The Thomas Paine Cottage and the Thomas Paine Memorial

Building are alongside North Avenue. Both are open Wednesdays through Sundays from 2:00 to 5:00 P.M. Admission is free. There is parking on Sicard Street for the cottage, and on Valley Road for the museum. Cottage and museum are within a few minutes' walk of one another.

On North Avenue, on a line with the cottage, is a marker commemorating the original burial place of Tom Paine. It was from this spot that his remains were exhumed by an admirer, stolen away, and subsequently lost.

Close by, at North and Paine Avenues, is the Paine memorial column, erected by public contribution on November 12, 1839, and superimposed with a bronze bust of Paine May 30, 1899. The column, paint-splattered and showing signs of erosion from weather and fumes, features quotations from the writings of Thomas Paine and Paine's motto: "The world is my country, to do good my religion."

The quotes are these:

"The pallaces of kings are built upon the ruins of the bowers of paradise."

Common Sense

* * *

"These are the times that try men's souls: The summer soldier and the sunshine patriot will, in this crisis, shrink from the service of his country; but he that stands it now deserves the love and thanks of man and woman. Tyranny, like hell, is not easily conquered; yet we have this consolation with us—that the harder the conflict, the more glorious the triumph. What we obtain too cheap, we esteem too lightly: It is dearness only that gives everything its value. Heaven knows how to put a proper price upon its goods; and it would be strange indeed if so celestial an article as freedom should not be highly rated."

Crisis I

* * *

"The times that tried men's souls are over, and the greatest and compleatest revolution the world ever knew gloriously and happily accomplished—in the present case. The mighty magnitude of the object, the numerous and complicated dangers we have suffered or escaped, the eminence we now stand on and the vast prospect before us, must all conspire to impress us with contemplation. To see it in our power to make a world happy, to teach mankind the art of being so, to exhibit in the theatre of the universe a character hitherto unknown, and to have, as it were, a new creation entrusted to our hands are honors that can neither be too highly estimated, nor too gratefully received.

"Never had a country more openings to happiness than this, her setting out in life, like the rising of a fair morning, was unclouded and promising. Her cause was good. Her principles just and liberal, her temper serene and firm, and everything about her wore the mark of honor. It is not every country that can boast so fair an origin; but America need never be ashamed to tell her birth, nor relate the stages by which she rose to empire."

Crisis XIII

* * *

"It is only in the Creation that all our ideas and conceptions of a *Word of God* can unite. The Creation speaks a universal language, independently of human speech or human language, multiplied and various as they be. It is an ever-existing original, which every man can read. It cannot be forged; it cannot be counterfeited; it cannot be lost; it cannot be altered; it cannot be suppressed. It does not depend upon the will of man whether it shall be published or not; it publishes itself from one end of the earth to the other. It preaches to all nations and to all worlds; and this *Word of God* reveals to man all that is necessary for man to know of God.

"Do we want to contemplate His power? We see it in the immensity of creation. Do we want to contemplate His wisdom? We see it in the unchangeable order by which the incomprehensible whole is governed. Do we want to contemplate His munificence? We see it in the abundance with which He fills the earth. Do we want to contemplate His mercy? We see it in His not withholding that abundance even from the unthankful. In fine, do we want to know what

God is? Search not the book called the Scripture, which any human hand can make, but the Scripture called the Creation."

Age of Reason

* * *

"I believe in one God, and no more; and I hope for happiness beyond this life.

"I believe in the equality of man; and I believe that religious duties consist in doing justice, loving mercy, and endeavoring to make our fellow-creatures happy."

Age of Reason

* * *

"It is necessary to the happiness of man that he be mentally faithful to himself. Infidelity does not consist in believing or in disbelieving; it consists in professing to believe what he does not believe."

Age of Reason

In New York City you can see a bust of Tom Paine in the Hall of Fame for Great Americans at New York University, Bronx campus. Washington is also in the hall, elected in the first class of twenty-nine "greats" in 1900. Paine was not elected until 1945, the tenth voting, after seventy-three other Americans had already been enshrined. The Hall of Fame is open daily from 9:00 A.M. to 5:00 P.M., admission free. It can be reached by way of the 179th Street exit of the Major Deegan Expressway or at the 180th Street stop (Burnside Avenue) of the Lexington Avenue IRT (Woodlawn Road Express).

But you had better hurry. The Hall of Fame has fallen on sad days. New York University and City University of New York recently announced an end to joint financing of the memorial structure, and no institution or foundation has rushed to take over supervision and maintenance of the property. Tom Paine and the other distinguished Americans enshrined there—their number is now ninety-six—may have to move on, if anyone will have them. Without removal elsewhere, or without a fresh influx of support money, the Hall of Fame seems destined to become another casualty of urban decay in America.

Chapter
Two

JAMES FENIMORE COOPER

Natty Bumppo, Where Are You When We Need You?

The indignities suffered by some of the world's best-known writers in the indelicate hands of posterity are saddening to contemplate. If James Fenimore Cooper could somehow see what is happening to the house of his young manhood in Westchester County he might reactivate his frontiersman-hero Natty Bumppo to draw a bead on posterity.

The building, near Mamaroneck Harbor's placid West Basin, is the eighteenth-century DeLancey House, where Cooper courted Susan DeLancey, where he was married in the west drawing room (playing chess before riding off in a gig-tandem for a honeymoon in Cooperstown), and where he and Susan visited for long periods thereafter. The building is shedding its history and slipping toward disaster. Despite fresh coats of paint, the structure has about it what critic Wilfrid Sheed would call "creeping New Jersey."

Fenimore Cooper deserves better than that. He was, after all, the first of the famous American romantic novelists, and he did point American writers away from imitating the British style. If he didn't write *War and Peace*, he did write *The Last of the Mohicans* and some other pretty good tales of the time when the Eastern slope of North America was wilderness.

One would hope for some more gracious reminder that Cooper lived and loved in Mamaroneck than a house that now harbors a restaurant (however good), a gas station (however indigenous), and three upstairs apartments, particularly since this is the last of the major physical associations with the author left in Westchester.

If there is the slightest ray of hope left for DeLancey House, no one sees it. The building is in private hands, and private hands shape their own values. Thus the restaurant (Cooper probably would not approve of an eating place bearing his name) and the gas station are

James Fenimore Cooper was married in this house in Mamaroneck, New York, in 1811. It is known as DeLancey House, after Mrs. Cooper's family, and was once one of Mamaroneck's grandest residences. That was when it sat on the brow of Heathcote Hill and commanded a sweeping view of Mamaroneck Harbor. The house was subsequently moved to the Boston Post Road, where it remains — a combination restaurant and gas station, with apartments upstairs. It faces the West Basin of Mamaroneck Harbor.

likely to be around as long as people eat and cars drink gas, or until something unforeseen does the building in. The gas station seems especially permanent. "It's been here since the beginning of time," says station proprietor Alfred Chmelecki, seeming to exaggerate not one minute. The station was operating when Chmelecki and his brother, Stanley, took the property over "fifteen years ago, maybe twenty," and perhaps always will be; most gas stations never die—or at least didn't before the energy crisis came along.

DeLancey House might be better off today than it was after the turn of the century when it sank so low it became a saloon, but it is a long whoop and holler from the glory days of the early nineteenth century. At that time it was a showplace and dominated the brow of Heathcote Hill, commanding a sweeping view of the harbor and Long Island Sound. It was an ideal house for the town's most historic rise. Heathcote Hill carries Caleb Heathcote's name. Heathcote in 1698 acquired (for 600 pounds) most of the property of John Richbell's widow; the widow Richbell had inherited it from her husband; her husband had purchased it from the Siwanoy Indians. "Mamaroneck Lands," as the property was known, was a vast tract lying between the English in Connecticut and the Dutch in New Amsterdam. It wasn't as good a buy as Manhattan Island, but not bad for fourteen shirts, twenty-two coats, ten pairs of stockings, twenty hands of powder, twelve bars of lead, two firelocks, fifteen hoes, three kettles and a little wampum.

The DeLanceys were prosperous members of the community when they lived on the hill, but their fortunes dipped, and DeLancey House slid downhill. Literally. In 1900 it was sold for removal to the Post Road at the foot of the hill. It was then that it became a saloon. "If I told you it was bought for twelve dollars and you discovered the real figure was fourteen dollars, you wouldn't call me a liar, would you?" said Judge Charles M. Baxter, Mamaroneck town historian, now deceased. "But that was all—twelve dollars or fourteen dollars. Of course, the land wasn't included, and there was the expense of moving the place down the hill."

The town of Mamaroneck wasn't interested in DeLancey House then, and given today's tight money and high tax rates, the town probably couldn't afford to take it over now. The best it has been able to do is hang a pale green historical marker on the house's exterior, near one of the gas pumps. It hasn't been able to prevent additions from being tacked on, and it could only wring its hands when the east corner of the first floor was sawed away so that cars could swing more easily in and out of the gas station. Mamaroneck has no landmarks' preservation law and, as former Town Supervisor Christine K. Helwig concedes, there are no restrictions on what can be done to any landmark property.

On the other hand, if you can overlook DeLancey House, Mamaroneck has done pretty well by Fenimore Cooper. Streets of the area recall his books, his characters, his name (Cooper dropped the James from his full name in 1826 at his mother's bidding; she was a Fenimore). The local amateur dramatic group, oldest in Westchester County, is appropriately named the Fenimore Players; a Warren Chase Merritt mural in the town library depicts the Cooper-DeLancey wedding in 1811; and the town's nature trail, which winds five miles over lands the Cross County Parkway was originally scheduled to run, is called Leatherstocking Trail—what else?—after the five *Leatherstocking Tales* that are the cornerstone of Cooper's reputation.

Likewise, in the Mamaroneck High School cafeteria are murals of Cooper's life and scenes from each of the *Leatherstocking Tales*. The biographical paintings are the work of Mimi Jennewein, a local artist. The Leatherstocking illustrations—huge, colorful arrangements—were painted in 1941 by students of the Yale School of Fine Arts: Albert Crutcher of Dallas, Donald B. Driscoll of Washington, D. C., Harold Thresher of Boston, Mary E. Stone of North Haven, Connecticut, and John Potter Wheat of Darien, Connecticut. The murals are perhaps too photographic to suit some artistic tastes, but they do convey the excitement of Cooper's novels. They are in excellent condition, especially considering their setting; high school cafeterias hardly making good or safe repositories for works of art.

Because these murals are in the high school, they are not readily accessible for viewing. Schools are not museums. They are closed summers, weekends, vacations, holidays—and when they are open they are not for wandering about in. Especially Mamaroneck High. It is a forest of corridors; a visitor almost needs Cooper's Pathfinder to make his way around.

Other Cooper points of interest in Westchester include two spots in Scarsdale, where Cooper moved to put distance between him and his in-laws and where he wrote his first great success, *The Spy*, published in 1821. The Scarsdale house, from which Susan claimed to be able to see the Sound and "the low shores of Long Island, with the famous pippin orchards of Newtown," is long gone—and so is the water view (which seems to have been Susan's fiction). A historical marker indicates the location of the house. Nearby is a large stone memorial with bronze plaque commemorating *The Spy*.

In that book, Cooper drew heavily on Westchester's Revolutionary War history, a history still to be appreciated in driving around Mamaroneck and Scarsdale. The principal road between the two communities is the very route taken by British troops of Maj. Gen. Sir William Howe on their way to the Battle of White Plains on October 29, 1776. On Weaver Street, "one of the oldest of America's highways," a marker recalls that a detachment of Howe's forces encamped on the site before the battle. Then, not far from the Cooper homesite in Scarsdale is the house that was Howe's headquarters after the battle. This is the Griffen-Fish house, circa 1701, at Mamaroneck and Garden Roads.

Cooper lived the baronial life during his years in Mamaroneck and Scarsdale and clearly regarded this as nothing less than he deserved. He was born in Burlington, New Jersey, in 1789 and taken the following year to upper New York State, where his father had acquired 50,000 acres of unsettled wilderness around Otsego Lake and the headwaters of the Susquehanna. Cooper père developed the tract into a manorial estate and attracted settlers to a community he modestly named Cooperstown. There, son James was reared in what one biographer calls "a certain aristocratic bias."

Young James entered Yale at thirteen, but left after three years under still cloudy circumstances. The father took him back home for two years, then "articled" him to the captain of a merchantman. This led Cooper into the United States Navy and a commission at age nineteen.

It was while on a navy leave that Cooper was introduced to Susan DeLancey, and theirs was a meeting to Cooper's instinctive liking. "Susan is the daughter of a man of very respectable connections and a handsome fortune," he confided to his brother, Richard, as if to say that money and good blood had deservingly found money and good blood.

On Susan's urging, Cooper resigned from the navy at the end of his wedding furlough, and the two settled in Mamaroneck. In 1814 Cooper dragged Susan off to Cooperstown, which was obviously his preference. In 1817 they were back in Mamaroneck, Susan's preference, for what was to be a six-month stay. The six months grew into five years and the house built in Scarsdale—on DeLancey land.

As befitted his station, Cooper enjoyed the genteel life "of a gentleman of wealth" in Scarsdale. He lived quietly on the land, was moderately active in the local militia, and kept abreast of the latest novels from England. While reading one day to Susan, Cooper cast a volume aside with the comment, "I could write a better book myself." A challenging rejoinder from Susan set Cooper to pen and paper, and in a few months' time he produced *Precaution*, an imitation of an English novel. The work was a failure as a piece of writing, but the exercise did reveal a writing talent to Cooper. At thirty he began serious work as a novelist.

The following year came *The Spy*, and in 1823, *The Pioneers*, the first of the *Leatherstocking Tales* of frontier life, when the frontier was practically next door in upper New York State. In *The Pioneers*, Fenimore Cooper introduced the reading public to Natty Bumppo, the pioneer woodsman who became the central character of the *Leatherstocking Tales* and so popular a character that, à la Sherlock Holmes years later, Cooper had to resurrect him from the dead after having dispatched him in *The Prairie*. (Natty wandered through Cooper's pages under a number of names, including Leatherstocking, the Trapper, and Hawkeye of *The Last of the Mohicans*.)

In 1826 Cooper packed himself, his wife and daughters off on a seven-year stay in Europe. Ostensibly he served as United States consul at Lyons, but in fact Cooper was a traveler and celebrity. It was during this period that he wrote his sea stories and plunged into the political and social tempests that were to involve him in contentions the rest of his days and eventually separate him from the sympathies of much of his public. Particularly alienating were Cooper's upper-class proclivities and his theories of a "landed gentry" as the lodgment of culture. Distrustful of commonalty and afraid of familiarity, he championed a gentleman class as "the repository of the manners, tastes, tone, and, to a certain extent, of the principles of a country." On his return from Europe in 1833, Cooper settled down inevitably as Squire of Cooperstown.

The last years in Cooperstown—Fenimore Cooper died in 1851—were sad. Cooper's vanity and irritability involved him in a seemingly endless series of lawsuits; his emotional reserve created distances between him and his old literary colleagues in New York City; his aristocratic instincts led him into foolish fights, such as seeking to save the baronial estate as the cornerstone of the ideal American social order.

Yet through all his battles, Cooper continued to write—and he wrote excitingly, if not always wisely and well. He never became the American Sir Walter Scott that some sought to make him. But Balzac admired his work, and so did Victor Hugo; that's pretty good company. Today Cooper is discounted artistically and socially, and pegged by some as a writer of stories for boys. But he still makes interesting reading. And *The Last of the Mohicans* is still good enough to have been selected by the British Broadcasting Corporation for eight-part dramatization on television, with showings on both sides of the Atlantic. Though tastes for him have obviously changed, Fenimore Cooper is not a literary fossil, at least not yet.

Which, among other things, is reason sufficient for a town like Mamaroneck to look to its Cooper shrines, and maybe worry if the major one has become a restaurant and a gas station.

If You Travel . . .

. . . on a swing through Fenimore Cooper's Westchester County, start at the Mamaroneck Public Library with its murals of the author's wedding to Susan DeLancey. The library is open Tuesdays through Saturdays.

A few blocks west on the Boston Post Road, at the foot of Fenimore Road, is the old DeLancey House, where the couple were married. If you continue west on the Post Road to Weaver Street and turn right, you can drive to the paint-spattered stone marker indicating the spot where British soldiers encamped during the Revolutionary War.

Leatherstocking Trail crosses Weaver Street, but there is no convenient place to park nearby. Persons interested in walking the trail should be dropped off and later picked up on Fenimore Road or Old White Plains Road in Mamaroneck.

From Larchmont, proceed to Scarsdale, along Route 125, to Mamaroneck Road. Approximately 150 yards past Scarsdale High School on the right is the historical marker indicating the site where Cooper built his Scarsdale home and wrote *The Spy*. Beyond the Cooper homesite is the Griffen-Fish house (1701), which was the headquarters of Maj. Gen. Sir William Howe after the battle of White Plains. Farther on, at the junction of Route 22, is a large stone memorial to Cooper.

In upstate New York, there is the museum of the New York State Historical Association at Cooperstown, featuring folk art, nineteenth-century American paintings, and the life of James Fenimore Cooper. The museum is located in Fenimore House. Nearby is the Woodland Museum with its dioramas from Cooper's *The Deerslayer* (1841). Fenimore House is open the year round; the Woodland Museum from May 1 to September 15.

Cooperstown is reached the more easily from lower New England and the New York City areas via the New York State Throughway. One should take Exit 29 at Canajoharie, then Route 5S to Fort Plain, then Route 80 into Cooperstown. The driving time from New York City is between four and five hours. For the less literary-minded, Cooperstown offers a number of museums, including the Baseball Hall of Fame. It is open seven days a week, from 9:00 A.M. to 9:00 P.M. during the tourist season, and from 9:00 A.M. to 5:00 P.M. thereafter.

Chapter
Three

WASHINGTON IRVING

Writing on the Sunny Side at Sunnyside

The road to Sunnyside drops sharply from U.S. Route 9 in Tarrytown, New York, and winds through woods that once knew only the footpaths of Indians. It's a dank stretch, even when the dry heat is on the land—dark by day, black by night. Rip Van Winkle could be asleep in the underbrush to either side, and pounding around the bend, hot after Ichabod Crane, could come Brom Bones in the get-up of the Headless Horseman, pumpkin in hand ready for the throwing.

At Sunnyside, the land levels off, and the trees open up to receive sun, stars, and moon. The Hudson River laps gently at land's edge, and its waters cast up the mists that enveloped early Dutch settlers in a sea of legends. The storm ship of the Palisades could be not far from that stretch of river, and so could Rambout van Dan, the ghost of Spuyten Duyvel, his oars heard though no boat seen. Upriver, beyond Tappan Zee, the keeper of the mountain at Donderberg, a Dutch goblin—what else?—could be raising his speaking-trumpet to summon the winds and the thunderclaps. On the other hand, those rumbles of thunder could be Hendrick Hudson and the Little Men resuming their bowling off in the Kaatskill mountains after their twenty-year interval.

This is Washington Irving country, and Sunnyside—a quaint architectural *ménage à trois* of the Dutch, the Gothic, and the Romanesque—is its capital. Sunnyside was Irving's home for the last twenty-four years of his life. If Irving hadn't lived here, his ghost would have to be established here, so complete is the identification between the man and his work, the home and the geography.

The Hudson is one of America's most glorious waterways, and by none was it loved more than by Washington Irving. "I thank God I was born on the banks of the Hudson!" he would write. "I think it an

31

invaluable advantage to be born and brought up in the neighborhood of some grand and noble object in Nature,—a river, a lake, or a
mountain. We make a friendship with it,—we in a manner ally
ourselves to it for life." That may be more Washington Irving roman-
ticism, but it has a particular application in his case. For, indeed,
Irving did ally himself to this historic river that the explorers once
thought would provide a northwest passage to China, and that the
Dutch imbued with their colorful legends—perhaps, as has been
suggested, because the spectacular Hudson Valley area unlocked
imaginations dulled by the flat, monotonous landscape of their
homeland. Whatever that, Irving grew up by the Hudson, traveled
it beginning as a teenager, hunted squirrels not far from its shore,
rowed on it as an older man, and never loosened it from his memory, even during his long years in Europe.

Yet as Irving was formed by the Hudson Valley's legends, so did
he help give them their final shape. Ichabod Crane, Parson Prim-
rose, Katrina Van Tassel, Abraham Van Brunt (Brom Bones, himself), and others are firmly a part of American folklore because of
Washington Irving. How authentically Hudson they are is another
question. Rip Van Winkle, for instance, is less a Hudson River
Valley and New Amsterdam original than an imaginative recasting
of Frederick Barbarossa, the person of long sleep in the German
legend that Irving came to know and draw upon.

Interestingly enough, the Rip Van Winkle character points up a
paradox of the Irving story: his place in American letters notwithstanding, Irving the writer is a mite less distinctively American
than is usually presumed—or at least *was* less distinctively American
during a certain phase of his career, both in focus and situation. A
seventeen-year removal to Europe that began when Irving was
thirty-two made him, in effect, the pioneer American expatriate
author. There being no tradition of American writing at the time,
much less a newly established school of American writers, Irving
was subjected to criticism for absenting himself so long from the
United States and for not devoting himself to the development of a
distinctly American literary idiom. Goethe, for one, preferred Fenimore Cooper as a writer to Irving, and felt that Irving was making a
mistake in neglecting American themes for European ones. Criticism of this sort cut Irving to the quick and very likely helped turn

Washington Irving cautioned a nephew against the financial precariousness of the writer's life, but Sunnyside, his home at Tarrytown, N.Y., was proof that the successful writer could live very, very well in nineteenth-century America.

him in later years to themes of the American West and to a long biography of George Washington. This change in focus mitigated the criticism, though its results did not crown his career with distinction. His fame was to rest on the pleasant folk fantasies that Irving suspected of being frivolous, but which can be read today with the same enjoyment as when they were written a century and a half ago. Curiously enough, the most popular of these tales were written during the expatriate period.

Washington Irving was born in New York City on April 3, 1783, the youngest of eleven children of William and Sarah Irving. The father was a native of the Orkney Islands; the mother, of Falmouth. They came to this country in 1763, settled on William Street when Manhattan Island still knew farms and orchards, and proceeded to raise their large family on the income of a hardware business. The father served in the Revolutionary War and developed a keen admiration for his commander-in-chief. It was he after whom the Irvings' last-born was named.

The hardware trade did not propel the Irvings into New York's new commercial aristocracy, but the family operation was prosperous enough to support a branch office in Liverpool and for the Irvings to afford a Scottish nurse. She it was—piety has it—who whisked Master Washington Irving into the presence of Mister George Washington, when Mr. Washington was in New York in 1789 for his inauguration as first president of the United States. Approaching the celebrated hero in a Broadway shop, the nurse reportedly remarked, "Please, Your Excellency, here's a bairn that's called after ye!" Washington patted the six-year-old tot on the head and ostensibly went about his presidential business. Washington Irving grew up not only remembering that pat, but coming to conceive of it as benediction and charge, the latter impelling him to the exhaustive biography that would end his career and—by some opinion—shorten his days. For that labor of love, long contemplated and belatedly tackled, turned into trial and cross. "When will this ever end?" Irving complained towards the last. Fate decreed that biography and life should end within a few months of one another. On March 15, 1859, Irving wrote the final page of the fifth and last volume; he died of a heart attack the following November 28. He was seventy-six.

Life was good to Washington Irving, and, whatever the effects of
the Washington biographical project, providentially generous by
way of longevity. As a youth, Irving was delicate and frail, and it
was feared that he might be carried away by consumption. Anxious
for his health—or at least anxious to make as pleasant as possible the
limited time seemingly allotted him—his older brothers sent him on
the Grand Tour in 1804. Washington Irving found health on the high
seas, and in Europe discovered pleasure, to which he was no
stranger anyway. (Earlier days would see him climb out a bedroom
window to attend the theater and slip in later for family prayers.) To
the disconcertment of his elders, Washington Irving neglected
many of the prescribed rituals of the Grand Tour—sightseeing, for
instance, in which he had little interest. He dallied and danced, and
indulged his wit, and toyed with the idea of becoming a painter. But
he also kept a daily journal, and he worked at character sketching,
and in terms of career this industriousness proved more important
than hopping on and off carriages heading for some new city or
wonder. The Grand Tour, accordingly, solidified Irving's determi-
nation to be a writer and launched him on the refinements of word
that he would build into an art.

Washington Irving had read law, and upon his return to the
United States in 1806 he was called to the bar. He had a minor role in
the Aaron Burr treason trial of 1807, but his interest in the legal
profession was minimal. The brothers—ever doting, as Washington
Irving himself was to dote later in life on nieces and nephews—
made him a nominal partner in their firm, but left him free to indulge
his fancies as a writer. It was in this period that, together with
brother William and James Kirke Paulding, he began producing the
satirical miscellany that comes down to us as *Salmagundi, or the
Whim-Whams and Opinions of Launcelot Langstaff Esq. and Others*. This
was followed by *A History of New York from the Beginning of the World
to the End of the Dutch Dynasty*, a witty burlesque on a current
guidebook to the city, but a burlesque that irritated city fathers and
proud patroons, while amusing most everyone else. Sir Walter Scott
enthused that he had never read anything so closely resembling the
style of Dean Swift. The *History* created the character of the phleg-
matic Dutchman and made the name Knickerbocker—the author's
pseudonym—a New York byword to this day. Irving, by the way,
was a man of many pseudonyms, moving from Jonathan Oldstyle,

to Anthony Evergreen, to Diedrich Knickerbocker, to Geoffrey Crayon. To his pseudonyms he appended "Gent.," perhaps to reinforce the view, not commonly shared by Americans of the day, that writing was in fact a gentleman's profession.

In 1815, Washington Irving was back in Europe as a "sleeping partner," so-called, in the Liverpool office of the family business. He had lost his betrothed to tuberculosis. He had edited a magazine that failed. He had idled away time in New York, Philadelphia, Richmond, and Washington. The brothers obviously felt a change was in order and the family business provided a perfect opportunity. But the Liverpool office proved no sinecure, and only briefly did it preoccupy the new hand. In point of fact the office proved to be foundering, and the youngest Irving was hardly the person to rescue it, try as he might. Books were Washington Irving's forte— but not account books. The business went down the drain, and Irving was forced to take up writing for a livelihood. The dilettante thus became the professional, and Irving's writing career was formally launched.

That 1815 trip to Europe was expected to last a year or two. In fact, it extended to seventeen. Irving's Knickerbocker reputation had preceded him to England, and doors swung open that would otherwise have been shut to Americans without letters or portfolio. He became a friend of Scott, Moore, and Byron, and his grace and polish made him an adornment at social gatherings. Meanwhile, he wrote, and in 1819–20 published *The Sketch Book of Geoffrey Crayon, Gent.*, containing the tales of Rip Van Winkle and Sleepy Hollow that were to solidify his name and render his memory imperishable. In 1822 there came *Bracebridge Hall, or the Humorists*, followed by, among others, *Tales of a Traveller*, a four-volume *History of the Life and Voyages of Christopher Columbus*; *A Chronicle of the Conquest of Granada from the MSS. of* [an imaginary] *Fray Antonio Agapida*; and the Arabesque-flavored *Alhambra*. The Spanish writings developed under quasi-official auspices of the American consul at Madrid, and the Columbus volumes particularly introduced valuable source material to the reading public.

For Irving, it was an extremely productive period, and a varied one both in travels and in interests, including even a venture into play writing in Paris in collaboration with John Howard Payne. The effort ended in something of a dead end for both parties. Payne was to write more than fifty plays, only to slip into history for a song—"Home, Sweet Home"—sung by the farmer's daughter in his *Clari, or The Maid of Milan*. Irving collaborated on two plays with Payne—*Charles the Second* and *Richelieu*—then, annoyed by the "traps and trickery" of the theater, he returned to prose writing, ultimately leaving to others the task of adapting *Rip Van Winkle* to the stage. (Joseph Jefferson, the actor, produced a script for the play around 1860, then had his script reworked by the Irish-American playwright Dion Boucicault. The revised version first played at London's Adelphi Theatre in 1864, was a smash success, and became the standard stage *Rip Van Winkle*. During the next four decades it played to audiences in the United States and Europe, with Jefferson in the role of Rip. The play may be seen nowadays during special summer runs in a tent theater at Sunnyside.)

Meanwhile, honors began to accrue. The United States government named Irving to a ministerial post in London. Oxford University conveyed a degree in civil laws. And New York welcomed him back home in 1832 with ceremonies that nearly overwhelmed him. It was before the day, of course, of ticker-tape parades, but there was a grand public dinner in the City Hall, and the bravos and handkerchief waving were such as to bring tears to Irving's eyes and crumble his emotional reserve. In time would come offers to stand for mayor of New York and for Congress, and to serve as secretary of the navy during the Van Buren administration, all of which were declined. He did, however, accept an appointment in 1842 as ambassador to Spain, and held the post for four years. For Irving, Spain was always a special love demanding special exceptions.

The last chapters of Irving's literary career were his most thoroughly American, but, as suggested, not necessarily his most dazzling. In 1832 he journeyed through the West and acquired the facts and insights that helped him produce first *Astoria*, a history of the fur-trading settlement founded by his friend John Jacob Astor, then *The Adventures of Captain Bonneville, U.S.A.*—the same Benjamin Bonneville, by the by, who stood with his mother at Tom Paine's graveside, when Paine was buried in New Rochelle in 1809. Bonneville had gone on to West Point, then to the West as an explorer of the Rocky Mountain regions. Both of these works benefited from popular reading tastes of the time, but neither enhanced Irving's reputation to a marked degree historically. The same is true of other writings of the period, including his *Life of Oliver Goldsmith* and *Wolfert's Roost*, a collection of tales and sketches that drew its title from the earlier name of Irving's home at Tarrytown. Even the biography of Washington—though warm and feeling, and infinitely less wooden than what had been done to date on Washington—in some critical opinion fell short of greatness. Certainly the biography is not a standard tool for today's researchers.

Some of this may seem to disparage Irving, but the assessment is not far removed from his own. Irving appears to have been much more realistic about the depth and quality of his work than his cultists tended to be, then or now. "My writings . . . may appear light and trifling in our country of philosophers and politicians," he wrote of *The Sketch Book*, "but if they possess merit in the class of literature to which they belong, it is all to which I aspire in the work." Even the weightier projects of biography and history left him without delusions. "I scarcely look with full satisfaction upon any," he said late in life when asked which of his books he esteemed the highest, "for they do not seem what they might have been. I often wish that I could have twenty years more, to take them down from the shelf one by one, and write them over."

Irving's writing during this final literary phase was done in the carefully preserved study at Sunnyside, a home that was to acquire a fame almost as unique as its master. Artists romanticized Sunnyside in crayon and oils, among them George Inness, Felix O. C. Darley, and George Harvey. Currier and Ives rendered it in lithograph, and the color reproductions were hung in homes across the nation. Photographers—a new breed—set up tripods and captured Sunnyside on film. Sightseers gawked at it from river boat and train, and visitors arrived at its gate, sometimes, it seemed, as much to see the property as to do homage to Washington Irving.

Irving bought the place—a four-room seventeenth-century farmhouse on ten acres of land—in 1835. He paid $1,800 for the tract. Much is made of Irving's poor business acumen, but Sunnyside was anything but a financial mistake. He broke down walls, added rooms and a Moorish tower, tacked on weather vanes, picked up fifteen more acres of land—then in 1849 sold a right-of-way strip to the New York and Hudson River Railroad for nearly double his original investment. Irving was unhappy about parting with that strip, as it deprived him of direct access to the river below his promontory. But $3,500 eased the anguish, and Irving was astute enough to take a portion of the amount in stocks that were to multiply in value.

These were comfortable years for Irving. A financial panic caused heavy burdens for a time, and there were some poor investments, but royalties rolled in regularly from his books, thanks largely to the wisdom of George Palmer Putnam in returning to circulation works that Irving's Philadelphia publisher had allowed to drop from print on the mistaken assumption that demand for them was gone. In his lifetime, Irving earned $205,383.34 from his writings; $88,143.08 came from Putnam's. It was a substantial amount for its day, though it did not leave Irving perfectly satisfied. "I hope none of those whose interests and happiness are dear to me will be induced to follow my footsteps, and wander into the seductive but treacherous paths of literature," he wrote one day to a nephew. "There is no life more precarious in its profits and fallacious in its enjoyments than that of an author."

It is difficult to take Irving seriously on the point. At Sunnyside, he had a cook, a gardener, two chambermaids, and funds sufficient to hire neighboring help for the planting and harvesting. Thanks to the "paths of literature," he lived splendiferously, and to his choosing—surrounded by Nature, family, books, and the sentimental memories of a glamorous youth and middle age. Irving valued the past, and he nurtured it as solicitously as the ivy from Abbotsford, Scott's home, that garlanded Sunnyside and the climbing wisteria planted in 1842, which to this day turn Sunnyside in the spring into a wonderland of blossoms. Indeed, if Irving had any complaint at Sunnyside—a nonserious one, at that—it was that time would not stand still and leave him forever happy in this Shangri-la.

Sunnyside enabled Irving to live in privacy, or at least apart from those not of his choosing. He was anything but a populist. Crowds annoyed him, and "inferior" breeds the more so. He would bristle over the "disagreeable beasts" with whom he once had to share a sea passage, and during a brief political excursion he would be turned off by the "mob—whom my heart abhorreth." More shockingly for one so usually sensitive and sweet of character, he carried a disdain for blacks that crossed into contemptuousness. As a young man of twenty-four, he professed to Mary Fairlie, the Sophie Sparkle of the *Salmagundi* papers, that he found the Negro "an abomination to me." Forty-four years later, in writing to John Pendleton Kennedy, the novelist, he would express the wish that "nature would restore to the poor negroes their tails and settle them in their proper place in the scale of creation." A low whimsical remark said offhandedly to a close friend? Maybe. But eight years later he would comment to his biographer, "I shouldn't mind about the Niggers if they only brought them over before they had drilled out their tails."

Such remarks diminish considerably one's respect for Irving, and make one thankful after all that he never involved himself seriously in political and sociological questions.

Sunnyside was virtually inundated by family during Irving's last decades. His unmarried brother Peter came there to live, and so did brother Ebenezer and his five daughters, motherless since Ebenezer's wife had died in 1827. Sister Catherine and her daughter Sarah dropped by, and various nephews. In fact, so crowded did the house become with kin that for a while Irving had to give up his bedroom and fit out sleeping quarters for himself in the draped alcove of his study.

If Sunnyside lacked one thing in these blissful years, it was a mistress. Washington Irving was a bachelor—and of a classical sort, wearing on his sleeve sorrow for the death of a young sweetheart. Matilda Hoffman, the love of Irving's long sentimentalizing, died in 1809 of tuberculosis, she being seventeen and he an already near-bachelor of twenty-six. "She died in the flower of her youth and of mine," he wrote years later in his journal, "but she has lived for me ever since in all woman kind. I see her in their eyes—and it is the remembrance of her that has given a tender interest in my eyes to every thing that bears the name of woman." This is the stuff of nineteenth-century romance, and it can be questioned that Irving was ever as permanently crushed as some maintain. He measured the beauty of each new country by the appeal of its females, and on at least one occasion he considered marriage—after meeting Emily Foster, an English beauty passing time in Dresden. The decision not to wed appears to have been hers, not his. In Paris there was a flirtation of sorts with Mary Wollstonecraft Shelley, the poet's widow, who came into latter-day fame as the author of *Frankenstein*. But theirs never reached the stage of the Foster relationship.

Irving was unlucky in love, but at the same time he could jest about love's pleasures, presumably unindulged. As a young man in France, he was once asked to give up his hotel room to a French chief engineer and his lady, the room evidently being the best in the house and known previously to the engineer, if not necessarily the lady. Irving was firm. As "an American gentleman of character and not inferior to any engineer in France," he announced that he would not give up his room. He did not wish to be unduly difficult, however, so he indicated a willingness "to share part of my room and some of my bed with the lady." As to her husband, he begged to be excused.

Today, there is about Sunnyside an air of formality that, for all Irving's own formalness, would probably surprise him. Visitors are shown about by guides in period clothing, and the grounds are as manicured as those of a country club. It is precisely as Irving would have things, but only what an affluent institution can afford. Sunnyside is owned and maintained by Sleepy Hollow Restorations, Inc., a nonprofit educational corporation chartered by The University of the State of New York and established under an endowment provided in large part by the late John D. Rockefeller, Jr. It is one of three historical properties in a Sleepy Hollow Restorations complex, all within ten miles of each other, close to the east bank of the Hudson River and along Route 9. The other two are Philipsburg Manor, an early 1700s gristmill trading center unit in North Tarrytown, and Van Cortlandt Manor, a Revolutionary War–era manorial estate in Croton-on-Hudson.

Irving called Sunnyside his "snuggery," and in every respect the home reflects his tastes and whims. He devised its sloping barrel ceilings, its ingenious arches and alcoves, as well as the Dutch stepped gables at either end of the exterior that accent an almost infinite number of pinnacles, angles, and corners. The house could be a fairyland manor in a Hans Christian Andersen story. Irving relished its every nuance. Forty years after Irving's death, family descendants attached an addition in the kitchen-yard area that served as museum and gallery. This was removed in 1959 as part of a restoration program, and the rear of the house returned to its original state. In this rear area are the icehouse (Irving had his ice cut from a pond on the property that he called his "Little Mediterranean"), root cellar, woodshed, and "necessary houses." Washington had hot and cold running water in his house, and a bathtub. The challenge of the indoor toilet had yet to be mastered.

Purists have labeled Sunnyside a Victorian banality, a jumble of styles and focuses. But Sunnyside was Irving—figuratively as much as literally. His career was like the architecture of his house, seldom retaining its focus for more than a limited span. As a writer he leaped from satire to history to biography—lampoon to essay to tract. This literary agility is probably why Irving ranks as the jack of many forms rather than the master of one, a writer of the second level rather than a regent of the first. Still, Washington Irving's place in literary history is assured. At least he had helped prove that coarse, upstart America could produce a writer whose books would be read around the world, then live into the far future.

If You Travel . . .

. . .to Washington Irving country, you will find Sunnyside, Irving's picturesque home, on West Sunnyside Lane in the town of Tarrytown, New York. It is one mile south of the Tappan Zee Bridge, just off U.S. Route 9, and can be approached by way of the bridge, the Saw Mill River Parkway, or the Cross Westchester Expressway. Via the Cross Westchester, one would take the last exit before the bridge and reach Route 9 by way of State Route 119 (bearing left on Route 119 and going right at the first light). Coming across the Tappan Zee Bridge from the north and west, one would take the first exit after the toll gate. The turn to Sunnyside from Route 9 is clearly marked.

At the entrance to Sunnyside Lane is a Washington Irving Memorial, featuring a bust of Irving flanked by representations of Rip Van Winkle, Irving's deep sleeper of the Kaatskills, and Boabdil, the last king of Granada. The memorial is the work of Daniel Chester French, who also did the Minuteman Monument in Concord, Massachusetts, and the statue of Abraham Lincoln in the Lincoln Memorial in Washington, D.C. It was erected in 1928 and was the gift of

Mrs. Henry Black of Irvingtown, the community adjacent to Tarrytown named in honor of Washington Irving.

Sunnyside—a National Historic Landmark under provisions of the Historic Sites Act of August 21, 1935—is open seven days a week the year round, except for Thanksgiving Day, Christmas, and New Year's Day. Hours are from 10:00 A.M. to 5:00 P.M., and there is a modest admission fee. Combination tickets, good all year, are available for Sunnyside and the nearby Sleepy Hollow Restorations' properties of Philipsburg Manor and Van Cortlandt Manor.

At administrative headquarters of Sleepy Hollow Restorations at 150 White Plains Road in Tarrytown is a fine Washington Irving library. To use it, one must write beforehand to the curator, Joseph T. Butler, at Sleepy Hollow Restorations, Box 245, Tarrytown, New York, 10591. There is also an excellent collection of Irving papers, books, and related materials in the New York Public Library on Fifth Avenue at Forty-second Street in New York City. Washington Irving was president of the city's first free public library—the Astor Library—a forerunner of the present institution. (In 1850, Washington Irving presided over the expenditure of $7,243 for books; in recent years, New York Public Library spending for books has been in the neighborhood of $2 million a year.)

Washington Irving's grave is on the south slope of a hill in Sleepy Hollow Cemetery among famed Hudson River Valley families—the Philipses, van Warts, Martlings, Couenhovens, Pauldings, Ackers. The cemetery adjoins the Old Dutch Church of Sleepy Hollow, made famous by Irving (it was in this church's choir that Ichabod Crane sang with lusty piety). The church is on Route 9, just above Philipsburg Manor, and is said to be the oldest ecclesiastical edifice in New York State. Close by is the "Headless Horseman" bridge.

Chapter
Four

HORACE GREELEY

In Chappaqua, Shades of a Sometime Prophet

You don't "go West" from Manhattan's editorial offices to find the shade of Horace Greeley, the celebrated newspaper editor who helped shape the nineteenth-century United States. You go north, some thirty-five miles above New York City, to the tiny village of Chappaqua. There the Greeley shade appears to be everywhere at once, much as "Uncle Horace" himself almost was. It's in the carved stone of the high school; in the business signs of such disparate industries as a gift shop, a country store, a sanitation service; it's on street posts; it's in the heroic bronze sculpture by William Ordway Partridge.

Still, the Greeley shade is elusive. Chappaqua was Greeley's country home the last eighteen years of his life. It was where the Greeley roots at last took tenuous hold after his seemingly endless wanderings as journeyman printer, journalist, sometime politician, and incessant controversialist. Yet there is no formal Greeley museum in Chappaqua, no grand memorial exhibition hall. The Greeley "house on the main road" is a gift shop. The Greeley retreat—the "house in the woods"—went up in smoke in 1875. The Greeley dream house—the "house on the hill"—burned down in 1890. The famous Greeley "stone" barn, reportedly one of the first structures of its type in the United States, still stands, but it is a private residence. The Greeley land—all seventy-eight acres—has been disposed of, the last thirty-two acres to a real-estate developer in 1954.

There is, however, a "shrine"—a room in the New Castle Town Hall, Chappaqua being a part of New Castle. In it are collected such relics as a belatedly sensitive community has been able to bring together: Horace Greeley's crib; his eyeglasses; a smattering of books from the Greeley library; the grill he invented in defense against the cooking he encountered on trips west; his desk from the *New York Tribune*, the paper that Greeley founded in 1841 and made into the major public-opinion vehicle of mid–nineteenth-century America. The room is under the care of the Chappaqua Historical Society.

There are in the room additional fragments of Greeleyana: busts and plaster casts, including one of the famed Greeley writing hand; C. C. Markham's portrait of Greeley; a printing stand from the shop in East Poultney, Vermont, where Greeley apprenticed; pictures, papers, and odd bits of memorabilia. It's not a whole lot. On the other hand, there might have been nothing at all. Much of what is on display was up for general sale in 1954 and was rescued from dispersal by a committee hastily organized by Douglas G. Graflin, principal of the high school and later superintendent of schools. The committee raised the funds that saved the Greeleyana for Chappaqua. The relics kicked around in the high school for several years, being consigned at one point to space next to the furnace room. They did not win complete safety until the Historical Society opened its room in the Town Hall in June, 1971.

The fate of the Greeley property provides a poignant afterword to the Greeley story, but maybe one in keeping with the valid historical dimensions of the man. Horace Greeley is an authentic American folk figure: the self-educated small-town boy (b. Amherst, New Hampshire, 1811) who dazzled the big city (New York) and the country at large as an editor and writer; who turned out a number of volumes of history, letters, and essays; and who fell just short of realizing the allegedly noblest of American ambitions, the office of the presidency. (He was nominated in 1872, but ran second to Ulysses S. Grant.) He was a folk figure down to his individualistic appearance: baggy suit, broad-brimmed square hat, askew necktie, and fuzzy throat whiskers that framed a perpetually youthful, innocent-looking face. Quaint old Uncle Horace. But he was a mover and a shaker, a legend in his own time. Greeley, Colorado, took his name. So did five other villages and towns of the United States. So did a number of public schools. And presidents once paused to think how a particular action of theirs would strike Horace's fancy, among them Abraham Lincoln.

The Greeley "house on the main road" is now a gift shop, but nevertheless it dominates the multiple Greeley associations in Chappaqua, N.Y. At the other end of town, Greeley "relics" are collected in a room of Town Hall.

History has taken its measure, however, and later generations of Americans are not nearly so awed by Horace Greeley as were his contemporaries. Today his name is associated mainly with a catch phrase, which he may or may not have coined, but which summed up a national optimism and an enthusiasm that Horace Greeley helped convey for life beyond the Alleghenies: "Go West, young man, go West." A catch phrase, alas, is not an imperishable claim on posterity.

Looking back, in fact, it is oftentimes difficult to fathom what the hosannas were all about. The cultism was indisputable. The *Tribune*, as roaming reporter Bayard Taylor wrote from one of his trips, "comes next to the Bible all through the West." And the *Tribune*'s high priest was, of course, Horace Greeley. But high priests are not always lovable and not always infallible. Certainly Horace Greeley wasn't. He wasn't particularly easy to work for or live with. He was a neglectful spouse, and sometimes it seemed his marriage endured primarily because of the social conventions of the period. More pertinently, Greeley lacked some crucial insights, and he managed to be wrong on many more issues than a truly great journalist-editor has a call to be.

In pre-*Tribune* days, as editor of a weekly journal of literature and the news named *New Yorker* (no ink lines to today's *New Yorker*), Greeley endured without marked outward indignation the New York race riots of 1834 and the food riots of 1836. When twenty-one journeymen tailors were arrested and fined for striking in 1835, he straddled a middle position between employer and employee.

It may be argued that tomorrow's prophet was still in the process of formation. But that prophet of tomorrow, fully formed, had embarrassing soft spots as well.

Greeley went west in 1859, and he saw the Indian—and the stereotype. The Indian is "a slave of appetite and sloth, never emancipated from the tyranny of one passion save by the ravenous demands of another," he wrote. "As I passed over those magnificent bottoms of the Kansas . . . constituting the very best corn land on earth, and saw their men sitting round the doors of their lodges in the height of the planting season . . . I could not help saying, 'These people must die out—there is no help for them. God has given the earth to those who will subdue and cultivate it, and it is vain to struggle against his righteous decree.' "

History would also judge Greeley a chauvinist. "We repudiate the doctrines advanced by [feminist] Frances Wright and her co-workers . . . of the rightful equality of the sexes in political privilege and in social conditions," he wrote; "not disputing the mental capacity of women, we yet insist that . . . [the wife] should yield a general and cordial though not servile deference to the husband." Greeley hired feminist Margaret Fuller as a *Tribune* literary critic, but he would also say that "two or three bouncing babies would have emancipated her from a good deal of cant and nonsense." Predictably, he was no enthusiast for women's suffrage.

But Greeley's greatest misconceptions may have been with respect to Abraham Lincoln. The two served together in Congress in 1849, and Greeley was not impressed. "A quiet, good-natured man, who did not aspire to leadership . . . noticeably tall, and the only Whig from Illinois—not remarkable, otherwise, to my recollection"; that was Greeley's assessment. In 1860, the two found themselves together in the young and promising Republican Party, with Lincoln a strong candidate for the presidential nomination. Lincoln was not Greeley's man. He backed Edward Bates, a St. Louis lawyer who creaked with age and in appeal. Bates was a veteran of the War of 1812, and his greatest achievement, perhaps, was the siring of seventeen children. He had freed his slaves, however, and was a great champion of development of the West. This made Greeley a disciple.

At the nominating convention in Chicago, Greeley maneuvered and badgered and helped scrape together forty-eight votes for Bates—nowhere near enough to secure the nomination, but, as it turned out, a crucial number in determining who would be the Republican nominee. On the third ballot, Greeley threw the Bates bloc to Lincoln. It was a deciding maneuver—though it was engineered less out of Greeley's enthusiasm for Lincoln than a desire to derail the candidacy of William H. Seward, a one-time Greeley associate in politics and publishing and now a Greeley foe.

The Greeley-Lincoln relationship blew hot and cold during Lincoln's presidential years. Greeley became convinced that Lincoln was indecisive on slavery, and Lincoln, for his part, seemed nettled by Greeley's almost perpetual editorial carping. Thus it was to Greeley that Lincoln wrote his famous letter of August 22, 1862: "If I could save the Union without freeing any slave, I would do it; and if I could save it by freeing all the slaves, I would do it; and if I could save it by freeing some and leaving others alone, I would also do that." Whether this sentiment reflected Lincoln's genuine feeling or whether it represented a strategy to be pursued until the proper moment for emancipation presented itself is an interesting parlor debate. In the context of this discussion, the letter's significance is the power of Greeley to evoke it.

When the Emancipation Proclamation came shortly thereafter, Greeley was rhapsodic. "GOD BLESS ABRAHAM LINCOLN!" cried the *Tribune*. There was no Pharisaism in those words. Greeley and the *Tribune* had fought the good fight on slavery almost from the very beginning. (The 1834 "finesse" was the only real blemish on an otherwise proud record.)

The Emancipation Proclamation was not enough in itself, though, to convert Greeley to Lincoln. Thus, as Lincoln's first term neared its end, Greeley was casting about for another person to thrust forward to head the ticket. He inclined towards Secretary of the Treasury Salmon P. Chase, switched off to General John C. Frémont, the explorer, then, like many others, was forced to stick with Lincoln after Union victory in the field. One doesn't battle success. There were reports of a cabinet post's being held out to Greeley in order to win his support, but the report may have owed more to Greeley's ambitions—and imagination—than to Lincoln's actual dispositions.

The historical Greeley is an easy foil in additional respects. The man could get caught up in fads. Thus he munched Graham crackers, sat in séance with spiritualists, and dabbled with Fourierism, the social system that would have organized society into a series of phalanxes and associations. Greeley was a frightful administrator and incompetent custodian of riches. Accordingly, while the *Tribune* made many people financially comfortable, Greeley was frequently struggling to make ends meet. (One of his failings—albeit a winning one—was that he was an easy touch, a quality that was to bring down on his head the wrath of multimillionaire Cornelius Vanderbilt, upset because Greeley persisted in befriending Vanderbilt's sick and uncompliant son, Cornelius, Jr.) Greeley was impetuous and many times wrongheaded. He let one of his crack political editors—Amos J. Cummings of newsdom's "man-bites-dog" aphorism—be fired for profanity, though he himself could turn the air blue on occasion.

Still, for all his quirks and his foibles and his impracticalities, there was about Greeley something of the genius—or at least of the erratic prophet. He fought slavery as a moral evil and an economic wrong. He contended with monopolies, railed against exploitive corporations, and deplored the selfish acquisitiveness of so much of what passed for American business. He championed labor unions (and in 1850 became the first president of the New York Printers' Union, later Typographical Union Number 6). He opposed capital punishment. He stood for a reasonable protective tariff, land reform, full equality for blacks, and amnesty for those who fought for the Confederacy. Principles invariably outweighed possible personal consequences. Thus in 1867 Greeley went bail bond for President Jefferson Davis of the Confederate States, who had been languishing in jail for two years with no sign of coming soon to trial. The action touched off a storm of reaction throughout the North. Protests poured into the *Tribune*, and orders dropped precipitously for Greeley's two-volume history of the Civil War, *The American Conflict*. The prestigious Union League Club of New York clinched public opinion by summoning member Greeley to appear before the full membership for possible censuring and ousting. Greeley refused and fired off a blistering letter: "I tell you here, out of a life earnestly devoted to the good of human kind, your children will select my going to Richmond and signing that bail-bond as the wisest act, and will feel that it did more for freedom and humanity than all of you were competent to do, though you had lived to the age of Methuselah." The Union League backed off. It was one of Horace Greeley's finest hours.

As an editor, Greeley had an eye for talent as well as issues. He drew heavily on participants in the transcendentalist experiment at Brook Farm that had fascinated him so much. Charles A. Dana, for years Greeley's managing editor and later editor of the *New York Sun*, came from there. So did literary editor George Ripley and Margaret Fuller. As the paper's fame grew, the *Tribune* attracted as contributors Henry Wadsworth Longfellow, Charles Dickens, Mark Twain, Bret Harte. (Edgar Allan Poe dropped around the office and stuck Greeley with an I.O.U. for $51.50.) For more than ten years the paper carried dispatches from London written by one Karl Marx.

Marx "has indeed opinions of his own, with some of which we are far from agreeing," the *Tribune* editorialized, "but those who do not read his letters neglect one of the most instructive sources of information on the great questions of European politics."

The world was Horace Greeley's; yet, at the same time, it wasn't.

What did Horace Greeley in at the end, very probably, was the ambivalence within himself as to careers. He was the most celebrated newspaperman of his time, a powerful moral force, a teacher listened to on any topic to which he cared to address himself. Still he was emotionally and intellectually unsatisfied. He hungered constantly for elective office and, in fact, would have taken almost any political appointment that he considered worthy of one of his exalted position. In 1849 he managed a ninety-day term in Congress through appointment to a vacancy, but all else was fated. He twice sought a senatorial nomination, without success. He reached out for the governorship in 1870; again no luck. In 1868 and 1870 he aspired unsuccessfully to the House of Representatives. Then, when all political opportunity appeared past, he was a presidential candidate, the 1872 nominee of the Liberal Republican and Democratic parties against the Republican incumbent, Ulysses S. Grant.

Greeley's was an unhappy political marriage bed. The master crank of periphery politics let himself be wooed and won by the wildest crank elements of the splintered Republican Party. Then he let himself be bedded down with the Democratic Party—a bigamous arrangement if ever there was one, but one that was thought to have a chance of stopping Grant. The match was the more incongruous because Greeley, as Whig and Republican, had spent most of his life attacking Democrats. ("I never said all Democrats were saloon-keepers," Greeley once remarked. "I only said all saloon-keepers are Democrats.") Wiser heads sought to keep Greeley from his folly. "Greeley is an interesting curiosity which everyone likes to see and to show, and in whom we all feel a certain kind of national pride," diplomat-editor John Bigelow told a mutual friend, "but I do not think anyone can seriously believe in his fitness for any administrative position whatever. If they do, they know as little of him as he knows of himself." But Greeley was not to be dissuaded. He plunged after the prize.

It was a fatal plunge, quite literally. The campaign was dirty and vicious, and except for occasional moments—like the grand picnic in

July when three hundred of Greeley's friends and campaign workers descended on Chappaqua for speeches and a banquet of lobster salad, potted pigeon, ice cream, fruits, and lemonade—it was unrelieved agony. Cartoonist Thomas Nast caricatured Greeley unmercifully in *Harper's Weekly*, and others chided him as traitor, fool, doddering tool of political opportunists. Greeley was moved to remark that he was unsure whether he was running for the presidency or the penitentiary.

The race was over before the votes were even cast. Greeley knew it, but was unprepared for the dimensions of his loss. He carried only six states, all southern and border. His popular vote was 2,834,761, against 3,598,235 for Grant. Grant's plurality of 763,474 was a record that stood until the McKinley-Bryan vote of 1900.

The rout came as a final blow to one who had taken every attack and insult personally. Effects were quickened by other developments. Just a few days before the election, Greeley watched his wife, Mary, die in Chappaqua. There was a vast gulf between the two, but that death triggered deep emotions of remorse for his part in the marriage's lack of success; there were also waves of self-pity and haunting remembrances of the seven Greeley children who had died (only two daughters lived, Gabrielle and Ida). After the election, Greeley returned to the *Tribune*, fully expecting to resume the role he had resigned while running for office. It wasn't to be. He found his old associates firmly in control and intending to remain so. Insult was heaped on indignity when a Greeley editorial—bitter and ill-conceived, to be sure—was suppressed by Whitelaw Reid, now in charge. Greeley was unwell, and his condition did not escape Reid's notice.

Greeley headed back to Chappaqua, broken in mind and in body. He had suffered from "brain fever" at times in the past, but nothing like now. He lapsed into what looked like a complete nervous breakdown. Greeley was rushed to the private residence-clinic of Dr. George S. Choate, a specialist in mental illnesses, in Pleasantville, three miles from Chappaqua. There, fluctuating between lucidity and delirium, he died on November 29, 1872, age sixty-one. Five days before, John Bigelow confided to his diary: "I think he has been crazy for years."

Funeral services were held in New York City, at what was the Church of the Divine Paternity at Fifth Avenue and Forty-fourth

Street. The president and the vice-president came from Washington. The chief justice was there, most of the cabinet, two senators, and the governors of three states. Henry Ward Beecher preached and the celebrated soprano Clara Louise Kellogg sang "I Know That My Redeemer Liveth." Crowds lined the processional route as the remains of Horace Greeley were moved to Greenwood Cemetery in Brooklyn. Greeley had preferred burial in Chappaqua—"in my favorite pumpkin arbor, with a gooseberry bush for a footstone." In death, as in politics, he did not get what he wanted.

Nor has posterity been particularly reverent. Walt Kelly, the late cartoonist, featured a character in his "Pogo" comic strip named Horrors Greeley. Horrors was a cow, who sang as she ambled westward:

> Oh, give me a home 'tween Buffalo and Rome,
> Where the beer in the cantaloupe lay—

Horace Greeley was a Universalist . . . and a teetotaler.

If You Travel . . .

. . .by automobile looking for Horace Greeley, follow the Saw Mill River Parkway north from New York City to Chappaqua—or hop a Harlem-Line train out of Grand Central Station. The train takes about an hour and deposits one in the center of Chappaqua, about a ten-minute walk from New Castle Town Hall, where the Greeley exhibit of the Chappaqua Historical Society is located. The exhibit may be viewed Wednesdays from 1:00 P.M. to 4:00 P.M., or by appointment.

In New York City, there is a memorial statue to Horace Greeley in City Hall Plaza, and another in Greeley Square, Thirty-second Street and Broadway. The Greeley grave is at Locust Hill in the Greenwood Cemetery, Brooklyn.

The Greeley birthplace in Amherst, New Hampshire, is in private hands and not open to the viewing public. Near the front entrance, however, is a commemorative granite boulder, with an inscription citing the high points in Greeley's life. It was placed there by the state of New Hampshire. Amherst is about twenty miles from the Massachusetts line, northwest of Nashua.

Chapter
Five

WALT WHITMAN

A Vision of America from "Fish-Shape Paumanok"

It is not easy to catch the pulse-beat of Walt Whitman's America at Walt Whitman's birthplace. Heavy traffic thunders by on an expressway just yards from the house. The landscape is overwhelmed with quick-food restaurants, gas stations, supermarkets, and the infinite variety of stores that keep a consumer society consuming. The caretaker's vegetable garden gives a hint in summer of the farm that once was, but the visitor is jarred back to the late twentieth century by the remaindered yellow school bus, tucked behind the barn, which serves as a toolshed.

The America of Walt Whitman's vision was an idealized place, broad and beautiful, where living was celebrated and where democracy had clean, noble vistas. Whitman's vision also was of himself as the voice of the common man, the seer of democracy. Yet for all his genius, he spoke but for a handful in his lifetime. And, of course, his idealized democratic way got out of control, aesthetically as well as politically. Before he died, Walt Whitman was to sense as much, and to take a strong stand against the gross materialism that gripped the soul and the spirit of burgeoning America. It is safe to say, however, that never in his wildest flights of fancy did Whitman envision the state as it would become. If the antidemocratic political revelations of the 1960s and 1970s did not mock the prophet in him, then assuredly the aesthetics of modern America did.

This is not to suggest that Walt Whitman was wedded to the concept of a simple, rural America, as were some poets of the age. He suffered more than enough setbacks to be cynical and morose. But he wasn't. Whitman loved America. He thrilled to the big city, its flavors and its culture; the newspapers, the theaters, the stimuli of busy streets, people, and pubs. He believed in the ocean-to-ocean destiny of the nation and sang mystical songs of poetry about the

The Walt Whitman birthplace at Huntington, Long Island, is a carefully kept New York State historical landmark. The house is a remarkable example of early American craftsmanship, but the area is twentieth-century America at its busy crassness.

sundry parts of the country, though most he knew only by romantic legend. Whitman wanted America to grow physically and be vigorous democratically, although at the same time he was anxious that its energy be spiritualized—not in a religious sense, for Walt Whitman was not that type of evangelist, but in the sense of a country whose culture is intellectual and whose people are liberated from economic and political repressions and human inhibitions, including the erotic.

His world view was large, but his roots were still deep in the land that Whitmans, going back to a great-grandfather, worked on Long Island. There he would retreat time and again to renew his soul. He wasn't much of a hand around the place; some said Walt Whitman was dreamy and lazy. If by dreamy they meant meditative, then Whitman surely was that. As for being lazy, he has more to show for his life than most Americans before or since. On Long Island he would wander the gentle hills, stretch out on the grass, hike to the shore, which was never far away. Refreshed by seashore and lilac scent—and family, with whom he was ever close—Walt would be ready to challenge the world again.

There would be precious little of the old refreshments for Walt Whitman on Long Island today. He would find the grass in patches, his walks blocked by soft-ice-cream stands and hamburger joints, and the seawater probably polluted. To the extent that Long Island was the inspiration for his poetry, he would have to write a different poem.

Walt Whitman's poem was *Leaves of Grass*, of course. It was a poem that grew and grew with the years and out of the author's gadfly experiences as teacher, reporter, editor, political worker, hospital visitor, friend, and lover of humankind. Whitman, as John Burroughs once remarked, was a law to himself, and so was his poem; still is, for that matter, if one can draw a conclusion from its different meanings for different times. For the nineteenth century, *Leaves of Grass* was the articulation of the philosophy of an expansionist America; young, energetic, bursting of muscle. For the first half of the twentieth century, when the democratic principle was under pressure from Naziism, Fascism, and, later, Communism, *Leaves* became democracy's testament through Whitman's almost encyclopedic formulation of patriotic and democratic slogans. More recently, in a personalist age, *Leaves of Grass* is the expression for the free spirit that resides in the individual and that seeks sensual as well as intellectual expression.

Walt Whitman was born thirty miles out on "fish-shape Paumanok"—the Indian name for Long Island that he preferred—on May 31, 1819. His father was a farmer and a carpenter; his mother, as he tells us in *Starting from Paumanok*, "perfect." The birth site was West Hills, in what is now the town of Huntington; the birthplace, a small, shingled farmhouse that the state of New York maintains as an historic monument. Walt Whitman spent his first four years in this house, then was taken by his parents to Brooklyn, where his father hoped to profit from the building boom in the New York bay areas. He didn't. Life in Brooklyn was a struggle. At least two of the father's houses were mortgaged and lost; the mother was in an almost constant state of childbearing (Walt was but the second of nine children, the oldest and youngest of whom were retarded). Walt carpentered and went to school, but schooling ended some time between his eleventh and thirteenth years, and at thirteen he was a printer's devil in the composing room of the *Long Island Patriot*. It was the beginning of a journeymanship with newspapers and magazines in Brooklyn and New York so bewildering as to have never been fully reconstructed.

Whitman's parents gave up on Brooklyn and returned to farm life. Walt joined them in mid–Long Island in 1836 and over the next five years taught in seven schools in as many towns. Meanwhile he founded and edited the *Long Islander* at Huntington in 1838–39. (Incidentally, no copy of a Whitman-edited issue is known to exist, and the present management of the *Long Islander* is on record as willing to pay $500 for a copy of a paper from the Whitman period.) In 1841, Whitman was back at the west end of Paumanok, contributing to newspapers and magazines in Brooklyn and New York before graduating to the editorship of the *Brooklyn Eagle* in 1846.

The *Eagle* was a Democratic-oriented newspaper, and Whitman wrote strong, party-line, chauvinistic editorials: "Yes: Mexico must be thoroughly chastised! . . . What has she to do with the great mission of peopling the New World with a noble race? Be it ours to achieve that mission!" Young Whitman celebrated "Beautiful Brooklyn, with its saucy-browned Heights"; supported progressive reform; stressed culture and the arts, reviewing some two hundred new books and giving generous space to theater notices. Whitman called the editorship of the *Eagle* his "best sit," but in January of 1848 he was unseated for refusing to accommodate his views to those of the Democratic party on the extension of slavery. His was an act of principle and courage, which helped counterbalance some Whitman family history—his grandfather was a slave-owner. But it was an act which also returned him to "drifter."

Walt Whitman

There was some travel, a short stint with the *New Orleans Crescent*, a return to Brooklyn, and more writing and editing jobs. On the surface this period of his life—which stretched on to seven years—seemed aimless and wasted. However, the great project of his life was being given shape, and in 1855 it sprang forth as *Leaves of Grass*, twelve poems in this original version and a preface stating a theory of poetry for America and democracy which Christopher Morley would one day describe as being as important in American literature as the Gettysburg Address is in American history. In Whitman's words, the poems were saturated "with the vehemence of pride and audacity of freedom necessary to loosen the mind of still-to-be form'd America from the folds, the superstitions, and all the long, tenacious, and stifling anti-democratic authorities of Asiatic and European past." It was a large concept, but one that was hardly overstated.

In *Leaves of Grass*, Whitman took moral, social, political, and patriotic questions, hammered them into unique shapes, and in the process made himself the champion of American intellectual independence. It was years and years, however, before the claim he staked out was to be generally recognized.

Leaves of Grass was not just Whitman's poem, it was his life. There were numerous editions—in 1855, 1856, 1860–1861, 1867, 1871, 1872, 1876, 1881–1882, 1882, 1888, 1891–1892. He was forever arranging and rearranging the work, adding sections, grouping and regrouping the various segments. For the early editions he had been his own printer, for reasons of economy as well as typographical appearance. (As a professional printer, he knew precisely the type and quality of the job he wanted done.) For some editions, he was his own publisher and distributor, though stories are apocryphal that have him scrounging around Camden and Philadelphia hawking *Leaves* from a basket slung over his arm. For some editions, too, he was his own best publicist, writing blurbs and planting glowing self-reviews of the book in journals such as the *Brooklyn Times* for September 29, 1855. Self-reviewing is professionally unorthodox and not a little vain. But then, Whitman was never to be accused of orthodoxy and modesty. Besides, what better way was there to help make a revolutionary book understandable?

Leaves of Grass mystified Whitman's contemporaries on the levels both of form and content. To begin with, the poets readers then knew and admired wrote in regular beats, on predictable themes, with "proper" emotional patterns, and with rhyming lines. But Whitman was no Longfellow or Poe; no Tennyson or Browning. He wrote in an unconventional free verse, using colloquialisms and employing lines of sometimes extravagant length. Even his punctuation defied the usual canons of writing. William Dean Howells, for one, denied that Whitman wrote poetry at all. But beneath the unorthodoxies were cadences and rhythms that were subtle and true, and an artistry that would prove itself permanent. Whitman was breaking with the past and with modes he considered unsuited for the expression of a free and open people. His was, in part, an ideological concept translated to art; the result was an originality of form and expression that one day would make Whitman the great poet of the so-called American ideal.

An even greater challenge to the times was presented, however, in the area of content. Whitman broached themes of egoism and sex with a directness that startled a genteel age. The egoism his contemporaries might have managed, had it stood alone. But the sensuality was something else—and ultimately not even to be separated from the whole because of the autoerotic and erethistic extensions of the poems. If this sensuality had been low and base, his critics might still have coped. But Whitman's songs to himself and to the body electric, his own and others, male and female, took on the quality of hymns. "Offensive" themes were not supposed to achieve such moral and artistic elevation. The reading public was confused, and large amounts of energy were expended denouncing Whitman and suppressing or censoring *Leaves*. Meanwhile, there was the question whether Whitman was homosexual or not. The very possibility that he might have been homosexual presented a major problem to the American social psyche, and over several generations Whitman enthusiasts, in praising his poetry, felt compelled to make their cases for Whitman's so-called normalness, as if the quality of his poetry was necessarily linked to his being heterosexual. Even such an otherwise sophisticated person as Henry Seidel Canby got sucked into the effort, with results that are now as comic as the reasons have ever been irrelevant.

Whitman made things easier for some partisans by boasting to John Addington Symonds in 1890 that he was the father of six illegitimate children. A rake and exploiter of women was so much easier to write about, to defend and promote, than an honest and inoffensive homosexual! Ironically, Whitman's parenthood boast was idle, as indeed certain romantic references in his poems were misleading. The manuscript version of *Once I Pass'd Through a Populous City*, for instance, reveals an attachment with a man, not a woman.

It was not until decades after his death that the question of

Whitman's homosexuality could be frankly discussed and the conclusion accepted that *Leaves of Grass* is no less a classic—and is
probably a more interesting social document—because of Whitman's sexual and psychological constructions. By the same token, it
was not until the 1970s that biographical facts about Whitman's life
could be put before the public at face value and not have to be
prejudiciously shaped in order to fit certain societal preferences.
Accordingly, Peter Doyle, the young streetcar conductor of Whitman's later years, no longer needed to be represented as some
simple, dependent kid who supplied companionship to a lonesome
old man; at last he could be represented, as in a 1976 network
television program and in a *New York Times* story, as "the poet's
lover."

Ordinarily, one would say that the decades-long controversy was
out of place, that a person's sexual orientation is no business of the
public and has no place in its reaction to the individual or his work.
But, of course, that was impossible in Whitman's case. *Leaves of
Grass* was a personal testament, and it continually probed the meaning of sexuality—at times, obliquely; at times, as a theme of its own.
In *Children of Adam*, for instance, the focus was "amativeness," or
heterosexual love; in *Calamus*, it was "adhesiveness," or homosexual love. To have ignored the sex in and of Whitman would have
been to talk of sea water as if it were without salt. The mistake,
rather, was in attempting to make the sex of *Leaves* and Whitman
more than it was—more specifically, other than it was.

Walt Whitman was forty-two when the Civil War broke out, well
above the average age of the Union recruits—but not too old to
enlist, as critics pointed out, particularly after Whitman's insistence
that *Leaves of Grass* have as its nucleus *Drum-Taps* and the Lincoln
poems. How, critics asked, could one given to such lofty patriotic
sentiment not shoulder a rifle himself? It was a tendentious, unfair
question. Whitman was a large and robust man physically; intellectually, the survival of the Union had a near mystical significance for
him. But his temperament was not that of a warrior, and he was
sensible enough to know that there were other, not less important,
means of service than the shooting of a gun. When his brother
George was wounded fighting for the Union, Walt went to Virginia
to care for him and found his own role in the war, one less arduous
and less dangerous only by degree than that of soldier.

In the Quaker tradition that so influenced his boyhood (although he himself was never a Quaker), Walt Whitman became a visitor in the hospital camps of the Washington area, bringing small gifts and his large presence to the thousands of wounded and sick. Walt Whitman read to the hospitalized, penned letters home for them, helped to nurse them, raised funds to purchase their small comforts. He wrote his mother that most days he went to the hospitals—there were as many as sixty of them around Washington—from twelve to four in the afternoon, and again from six to nine in the evening. "Mother," he said, "I have real pride in telling you that I have the consciousness of saving quite a number of lives by saving them from giving up—and being a good deal with them; the men say it is so, and the doctors say it is so—and I will candidly confess I can see it is true, though I say it of myself."

This service was totally of his own devising and on his own initiative. Whitman had no official status, no backing. Yet he became such a familiar and respected figure about the hospital camps that guards saluted when he passed. He paid his way with a small salary earned by copying documents for the Department of the Interior—until 1865, when his superior discovered that this minor clerk was the "notorious" author of *Leaves of Grass* and summarily fired him. Walt went on to a clerkship in the office of the attorney general.

According to Whitman, there were twice as many sick as there were wounded in the military hospitals—men suffering from smallpox, dysentery, and various other forms of contagious disease. Very many would lie around for days unattended, their wounds festering, their diseases becoming more contagious. Whitman moved about these men selflessly, and ultimately to his own physical disabling. His health broke down and a paralysis of his arm and leg in later years was traced by some to debilitations resulting from his war service.

The last years were spent in Camden, New Jersey—at first in rooms of George Whitman's house at 322 Stevens Street; then, after George moved from Camden, in a small house Walt was able to buy for himself at 328 Mickle Street. (That house, incidentally, is now a Whitman museum.) The creative gifts gradually diminished, but Whitman continued to tinker with *Leaves* to the very end. In 1881, the poems were given their final rearrangement, and in 1892, the year of Whitman's death, they got their final text. There were those who felt that *Leaves*, having grown over decades like an ungainly tree, needed some select pruning. Whitman forbade it. After his death, with no one to object, poems of lesser vitality were dropped from various editions in order to strengthen the effect of the whole. However, to understand Whitman fully, to see and appreciate him at full growth, the reader must still go to the unabridged version.

Death took its time claiming Walt Whitman, not that he was particularly old when he died—seventy-three—but that he was decidedly infirm. During the last four years he was by one description only "half-alive," suffering in addition to the paralysis almost constant headaches and abdominal distress. He was not so unwell, however, that he was unable to greet the visitors who, in the recognition at last of his genius, now beat a path to his door from all over the United States and England as well. The reprobate was at last a revered old man, no longer "lusty, brawling," but still "hirsute" and newly lovable . . . and respected as poet.

When death did come, it came quietly toward the close of a soft rainy Saturday afternoon, March 26, 1892. The autopsy revealed extensive tuberculosis and a wide disintegration of vital organs. The magnificent, healthy body that Whitman had celebrated for its sensualness and taken pride in as physical specimen was pitiably wasted.

Walt Whitman died with apologies for taking so long and was buried in Camden's Harleigh Cemetery under a monument of his own planning. Some thought the monument ostentatious and felt that maybe there was a gesture of defiance to the world in its selection. It is very doubtful that that is so, though if anyone was entitled to a defiant gesture in death, it was the author of *Leaves of Grass*.

As for farewell, Whitman set one down years before in the concluding poem of the "Songs of Parting" section of *Leaves*:

> Dear friend whoever you are take this kiss,
> I give it especially to you, do not forget me,
> I feel like one who has done work for the day to retire awhile,
> . . . *So Long!*
> Remember my words, I may again return,
> I love you, I depart from materials. . . .

If You Travel . . .

. . .to the birthplace of "the Good Gray Poet," cross the Whitestone Bridge to Long Island and drive east on either the Long Island Expressway or the Northern State Parkway to State Route 110 in Huntington. Drivers should proceed north on Route 110 to Schwab Road, where they should turn left, then right on Walt Whitman Road. Walt Whitman House is number 246 and is clearly marked. (The house is behind a King Kullen store, which, in turn, is across from a Korvette Shopping Center on Route 110.) The distance from the Whitestone Bridge to the house is thirty miles.

The Walt Whitman birthplace sits on an acre of carefully kept land. The house was built about 1810 by Whitman's father, Walter (Walt's name, too, before he shortened it). The house is firmed up with hand-fashioned beams held together by wooden pegs. The exterior is shingle, and the whole is considered an outstanding example of native American craftsmanship. On the first level are kitchen, parlor, and "borning room," all consistent with the original architecture of the house. Upstairs is considerably revamped and is given over to exhibit rooms and library. The house features some Whitman memorabilia, including a desk from the Woodbury School, where Walt Whitman taught, his mother's slat-back tulip chair, and his father's whiskey jug. Many of the Whitman possessions vanished as the family moved among West Hills (Huntington), Brooklyn, and Camden, so that most of the furnishings in the house now are of the period rather than of the family.

Walt Whitman House was almost demolished after World War II for a road-widening project, but was saved by public reaction to the proposal. In 1949, the Walt Whitman Birthplace Association came into being, and it acquired the house for the specific purpose of preserving it as a literary shrine. In 1957, the property was turned over to the state of New York, which maintains it as an historic site. The Association's interest continues in the house, however. It promotes study and attention to Whitman's life and work, and has assembled in the upstairs library a collection of several hundred volumes, monographs, and catalogues dealing with Whitman. The Association also mounts exhibits and sponsors publications and lectures.

Walt Whitman House is open from 10:00 A.M. to 4:00 P.M. Wednesday through Sunday, the year round. Monday and Tuesday it is closed, as well as Christmas, New Year's, and other "special days." Library hours are from 1:00 to 4:00 P.M., Wednesday through Sunday. There is no admission charge.

An average of 10,000 visitors come to the birthplace each year, many of them school groups. The house is small and can accommodate but limited numbers at one time. Large contingents of visitors are advised, therefore, to make arrangements beforehand (516-HA7-5240). There is ample off-street parking. Food, beverages, and other accommodations are available nearby.

Chapter Six

When You're in the Vicinity of . . .

THE BRONX, New York

Edgar Allan Poe

In the busy, bustling Bronx, on the Grand Concourse at Kingsbridge Road, is a small frame cottage, a reminder of the time when the Bronx was country and people gravitated here from Manhattan for clean air and more spacious living. One such person was Edgar Allan Poe. He came to the Fordham area of the Bronx from Greenwich Village in 1846, with a wife suffering from tuberculosis and with a mother-in-law, and took over the cottage and an acre of land for a yearly rental of $100. His wife—the cousin, Virginia Clemm, whom he married when she was thirteen—did not recover, dying in the first-floor bedroom and plunging Poe into a long siege of melancholy.

For three years Edgar Allan Poe lived in this cottage in the Bronx, and though Virginia's illness was said to have diminished his will to work, Poe nevertheless managed to write "Annabel Lee," "Ulalume," "The Bells," and "Eureka" while here. Fordham University, then known as St. John's College, was nearby, and Poe enjoyed wandering about the campus and mingling with the Jesuit fathers. To him the Jesuits "were highly cultivated gentleman and scholars, [who] smoked, drank, and played cards like gentlemen, and never said a word about religion."

In Poe's time, there was a view from the cottage of the Hudson River. Poe was happy here. "It was the sweetest little cottage imaginable," Maria Clemm, the mother-in-law, was to recall later. "Oh how supremely happy we were in our dear cottage home! We three lived only for each other. Eddie rarely left his beautiful home. I attended to his literary business; for he, poor fellow, knew nothing about money transactions."

In the fall of 1849, Edgar Allan Poe left on a trip to Richmond and never made it back to the Bronx. He was found dead in Baltimore on

Edgar Allan Poe moved from Greenwich Village to the Bronx for clean air and more spacious living. The cottage remains, in a small park off the Grand Concourse and nearby Fordham University — then St. John's College. Virginia Clemm, Poe's cousin, whom he married at 13, died here.

October 7, 1849, the victim of acute alcoholism. One theory has it that en route home, he fell into the hands of election thugs, who kept him plied with liquor in order to use him as a voting repeater. It was a not uncommon fate of derelicts of the day to be kept drunk by unscrupulous ward heelers and dragged from poll to poll to cast another vote. Poe was buried in Westminster churchyard in Baltimore. Mrs. Clemm stayed on briefly at the cottage, then went back south.

The Poe cottage has had a precarious existence, several times nearly succumbing to demolitioners and to vandals. New York City acquired the cottage in 1912 and moved it the following year from a wedged site between two large houses to a new park across the street named for Poe. There the house was restored by the Bronx Society of Arts and Sciences. Still, the cottage's future was anything but secure. As late as 1974, there was no permanent custodian of the cottage, and the cottage was a regular target for vandals and looters. A number of Poe mementoes had been moved into the cottage, and some began to disappear, including an unsigned nineteenth-century portrait of Poe and a black carved figure of a raven, the bird of Poe's famous poem, "The Raven." In 1975, the Bronx County Historical Society took over maintenance and administration of the cottage, and matters have improved. There is a permanent custodian now for the cottage, and there are guides to conduct tours.

The visitor is shown through the downstairs rooms of the cottage: kitchen, sitting room, and bedroom, where Virginia died. There is a two-room attic, where Poe did his writing, but it is closed to visitors because of the sharp pitch of the stairs. The cottage has several original pieces from the Poe occupancy, such as the hutch in the kitchen, a rocker, and Virginia's deathbed, including its straw mattress and down pillow. Among other items in the cottage is Edward G. Quinn's bronze bust of the poet, short-story writer, and essayist.

Poe cottage is open Saturdays from 10:00 A.M. to 4:00 P.M.; Sundays from 11:00 A.M. to 5:00 P.M.; weekdays, by appointment (212-881-8900). There is a modest admission fee. School groups enter free. About one hundred people visit Poe cottage on the average weekend. In addition to seeing, they hear a tape of Malachy McCourt reading Poe's poems.

By automobile, one may reach the cottage via the Major Deegan Expressway, east to Fordham Road, north on Kingsbridge; or, the

Bronx River Parkway to Fordham Road, then north on East Kings-bridge Road. By subway from Manhattan, one would take the Sixth Avenue D Express to Kingsbridge Road; or, the Lexington Avenue No. 4 Woodlawn-Jerome Express to Kingsbridge Road. The cottage is above the subway stop.

A number of public transportation buses run by or near Poe cottage, including Bx 1 and Bx 2.

ROSLYN, Long Island

Christopher Morley

It is recorded that Christopher Morley regarded himself primarily as a poet who was overpraised in his early career and underpraised in his maturity. True, his career did take a curious turn downward. But it is also true that Christopher Morley was more than a poet. In fact, he left behind more than fifty books, including novels, essays, and fantasies. He was, in a word, an all-around man of letters—indeed, one of the most famous of his day. Today, alas, he is remembered mostly for *Kitty Foyle* (1939), a book which a *New York Times* reviewer recently alluded to as a potboiler, but which is nevertheless an accurate depiction of the then-modern, self-sufficient working girl. Other Morley books include *Parnassus on Wheels* (1917) and *Thunder on the Left* (1925). He was also the editor of the revised edition of *Bartlett's Familiar Quotations* (1937).

Christopher Morley (1890–1957) was a native of Haverford, Pennsylvania, a Rhodes scholar as a young man, and a writer with a gift for whimsical urbanity; he was right at home in New York. He did his writing in an office, which he called his "Kennel," on Nassau Street, in the heart of the city's financial district, and the exact location of which he kept a guarded secret from all but a few close friends. Later his favorite writing place was "The Knothole" in Roslyn. It was a small building crammed with books, with room for little more than his writing table, some bunk beds, and a Dymaxion bathroom that Buckminster Fuller and the Phelps Dodge Corporation had introduced to the world with such fanfare. (It consisted of four basic sections designed to be dye-stamped out of sheet metal. Tub-shower and lavatory-toilet occupied a floor space of five square feet, cost about $300 to manufacture, and weighed only 420 pounds—about the weight of one standard bathtub. Christopher Morley bought two of them; Buckminster Fuller, after all, was a close friend. The Dymaxion bathroom was supposed to revolutionize the business—or should the word be trade? It never did.)

"The Knothole" is situated in Roslyn's Morley Park and is maintained as a literary visiting place by the Department of Recreation and Parks of Nassau County. Roslyn is on Long Island, about twenty-four miles from mid-Manhattan. Morley Park is a half-mile north of the Long Island Expressway, at the Searington Road exit. "The Knothole" is open from mid-April to mid-October, on Thursdays, Fridays, Saturdays, and Sundays. Hours are from 1:00 to 5:00 P.M. There is no admission charge.

WEST PARK, New York

John Burroughs

John Burroughs (1837–1921) lived quietly and wrote prolifically. He turned out thirty-one books, most of them dealing with nature and some sometimes achieving what one evaluator—Norman Foerster in the *Dictionary of American Biography*—calls "an accuracy of observation superior to that of Thoreau." Unlike Thoreau, Burroughs does not loom giantly in American literature. But he was important in his day, and, as Foerster notes, he was instrumental in establishing the nature essay as literary genre. During the last twenty-five years of his life, he wrote in a cabin called Slabsides that he built in 1895 in the hills of West Park, about a mile from his home near Esopus. Here he could study nature almost in nature's very womb, and here he could entertain friends and fellow nature-lovers. Theodore Roosevelt came to visit. So did John Muir and Walt Whitman.

Burroughs had been a friend of Whitman from their time together in Washington. Burroughs worked for the currency bureau of the treasury department; Whitman was engaged in his voluntary service in the military hospitals among the wounded and sick of the Civil War. Burroughs occasionally accompanied Whitman on his rounds, believed in Whitman as a poet, and wrote his first book about him—*Notes on Walt Whitman as Poet and Person* (1867). The book is of interest today, but probably less for Burroughs's authorship than his admission in 1920 that "half the book" was Whitman's. In 1896, Burroughs updated his appreciation, issuing *Whitman, A Study*. It is a book that confirms his prescience with respect to Whitman's worth and that is a useful reference tool still for students and scholars.

Twice a year—on the third Saturday in May and the first Saturday in October—open house is held at Slabsides, with a program of talks at 11:00 A.M. and nature walks, with leaders, in the early afternoon through the 175-acre John Burroughs Sanctuary. For clubs and student groups, the cabin is open at other times by arrangement with the caretaker, Mrs. Elizabeth Burroughs Kelley of West Park, New York, 12493. Mrs. Kelley is the granddaughter of John Burroughs and herself the author of a Burroughs biography, *John Burroughs: Naturalist: The Story of His Work and His Family by His Granddaughter* (New York, 1959).

The John Burroughs Sanctuary is open to visitors at other times of the year, but the John Burroughs Memorial Association insists that nothing be removed or disturbed, and that there be no hunting, fishing, smoking, or fires. "The sanctuary is to be enjoyed for nature study in the spirit of John Burroughs," says the Slabsides Committee.

West Park, New York, is eighty miles from New York City. It rests in the Hudson River Valley and the lower pastoral regions of the Catskills that Burroughs loved so much. From New York City, drivers should take the New York State Throughway (Interstate 87) north to Exit 18, or U.S. Route 9W north. Slabsides, a national historical landmark, is one mile west off Route 9W.

John Burroughs is buried five miles to the west at Roxbury, New York. Take State Route 28 west from Exit 19 of the Throughway (87) and connect with State Route 30 north into Roxbury.

Burroughs stated in his will: "It is my wish to be buried upon the old farm where I was born, at Roxbury, in the county of Delaware, and I hereby direct that my body be buried beside the rock on the hill above Woodchuck Lodge." Grave and rock are now a New York State historic site. A bronze plaque depicts Burroughs and recalls lines from his poem "Waiting":

> I stand amid eternal ways:
> And what is mine shall know my face.

Woodchuck Lodge, where Burroughs did some of his finest writing, is open only on special occasions. The lodge is a National Historic Landmark, but it receives no federal nor state aid, and no systematic maintenance and preservation work has been done on it for some years. The John Burroughs Memorial Association *Bulletin* appealed to its membership in 1976 for contributions for the preservation of Woodchuck Lodge. Inquiries about helping, membership, and other matters may be had by writing the John Burroughs Memorial Association, c/o American Museum of Natural History, Central Park West at Seventy-ninth Street, New York City, New York, 10024.

EAST AURORA, New York

Elbert Hubbard

Elbert Hubbard (1856–1915) does not rate as a literary figure in the strict understanding of the term. He was a social visionary of sorts who dreamed of a community, or association, in which young people could make articles of worth in an atmosphere of learning. Thus he established in East Aurora, New York, the Roycroft Shops, so named for a seventeenth-century English printer, and from there he turned out fine books as well as copper and leather articles and furniture.

Understandably, the emphasis was strongly on the printing crafts. Hubbard was a writer, and he founded and edited a monthly magazine called *The Philistine*. In the March, 1899, issue of that journal, he scored the great success of his career as writer, lecturer, entrepreneur. This was his inspirational essay based on an incident in the Spanish-American War involving Garcia Iniguez, the Cuban lawyer, soldier, and revolutionist who was a leader in the Cuban fight for independence from Spain. The essay was intended as a lesson in duty and efficiency, and the New York Central Railroad thought enough of it to have it reprinted in pamphlet form for the reading racks of its passenger trains. Suddenly, Elbert Hubbard was propelled to fame. Over the years, more than eighty million copies of the essay were printed in eleven languages. For decades there was hardly a child who went through grade or high school in this country without having read Hubbard's essay. Its name? "A Message to Garcia."

Elbert Hubbard did more writing—in a second Roycroft journal called *The Fra*, and in chapbooks issued also from his presses under the title, *Little Journeys*. These were monthly sketches, chiefly biographical, informational, and again inspirational, built about visits "to the homes of the great"—and the near-great. All told there were 170 sketches, and ultimately they filled fourteen volumes. Hubbard's style was popular, and he was ever on the watch to spin some of his own homely, common-sense philosophy.

Elbert Hubbard died tragically, going down on the S.S. *Lusitania* on May 7, 1915, en route home to report from the battlefields of World War I. His son, Elbert Hubbard II, continued the Roycroft activities until they outlived their times. In 1938, the operation shut down, the victim of the Depression.

In East Aurora is the Elbert Hubbard Library-Museum, featuring books, bound holographs, and other items related to Hubbard and the Roycroft Shops. Owned by the village of East Aurora and staffed by members of the Aurora Historical Society, the library-museum is located in the Village Hall, corner of Main and Paine Streets. It is open from June 1 to November 1, Wednesdays, Saturdays, and Sundays, from 2:30 to 4:30 P.M.—other times by appointment.

East Aurora is a suburb of Buffalo, in the so-called Niagara Frontier area of New York State. Buffalo is 438 miles from New York City.

Robert G. Ingersoll

Robert G. Ingersoll (1833–1899) was one of the most controversial men of his time. He was a well-known trial lawyer; a spellbinding political lecturer who helped elect three Republican presidents; and a militant agnostic who took to the platform to rescue the reputation of the Deity from "the aspersions of the pulpit." Ingersoll served as attorney general of Illinois, and it is speculated that he might have become governor of the state but for his agnosticism. He was an earnest, humane man, but to millions he was a "notorious infidel" because of public lectures attacking the Bible and a variety of Christian views. People flocked to hear him, nonetheless, and, according to one lecture-manager, he was the "best card" in America.

Ingersoll was born in Dresden, New York; lived in Wisconsin and Illinois; practiced law for a time in Washington, D.C.; and died in Dobbs Ferry, New York. His major lectures and speeches were published under the titles, *The Gods and Other Lectures* (1876), *Some Mistakes of Moses* (1879), and *Great Speeches* (1887). The lectures of his that attracted particular attention were "The Bible," "Ghosts," and "Foundations of Faith." The year after his death, his complete works were published in twelve volumes and were reprinted in 1902, 1909, and 1910.

At the junction of state routes 14 and 54 in Dresden is the Ingersoll birthplace. For a number of years the birthplace was a public visiting place, featuring oil paintings, photographs, letters, and manuscripts of the famous orator and agnostic. In 1975, the then-owner of the property—the Illinois Historical Society—sold the house to Timothy D. Potter of Brooklyn, a private party with an interest in historical properties. Mr. Potter has returned the Ingeroll house to private residence. Some time in the future, after restorations, he expects to open the house again to the public, although the emphasis then may be more on the eighteenth-century architecture of the structure than on the Ingersoll association. If he wishes to accent the Ingersoll association, however, he has a strong starting point with books and an upright square piano left behind by the Illinois

Historical Society.

The village of Dresden is on Seneca Lake, south of Geneva, in the Finger Lakes district of the state of New York. The nearest sizable community to Dresden is Penn Yan.

Robert Ingersoll is buried in the same Sleepy Hollow Cemetery in the Hudson River Valley town of Tarrytown where Washington Irving and other notables rest.

PART TWO

NEW ENGLAND

Chapter
Seven

BRONSON ALCOTT AND FRUITLANDS

Mirror on a Divine Insanity

Visiting Fruitlands in the town of Harvard, Massachusetts, is like stumbling into a penny-candy store as a child with a fat buffalo nickel and an extra sweet tooth. There's so much to choose from, you hardly know where to start.

There's an American Indian museum, crammed with Indian artifacts and animated by dioramas of New England Indian life, such as the "redemption" of Mary Rowlandson from the Wampanoag sachem Metacomet (King Philip) at nearby Princeton in 1676. Flanking the museum, like lost warriors from the past, are life-size bronzes by Philip S. Sears of Pumunangwet ("He Who Shoots the Stars") and Wo Peen ("The Dreamer").

There's a 1790 Shaker house, removed to Fruitlands from the old Shaker village near Harvard Center, beautifully preserved and forming the setting for products of Shaker handicrafts and community industries. Outside is the mounting stand from which celibate Shaker women could step into the high-slung Shaker carriages without being helped aboard by any overly chivalrous Shaker male hands.

There's also an art museum featuring landscapes from the Hudson River School and primitives by early American itinerant artists, some of whom, like Chester Harding and Francis Alexander, brushed their names into history as portrait painters.

But the prize of all—like that extra-long licorice stick tucked way to the back of the penny-candy display case—is the 1740 ochre red farmhouse at the end of the Fruitlands lane. It's square and plain and typical of the period: four rooms down, four up, sleeping space in the attic, with a first-floor ell added later. Yet this is no ordinary Massachusetts farmhouse.

Here in 1843–44 Bronson Alcott and Charles Lane conducted their

Bronson Alcott and his small band of Transcendentalists lasted only seven months on the communal farm in Harvard, Mass., that they called Fruitlands. But Fruitlands survives as the purest — if most foolhardy — application of New England's Transcendentalism.

experiment in communal living that rivaled the more famous Brook Farm and which was envisioned as the purest application of New England transcendentalism and, by extension, of the philosophical school that fixed its center in the Concord of Ralph Waldo Emerson. New England transcendentalism claimed Emerson, however tenuously, and a long list of the day's worthies, including Henry David Thoreau, William Ellery Channing, Margaret Fuller, and Orestes Brownson.

Fruitlands never became the New Eden envisioned by Alcott, its intellectual theoretician, or by Lane, its primary funder. It lived through a fitful summer and fall in 1843, and died, after barely seven months of existence, in the cold January snows of 1844. Nevertheless, Fruitlands stands as a memorial to some of the most interesting people of the age and to the dream-turned-delusion that the perfect society could be formed in America from some model of correct social, intellectual, and religious theory.

The American countryside was liberally dotted in the early decades of the 1800s with searchers for Utopia—from Harvard in Massachusetts, to Oneida in New York, to New Harmony in Indiana, and beyond. All had their magic formula. At Fruitlands it was to construct a social order in which neither man nor beast would be exploited and where mind and soul would soar to new heights under a regimen of work, study, meditation, diet, and, alas, cold baths (hydropathy being an "in" science at the time). Fruitlands' failure was spectacular. There wasn't a solid ounce of business sense in the whole community. There were rifts. Lane came to regard Alcott as "despotic"; Alcott looked on Lane as extremist for urging on him both celibacy and the dissolution of his family. (Alcott loved his wife and his four "little women" too much for that. Louisa May was a special favorite. "Duty's faithful child," Alcott called her, and such she always was, whether as a tot at Fruitlands or as the eminent author of *Little Women* and other books.)

Failure though it was, Fruitlands has a place in history as the reflection of a philosophy that helped shape the New England conscience, and of a movement that infused American literature of the period with its unique moral tone. Fruitlands, as an experiment, was not as important as the longer lived (1841–46) transcendental community at Brook Farm in West Roxbury, Massachusetts. Brook Farm, however, has long since been lost to urbanization. Fruitlands, in the folds of the still magnificent Nashua Valley and protected by distance from Boston sprawl, survived as a physical property to become the spiritual reminder of what New England transcendentalism was all about.

Transcendentalism took its name from the *Critique of Pure Reason*, Immanuel Kant's 1781 treatise in which he used the term "transcendental" to refer to ideas received by intuition rather than through the experience of the senses. The transcendental principle crossed to England, where it was popularized by Coleridge, Wordsworth, and Carlyle, and took root in New England through Unitarianism, which was then making its break with Puritan formalisms. The transcendental notion of a God immanent in nature and the individual soul had an instant appeal to Unitarian intellectuals suddenly in revolt against the old concepts of a wrathful God and a depraved human nature.

New England style transcendentalism, as much literary as it was philosophical, dates from an 1833 essay on the thought of Coleridge by Frederick Henry Hedge, the philosophical theologian, in *The Christian Examiner*. In 1836 the Transcendental Club was established in Boston, and around it and its thought grouped the northeast's intellectual élite: Emerson, Thoreau, and Alcott (who had an international reputation as an educator before going to Fruitlands); Dr. Channing, Theodore Parker, and James Freeman Clarke, luminaries of Harvard College; Margaret Fuller, noted feminist and editor, with Emerson, of *The Dial*, transcendentalism's famed quarterly; Sophia Peabody, who was to become Nathaniel Hawthorne's wife in 1842; Hawthorne (until his "deconversion"); Charles Dana, subsequently editor of the *New York Sun*; Parker Pillsbury, the abolitionist; George Bancroft, historian; Isaac Hecker, future Catholic and founder of the Paulist Fathers.

There were more disciples of the movement, but also some skeptics. Fenimore Cooper sounded warnings from Cooperstown, New York, against transcendentalism's excesses, and Herman Melville placed in Captain Ahab's mouth a distinct distaste for the transcendental philosophy. The movement had run its course by mid-century, but as late as 1886 Henry James was zeroing in on it in *The Bostonians*, a detail that prompted one writer to speak of "the durability of transcendentalism as an object of ridicule."

What was it, this transcendentalism?

Basically, New England transcendentalists asserted the immanence of divinity in man and in nature. Definitions were strategically left vague, so that each adherent was free to add to the general philosophy something of the intellectual tradition he or she found most congenial. Thoreau exalted nature; Emerson espoused the natural adequacy of man; Parker embraced social reform, particularly abolitionism. With such openendedness, New England transcendentalism became an amalgam of German philosophy, French sociology, literary outreach, and social reaction against slavery, the mercantile civilization, and other institutions of the times. Its doctrines included self-reliance, individualism, self-culture, absolute optimism, a disregard of external authority, and an indifference to tradition. *The Dial*, which was published from 1840 to 1844, was the movement's chief literary manifestation. Brook Farm and Fruitlands were the testing places of sociological and economic theory.

Brook Farm attracted the larger numbers and, in some respects, the larger names (Hawthorne, Dana, Peabody, Hecker, etc.). Fruitlands had only a dozen pair of hands, but no one in the group doubted for a minute that it would be the New Eden, where the so-called Con-Sociate Family would mesh and live the holier life. By Alcott's plan, the Fruitlands community would "live independently of foreign aids by being sufficiently elevated to procure all articles for subsistence in the productions of the spot, under a regimen of healthful labor and recreation; with benignity toward all creatures, human and inferior; with beauty and refinement in all economics; and the purest charity throughout our demeanor."

Toward this end Alcott and Lane located a promising farm and moved into it a library said at the time to be the richest collection of mystical texts existing anywhere in America. As it turned out, they would have been better off with items on the art of agriculture. The library numbered 1,000 volumes and covered 100 feet of shelving. Books would elevate the mind. The body, meanwhile, would be brought under "utter subjection" to the soul by sacrifices and strict rule. Thus there would be no eating of fish, flesh, fowl, butter, eggs, milk, or cheese. These were unhealthy for the body and, since "exploitive" of animals, for the spirit as well. Anne Page, Mrs. Alcott's helper, was summarily banished from Fruitlands for harboring cheese in her trunk and eating fish at a neighbor's table. Leather and wool were obtained by depriving animals of their covering, so the community would dress in linens and search for leather substitutes for shoes, belts, and the like. Molasses and rice were eschewed as "foreign luxuries," cotton as the product of Southern slavery, tea and coffee as corrupting stimulants.

The chosen of Bronson Alcott's New Eden would subsist on native grains, fruits, herbs, and roots. The sole beverage would be spring water. There would be daily cold baths; "deep-searching conversation giv[ing] rest to the body and development to the mind"; occupation according to the season and weather; and after evening meal, assembly "in social communion, prolonged generally until sunset, when we resort to sweet repose for the next day's activity."

It was all very beautiful, and all very impossible. There were, to begin with, not nearly enough hands to work Fruitlands' ninety acres, so a quick compromise was made under the influence of "blistered hands and aching backs" to employ animals to ready the land. An ox and cow team was brought in from No Town, outside Fitchburg, Massachusetts, for the job. There also was some compromise as to crops. Originally preferences were to grow "aspiring vegetables," those that grew upwards, and spurn degraded varieties that "burrow into the earth." Yet potatoes were planted in two acres, and a supply of turnips and carrots was put in. There were few other concessions, however. The community, for instance, held fast against manures, on the theory that Mother Nature knew what was best and would generously supply their needs. She didn't, although no one could blame her entirely for the sorry yield. The Fruitlands community planted late in the season and recklessly, even sowing one field twice with different grains—a singular feat.

Still, there was early promise. Emerson dropped by on July 4, 1843, after a temperance-meeting lecture in the town of Harvard, and was impressed, however guardedly. "I will not prejudge them successful," he wrote in his journal for July 8. "They look well in July. We will see them in December. I know they are better for themselves than as partners." If Emerson was suggesting that the

Fruitlands people were too cerebral for so physical an undertaking, he was accurate. The crops grew among weeds, and then in the fall, about the time the fruits and vegetables were ripe for harvesting and the grain ready to house, the men, heeding "some call of the Oversoul," wandered off on a visitation to Brook Farm and the near-transcendental communities at Hopedale and Northampton. Alcott had hoped to pick up a convert or two on the trip. In fact, he picked up nothing but grief. Early frosts socked Fruitlands, and little of the crops was saved beyond what Mrs. Alcott, Lane's son, William, 10, and the older Alcott girls, Anna, 13, Louisa, 12, and Elizabeth, 7, could drag to cover in clothes baskets and linen sheets. (Abba May was still a toddler.) That apparently wasn't a whole lot, as the community was speedily reduced to a diet of barley.

The harvest debacle was the end for Fruitlands. Lane threw up his hands and on January 8 went off with William to the Shaker community at Shirley, "where," Louisa confided in *Transcendental Wild Oats*, her fictionalized account of the Fruitlands experience, "he soon found that the order of things was reversed, and it was all work and no play." The others went in as many directions, and Alcott took to his bed in despair. For days and nights "neither food nor water passed his lips," and for a time "there seemed no passage through" Alcott's deep waters. "But," records Louisa, "the strong angels who sustain and teach perplexed and troubled souls came and went, leaving no trace without, but working miracles within."

In mid-January neighbors rescued the Alcotts, now alone at Fruitlands, from hunger and the winter colds, and took them into their house. A short time later the Alcotts were moved to Concord by Emerson, where they lived for years—often on Emerson's bounty. In 1859 Alcott became superintendent of schools in Concord, but the family's financial strains were not fully relieved until Louisa published *Little Women* in 1868. The book made Louisa famous and the Alcotts affluent. Louisa never married—in fact, seems never to have had a beau. "Duty's faithful child" looked after the family and eventually purchased a house in Boston's Louisburg Square, into which they all moved. It was there that Bronson Alcott died in 1888, an old man of eighty-nine.

Lane, meanwhile, was back in his native England, writing letters seeking to recoup something from his Fruitlands investment. Lane had put up money for the library and the $1,800 that bought Fruit-lands. (The owners had wanted $2,700 for land, house, and barn, but settled for the lower figure.) Joseph Palmer, a Fruitlands resident, took over the property after the collapse of the experiment, but Lane seems not to have recovered much of his investment beyond proceeds from sale of the library. Emerson bought some of the books, and these are preserved at the Houghton Library at Harvard University. Thoreau took the rest of the library to New York and sold it there for Lane's benefit.

Much has been written about Fruitlands and the transcendentalist experiment in the Con-Sociate Family. But the full story has never been told, and perhaps never will be. The Alcotts were assiduous diarists, but Bronson Alcott, in abiding disappointment over his failure, destroyed his journal covering the period. He also tore numerous pages from Anna's diary telling of the last painful months. (The presumption is that it was the father who did the censoring of the daughter's diary; his handwriting on surviving pages indicates that he had access to the diary.) Louisa's diary disappeared, but eight pages turned up recently behind a partition in a house in Walpole, Massachusetts, where the Alcotts once lived, sparking hopes that the complete diary may yet be recovered. It would be a fuller account, it is believed, than the one in *Transcendental Wild Oats*.

Meanwhile, the story stands where it is. The failure of Fruitlands preceded by two years the failure of Brook Farm. And the failure of both foreshadowed the eclipse of transcendentalism as philosophical and social alchemy. Fruitlands, however, survived physically, and after seven decades became a monument to an idea (however kooky) and a shrine to what Longfellow once sweepingly termed the "divine insanity of noble minds."

Thoreau's desk is at the Fruitlands farmhouse, as is a fistful of his pencils and an assortment of rocks and Indian relics that he picked up on his walks. His "parson-style" bookcases, made of driftwood, are also at Fruitlands. And Hawthorne's solid, upright bookcase. Likewise there are scores of manuscripts—by Alcott, Lane, Thoreau, Emerson, Fuller, and Hawthorne. There, too, is Louisa's pouring jug from her days as a nurse at the Union hospital at Georgetown during the Civil War and sketches and paintings by

Abba Alcott, who as an adult dropped her first name in favor of her middle name of May, her mother's maiden name, which she shared with her sister Louisa. May specialized as a copyist of Turner and was good enough to win the praise of art critic John Ruskin.

Credit for preserving Fruitlands goes first to Clara Endicott Sears, author and transcendental enthusiast. She took it over, derelict and crumbling, in 1914 and began the work of restoration. In 1949 she signed on as director William Henry Harrison, whose family tree includes a signer of the Declaration of Independence and two U. S. presidents (it is impossible to elude history on any level at Fruitlands). Miss Sears died in 1960, at the age of ninety-seven. Harrison now directs Fruitlands under a board of trustees headed by Judge Bailey Aldrich of Boston, and runs it in a way so that Fruitlands retains an almost transcendental solemnity. It is a solemnity that respects the wishes of Fruitlands' late benefactor. "There are public places given over to recreation," Miss Sears once wrote. "This place [Fruitlands] is not meant for recreation. It is meant for inspiration." Bronson Alcott could have written the same no-nonsense words—and maybe did.

If You Travel . . .

. . .on a pilgrimage to Fruitlands, follow State Route 110 north seventeen miles from Worcester, or State Route 2 north thirty-four miles from Boston, and you will arrive in the town of Harvard. Fruitlands is on Prospect Hill Road, due west of the center of town. There is a modest admission fee, which covers entrance to all Fruitlands' facilities. Fruitlands is open daily, except Mondays, from May 30 to September 30. (If a holiday falls on a Monday, Fruitlands stays open.) The hours are 1:00 to 5:00 P.M. Students and researchers may visit at any time during the year by making arrangements with the director.

Chapter Eight

RALPH WALDO EMERSON

Squire of Concord,
Sage of New England Transcendentalism

Of Concord's large and colorful nineteenth-century literary family—Nathaniel Hawthorne, Bronson Alcott, Louisa May Alcott, Henry David Thoreau, among others—Ralph Waldo Emerson stands foremost. He was the most purely intellectual of the group, a guru of sorts for many in and beyond Concord, and the ranking divine of American transcendentalism, though he eschewed the transcendentalist label for himself. Emerson meditated on Plato; expounded on self-reliance, friendship, behavior, nature; and as a once-upon-a-time clergyman managed to rattle religious orthodoxies as no American had before him. Withal, he was warm and approachable, and as comfortable talking about the fruit trees of his orchard and the hay of his fields as on any of the lofty philosophical thoughts that crowded his busy mind. He was a philosopher, but not in the systematic sense; he dealt rather in perceptions, and with a disarmingly simple observation could elucidate profound theory. He was also lecturer and poet, and many of his metered lines and platform epigrams slip yet into the speech of those who use the English language with wit and grace.

> By the rude bridge that arched the flood,
> Their flag to April's breeze unfurled,
> Here once the embattled farmers stood,
> And fired the shot heard round the world.
> "Concord Hymn: Sung at the Completion
> of the Battle Monument"

99

So nigh is grandeur to our dust,
So near is God to man,
When Duty whispers low, Thou must,
The youth replies, I can!

"Voluntaries"

This patriotic poetry—the first recalling the Revolutionary War; the second reflecting Civil War sentiments—is Ralph Waldo Emerson's. So are these epigrams:

The only reward of virtue is virtue; the only way to have a friend is to be one.——"Friendship."
Every hero becomes a bore at last.——Representative Men; "Uses of Great Men."
The hearing ear is always close to the speaking tongue.——English Traits; "Race."
Hitch your wagon to a star.——"Civilization."
Can anybody remember when the times were not hard and money not scarce?——"Works and Days."
Finally, and prophetically, from "Self-Reliance": *To be great is to be misunderstood.*

No short sentence sums up a complex man more perfectly than the last epigram. Emerson was a gentle soul and never argumentative. Yet, as a fiercely independent thinker, he could excite passions as a demagogue might. Except Emerson was no demagogue either. He spoke modestly, almost as if to himself. The world heard, and many of his associates were exasperated. But if they were not won over eventually by his logic, they were by his lovableness. He was a good man, Emerson was—and he was one of the most significant liberalizing personalities of the nineteenth century.

Misunderstanding of this great man began at home. His family loved him dearly, but there were ambiguous moments. Mrs. Emerson, for instance, did not share his theology, and she and the Emerson children—notably Ellen, who taught in the Unitarian Sunday school—were pillars of the church; Emerson not only gave up the ministry but church-going as well. (He was a respecter of conventions, however, and would remain out of sight until worshiping Concord was securely in the pews. Then he would set off, as with

Ralph Waldo Emerson purchased this house in Concord for $3,500 in 1835, and almost lost it in 1872 when a maid prying about the attic in an early morning hour set the place ablaze with her lantern. "Daring boys" darting in and out of the house with baskets and blankets saved most of Emerson's books and manuscripts. Emerson went abroad while the house was restored.

Nathaniel Hawthorne and George S. Hillard, on a brisk walk to Walden Pond or some other destination.) Wife and children could live resignedly with Emerson's nonconformism, but not Aunt Mary Moody Emerson, the intellectual mentor of Emerson's formative years. She was convinced that her nephew had slipped into atheism—Emerson was a deist, actually—and she once regretted that he "had not gone to the tomb amidst his early honors." Even Harvard found Emerson's theology unpalatable and drew the hard line after Emerson's shattering Divinity School address of 1838 attacking the pretensions of theological orthodoxy. The Harvard breach took years to heal—almost thirty, as a matter of fact—but when it was healed, it was with magnanimity. Harvard awarded Emerson an honorary doctor-of-laws degree in 1866 and a year later elected him an overseer of the university. Emerson, for his part, joined the faculty as a lecturer.

Similarly, there were misunderstandings involving close friendships. For long months Emerson extended bed and board to Thoreau "for whatever labor he chooses to do." He even provided the land at Walden Pond, a mile and a half south of the village, for Thoreau's little cabin. But Emerson never went to jail for principle, as did Thoreau. He was as mystified by Thoreau's unwillingness to pay his poll tax as he was by Thoreau's disinclination to put his Harvard education to more practical uses. He made no secret of the point to Thoreau. How could men so close be in fact so different with respect to an act of civil disobedience against war and over the application of one's life?

The answer, quite simply, was in their respective styles, not in the greater sensitivity or superior witness of one over the other. Emerson invariably sensed where evil resided and justice belonged; he differed, at least for the moment, on means of expression. Civil disobedience was fine for Thoreau. Emerson found it mean and skulking, and preferred the lecture platform or the written word, where feelings could be given an intellectual dimension. For some, this option to intellectualize might have been a convenient way of remaining above the heat and smoke of battle. But not where Emerson was concerned. He lived by the lecture platform, not by the royalties of his writings, which were forever meager (at the peak of his career, book royalties ran to no more than $600 a year). Accordingly, he had to carry body as well as thoughts constantly before audiences that were not always friendly. He preferred to shun political topics and political meetings, but not at the sacrifice of principle. Emerson went before an audience at an antislavery meeting in Boston's Tremont Temple on January 24, 1861—and was harassed off the platform because of his attitudes towards slavery.

Emerson supported women's suffrage and was receptive to liberal reforms, but antislavery was the single dominant political issue of his life. He regarded the Fugitive Slave Law as a "filthy enactment," and, with marked lack of intellectual consistency to his earlier position on Thoreau's civil disobedience, he swore "by God" not to obey it. He denounced the Kansas-Nebraska Bill of 1854 for vitiating the safeguards of the Missouri Compromise, and he looked upon the Civil War as the nation's opportunity to be fully honest to its ideals. He supported patriotic causes; revered John Brown, saying that he had made the gallows as glorious as the Cross; and though he once harbored reservations with respect to Lincoln, these disappeared with the Emancipation Proclamation. Emerson, in a word, was in full sympathy with the concept of freedom for the black person. Yet, for all his rectitude and intelligence, he could speak wistfully of the possibility of "a rose-water that will wash the negro white."

The Emerson name is virtually synonymous with Concord, but not alone the name of Ralph Waldo Emerson. Grandfather Emerson—William, a minister of Congregationalist suasion and Puritan trappings—came to Concord in the mid-1760s, built the Old Manse, and from one of its windows witnessed the encounter of April 19, 1775, at North Bridge that helped set the course of American independence. This Emerson went off to the Revolutionary War as a chaplain, contracted a "Sort of mongrell Feaver & Ague" at the Ticonderoga encampment, and died in Rutland, Vermont, en route home. After a decent interval, Grandmother Emerson married Ezra Ripley, who moved into both the Concord pulpit and the Old Manse, as well as the affections of all the Emersons.

Ralph Waldo Emerson was born in Boston—May 25, 1803—but the Old Manse was ever a second home. As a boy, he lived there for several months when his widowed mother was forced to lean on kin while readjusting her life. Young Ralph (he actually preferred the name Waldo) revisited often, but then would be back in Boston for schooling. He entered Boston Public Latin School when he was nine, and Harvard when he was fourteen. Entrance to Harvard was facilitated by his being named the "president's freshman," or orderly, for which services he received free lodging in President John Thornton Kirkland's house. It was a minor grant, but a helpful one to a family that knew nothing but financial struggle. At graduation four years later, Emerson was class poet, an honor rather less than might be expected—six others, it is said, declined the role. Ralph graduated an undistinguished thirtieth in a class of fifty-nine.

In 1834, Ralph Waldo Emerson returned to Concord to stay. He was briefly at the Old Manse as a boarder, then in 1835 purchased for $3,500 the white frame structure at Lexington Road and Cambridge Turnpike erected a few years before by one of the Boston Coolidges. Emerson settled in with a new wife, Lydia Jackson of the Plymouth Jacksons, and an uncertain future. Behind him were two abandoned careers (teaching and the ministry) and one buried wife. (In 1829 Emerson had married the frail Ellen Louisa Tucker, of Concord, New Hampshire, who died in 1831, leaving him a saddened but ultimately recompensed widower—though there were long and vexing court struggles before Ellen's share of the substantial Tucker legacy came to him.) Emerson euphonized his new wife's name—henceforth she would be Lidian—and sunk roots as country squire and sage. The man of loose ends and hitherto indifferent public impression speedily became local dignitary as well as international celebrity.

Not that Emerson was not already well known. He had touched nerves and set tongues wagging when, as the rebellious young minister of Boston's Second Church, he decided he could no longer administer the Lord's Supper rite, on grounds that the modern observance was without valid historical and theological legitimacy. He had related doubts about other dogmas, about religious formalism in general, and about the claims of religious institutions over individual consciences. But the bread-and-wine issue was the lightning rod. Personal principle and parishioner pressure resulted in his resignation in 1832 from his pastorate and, it eventually developed, from the ministry. The decision may have surprised Boston and shocked Aunt Mary, but it was hardly a precipitous one. "I have sometimes thought that in order to be a good minister it was necessary to leave the ministry," he confided to his journal. "The profession is antiquated."

That December, Emerson sailed for Europe on a year's visit that was to bring him into the company of Coleridge, Carlyle, and Wordsworth, and more directly under the influence of philosophers—Goethe, Hume, Locke, Montaigne, Swedenborg—whose points of view were to shape his and the transcendentalist school of thought. So it was that when *Nature*, Emerson's first book, was published in 1836, transcendentalism took on philosophical flesh in New England, and Emerson became the sage of a movement which was to catch up Alcott, Margaret Fuller, Theodore Parker, Orestes Brownson, James Freeman Clarke, and other intellectuals. Emerson's captivating conviction was that the individual is in direct communication with God in and through nature, and that the key to life and universality was to be found in self-reliance and nonconformism.

The extension of these principles, first to secular scholarship, then to theology, confirmed Emerson as philosophical maverick and brought on the Harvard trouble. The fuse was placed with the Phi Beta Kappa lecture of August 31, 1837, in which Emerson urged an end to "our long apprenticeship" to other lands and other cultures, and a development in America of a new world of ideas and relationships for the mind and the spirit. "Our intellectual Declaration of Independence," Oliver Wendell Holmes called the talk. The explosion came a year later when Emerson extended the principles of that lecture to theology. The shock was felt most strongly when he scored modern Christianity's preoccupation with ritual, its "noxious exaggeration about the *person* of Jesus," its myth-making. Emerson did not deny the existence of a God, but he declared the church as known and experienced to be dead and argued that a new revelation was to be sought. He predicted that that discovery would be found in self-reliance and in daring to love God without a mediator.

Harvard was unamused and banished him from its friendship. The press cried blasphemy, and, as the controversy raged on, Emerson feared that his new career as lyceum lecturer would be prematurely ended. He need not have worried. When he showed in Boston for his next series of lectures, he found himself personage as well as person.

This was the day, of course, of the lyceum, that nineteenth-century tool of popular education that flourished in the absence of extensive public schooling, radio, films, and television. In its own way the lyceum was precursor to all. In 1826, the lyceum movement was spurred by Josiah Holbrook's recommendations on adult education, and it flourished in the years of mid-century. By 1839, there were 137 lyceums in Massachusetts alone, drawing an estimated 33,000 persons to concerts, debates, and lectures on the arts, sciences, current events, and philosophical topics. Emerson was one of the "stars" of the circuit, and it had to be for substance rather than flair, for Emerson disdained rhetoric and dramatics, the tools of others, for a style that smacked of diffidence and a posture that was stiff and formal. One observer likened his platform presence to that of "a great overgrown schoolboy, saying his task."

Emerson had always been available for the occasional lecture, but lecturing did not become his career and means of livelihood until November of 1835, when he presented the first of a series of ten lectures on "The Best Mode of Inspiring a Correct Taste in English Literature" to the Society for the Diffusion of Useful Knowledge, in Boston's Masonic Temple. He received $200 for the ten lectures, a modest sum even for those days. But shrewdly he capitalized on his lectures, if not his creativeness, by repeating the lectures elsewhere, as in Lowell and Salem. Fees improved as his reputation grew, and though these gave him some affluence, they never made him particularly rich. Lecturing was, in fact, a hard way to make a living, for Emerson inevitably exhausted the convenient lyceum circuit of New England and had to push out for audiences to Baltimore, Philadelphia, New York, Brooklyn, and places more distant. Demand for appearances in time crossed the Atlantic, and in the fall of 1847, he took talents and texts to England and Scotland, where he spoke on "Napoleon," "Domestic Life," "Shakespeare," "Powers and Laws of Thought," "Natural Aristocracy" and other popular topics for nineteenth-century audiences.

It was a wearying occupation, and before it was over, Emerson was a broken man, plagued with memory losses and giving fits of worry to daughter Ellen, who in his seniority had become guide, companion, and executive secretary. Still, audiences came reverentially to his lectures—a course of lectures in the spring of 1872 netted him some $1,400. But more and more it was apparent that people were coming for sentiment's sake, to see rather than in the expectation of being intellectually challenged. Emerson was hardly unknowing, but he was serene in the face of decline, remaining unperturbed, for instance, when in mid-address he would encounter misshuffled pages in his prepared texts—a not unknown phenomenon in the best of days. Characteristically, he would pause momentarily, then blithely continue on with the out-of-order page, innocently dramatizing the Emersonian dictum that the force of a sentence is in considerable part the man behind it. Under the circumstances, the ability to live easily with his ailments was probably the best of prescriptions.

Emerson's decline was hardly helped by the fire that ravaged his Concord home in the early hours of July 24, 1872. A maid, prying about an attic trunk around two in the morning, either set her lamp too close to the roof rafters or else knocked the lamp over. In any case, Emerson and his wife—the children were away at the time— awoke to find the house in flames. The alarm was sounded, and heroic work by neighbors spared a disaster. There was serious damage to the house, but all, or most, of Emerson's manuscripts and books were saved—thanks, it is said, to "daring boys" darting in and out of the house with baskets and blankets into which they piled this treasure. Some family letters stored in Ellen's closet were destroyed, but others survived the fire with charring at the edges. Word of the fire spread, and Emerson's friends rallied to his assistance, raising a sum of $17,000—more than enough to restore the house. (The restoration, in fact, cost $6,500, and insurance covered 40 percent of that amount.) The financial cushion was welcome, but Emerson would have been more grateful no doubt to have been spared his ordeal. He never regained the old self.

Emerson lived on for ten years. There was a stimulating trip to Europe, where he revisited old haunts, renewed old friendships, and crossed the Mediterranean to Egypt for a voyage up the Nile to antiquities he had long desired to see. There was an equally stimulating return to Concord after seven months abroad. Concord had missed its famous citizen and grandly received him back. The Fitchburg train from Boston whistled mightily all the way from Walden Woods into Concord station, and Emerson stepped down to be greeted by band and baritone, village fathers and schoolchildren—in fact, just about the whole of Concord. The children sang "Home, Sweet Home," and Emerson passed under an arch of welcome to cheers and salutes. Lidian awaited him at the east door of his home, now repaired and renovated, and as comfortable as ever. The crowd lingered on the main road and dispersed only after Emerson walked to the front gate and expressed a thanks to more cheering.

In 1875, *Letters and Social Aims*, Emerson's tenth book, rolled from the presses, but it was more compilation than new thought, and as much the collaboration of James Elliot Cabot and Ellen as it was the result of his own creativity. Those powers of incisive intellect which had arrived tardily had now ebbed, stranding him in the fullness of his years. "It must be mortifying," commented Alcott, who was older still, "to one of his accurate habits of thought and speech and his former tenacity of memory to find himself wanting in his once ready command of imagery to match his thought instantly." Emerson did his best to cover up memory lapses with circumlocution, but he became less and less successful at the effort. He once managed the word hen only after detouring through cat, fish, bird, and cock. Another time he could get no closer to specifying the Capitol in Washington than by speaking of it as "United States—survey of the beauty of eternal Government." Emerson was unblushing and undaunted, however. Biographer Ralph L. Rusk notes that just four years before his death, Emerson had the courage to read before a gathering of the Concord lyceum a lecture entitled "Memory."

He was active to the end, though eventually he was barely conscious of times, places, and people. The summer before he died he visited with daughter Edith, married to Col. William Forbes, at their home on Naushon, one of the Elizabeth Islands off the Massachusetts coast. In February, he was struggling through snowdrifts to hear Franklin B. Sanborn read from his newly completed biography of Thoreau. In March he was present at a meeting of the Social Circle, a favorite Concord club.

Next month the end came quietly and painlessly, four weeks short of Emerson's seventy-ninth birthday. A cold grew into pneumonia, and on the twenty-second he took to his bed. The Emerson story had been writ, but death waited patiently for five days before placing its period, almost as if to give friends and neighbors time for a last farewell. The dearest called: Cabot, Alcott, Sanborn, Ellery Channing, Judge Ebenezer Rockwood Hoar, jailer Sam Staples.

Staples bore a bottle of brandy and announced good-humoredly that he was ready to take care of Emerson at any time. Sedated by ether, Emerson breathed his last at 8:50 P.M. on April 27, 1882. The village's church bells tolled seventy-nine times. The world learned that Ralph Waldo Emerson was gone.

Three days later was the funeral. There was a private ceremony in the home with William Furness, a boyhood friend, in charge. A public service was held in the Unitarian Church, with James Freeman Clarke preaching and Alcott reading a sonnet. Burial was on authors' ridge in Sleepy Hollow Cemetery, not far from the graves of Thoreau and Hawthorne. Samuel Moody Haskins, Emerson's cousin and rector of St. Mark's Church in Brooklyn, conducted the committal service—and as the coffin settled into place, he cast ashes from the fireplace of Emerson's study, mixed with gravel from the front walk. James Russell Lowell's "least vulgar of men, the most austerely genial and the most independent of opinion" was at rest.

If You Travel . . .

. . .to Concord, you cannot miss Emerson's home. It stands behind a white picket fence at the junction of Lexington Road and Cambridge Turnpike, cater-corner to the Antiquarian House. The home is only a short distance from Concord Square. Emerson House is open from April 19 to November 1, daily except for Mondays. Weekday hours are from 10:00 A.M. to 5:00 P.M., and Sunday hours from 2:00 to 5:00 P.M. There are half-hour tours of the house, the last of which begins at 4:30 P.M. There is a modest admission fee, and children under six years of age enter free of charge.

Emerson House breathes the memory and the spirit of its famous nineteenth-century occupant, even though some of the furniture is reproduction and many of the books are substitutes or those of his children rather than Emerson himself. Not that Ralph Waldo Emerson's possessions have gone astray. Rather, the originals have been moved to safer places, such as the Antiquarian House. (Memories are long of the 1872 fire at Emerson House.) Emerson's papers are, in the main, at the Houghton Library of Harvard University; some are at the Concord Public Library and with the Concord Antiquarian Society.

Not all of Emerson House is open to visitors, but more than enough to convey fully a feeling for the man and his times. Tours move from the study, with its replica furniture; through the parlor, with its Thomas Carlyle mementos (a steel engraving of "Aurora Bringing in the Dawn" and a candle-mirror); through the dining room, with its table opening out to seat eighteen persons; through the downstairs bedroom with its mighty cannonball bed where Emerson's four children were born. Upstairs are three more bedrooms. In stairway and hallways are such Emersoniana as fire buckets, family Bible, walking hat, and "Sunday chair"—that unique Thoreau contrivance with a draw beneath the seat, where Emerson's scarf and gloves could be kept for quicker scooting off to church services . . . when and if Emerson went, of course, which was not very regularly after 1838.

The house, in a word, is much as Emerson left it in 1882. So are the grounds. The horses and cows are no longer grazing about. But the barn stands, and as Emerson's prized trees go down from wind or age, they are replaced in position by younger ones of the genus. Even the meadow that reaches towards Walden Pond is much as it was when Emerson trudged across it and let passing Indians and gypsies use it as a camping site. Less sensitive guardians of the Emerson heritage might have built a parking lot here, but one leaves one's car along the gravel shoulder of the main road when visiting Emerson House.

Concord is within fifteen miles of Boston and is accessible by automobile, bus, and train. After crossing Harvard Bridge from Boston, drivers have a choice of Route 2 (Memorial Drive), the direct route to Concord, or Route 2A, an alternate route through Cambridge, Arlington, and Lexington.

From the north, Concord may be reached via Lowell, Chelmsford, and Carlisle. From the east, via Route 20 from Watertown, through Waltham, turning north on Route 128 and west at Route 2. From the south, via Route 126 from Framingham, past Walden Pond, and across Route 2 to Concord Center. From points west (Connecticut, New York, etc.), drivers should get on the Massachusetts Turnpike and depart at the exit for Route 495, then head north to Route 2 and Concord.

Buses to Concord leave Harvard Square in Cambridge and arrive in Concord by way of Lexington and Bedford Airport.

Trains run daily to Concord from Boston's North Station.

Chapter
Nine

HENRY WADSWORTH LONGFELLOW

A Yankee on Olympus

Few poets have been forced to dodge more slings and arrows of outrageous critics than Henry Wadsworth Longfellow. His poetry has been labeled didactic, flaccid, trite—he, a mere rhymer, a romanticizer, even a plagiarist (by Edgar Allan Poe, yet). Critics predicted that his fame would never again be what it was in the nineteenth century—when, for instance, fifteen thousand copies of *The Courtship of Miles Standish* would be snapped up on publication day in Boston and London, and when Britons would erect a commemorative bust in his honor in Poets' Corner of Westminster Abbey, the first American to be so honored. "Our hemisphere cannot claim the honor of having brought him forth," Nicholas Cardinal Wiseman commented when Longfellow was at mid-career, "but he still belongs to us, for his works have become as household words wherever the English language is spoken." To Wiseman, Longfellow embodied genius. But critics clamored back that he was unworthy of immortality and that his admirers ought to be about the appreciation of more authentic talent. Critics, however, seldom have the final word—there is still popular taste. Longfellow was to endure; indeed, more than endure. His popularity grows with the decades. He is read, memorized, recited—and he is visited.

In the old days, young writers like William Winter would walk the bridge over the Charles merely to touch the latch of Longfellow's gate. Today they come from great distances and by the thousands—to Craigie House in Cambridge, the Longfellow residence at 105 Brattle Street, not far from Harvard Square; to the Longfellow ancestral home in Portland, Maine; to the fabled Wayside Inn in Sudbury, Massachusetts, setting for the *Tales of a Wayside Inn* with its typically Longfellowian warmth and homey opening:

> One Autumn night, in Sudbury town,
> Across the meadows bare and brown,
> The windows of the wayside inn
> Gleamed red with firelight through the leaves
> Of woodbine, hanging from the eaves
> Their crimson curtains rent and thin.

These visitors—22,046 to Craigie House alone in 1974—may not come away as authorities on or worshipers of Longfellow. A visit is still only a visit; a tour, only a tour. But most undoubtedly depart the more convinced that a special talent resided in this man who, then as now, could be as easily maligned as idolized.

As a conscientious developer of American themes and celebrator of basic virtues—goodness and honesty and hard work—Longfellow has always had a natural appeal for a large audience of readers. His poetry brimmed with ready-made nostalgia, and when he rhymed of hearth and nation, he furnished ideal material for jingoists and chauvinists of various genre. Naturally he would be a favorite during the nation's Bicentennial period, and naturally President Gerald Ford would take to quoting him, although with mixed success. During one Ford visit to Boston, Longfellow's line about those lanterns to be hung in the tower of the Old North Church emerged as "One, if by day, and two, if by night."

President Ford's rendition was not parody, though if it had been, it would have been in a long and, for Longfellow, vexing tradition. Perhaps no poet has been parodied more. Longfellow was unamused by most of the efforts, ostensibly for the irreverence involved, but maybe, too, in the suspicion that vulnerability to parody betrayed a simplicity of style and commonplaceness of theme and sentiment. He need not have been so sensitive. Indeed, he was at times simple and commonplace. But he was eternally clear and understandable—which helps explain why he is yet the most recited of American poets. Henry Steele Commager has named Longfellow among the "Founding Fathers of American literary nationalism" (along with Irving, Cooper, Hawthorne, Whittier, and a handful more). Biographer Edward Wagenknecht has typed his work as

C.J. PUGLIESE

Craigie House — the Longfellow home in Cambridge — was ever a showplace, and the Longfellows were blissfully happy here, until.... The tragedy that befell them shocked their wide circle of friends, including Oliver Wendell Holmes, who seemingly had a premonition of something happening. He passed Craigie House one day in 1861, and reportedly trembled to look at it, sensing that "those who lived there had their happiness so perfect that no change... could fail to be for the worse."

"our best American poetic storybook." And Van Wyck Brooks has written that no one who experienced Longfellow's poems can "quite forget their dreamy music, their shadowy languor, their melodious charm, their burden of youthful nostalgia." There can be little argument.

For all of that, Longfellow is not an entirely reliable poet. *The Song of Hiawatha* has been judged to reveal more the poet's appreciation than an anthropologist's knowledge. Nor did Longfellow bother much about exhaustive research. He had no experiential acquaintance with many of the scenes he chose to landscape, not even troubling to go to Plymouth, an easy journey from Cambridge, before writing *The Courtship of Miles Standish*. Even facts eluded him. *Tales of a Wayside Inn*, for example, gives Paul Revere considerably more dash and color than history justifies. Revere did not receive the steeple signal that night in April of '75; the people of Charlestown did. Revere went over to Charlestown by boat, exchanged information with people there about British troop movements, and only then mounted a horse for his ride through every Middlesex village and farm—well, not quite every. Revere never reached Concord, as credited. Samuel Prescott did. Revere was intercepted by a British patrol the other side of Lexington, and he told all he knew.

Alas, even that spreading tree under which the village smithy stood wasn't an honest-to-God chestnut. It was quite a different type from the prized American chestnut that supplied hardwood to the builder and autumn nuts to the connoisseur before disappearing in the blight that completed its work around 1940. It was, rather, a horse chestnut, native to Europe, not America, with an inedible nut something like that of the native buckeye.

Many of these complaints are quibbling, of course. Exactness is the historian's charge; license, the poet's privilege—and Longfellow indulged it. No one is the worse for it. From student days at Bowdoin College in Brunswick, Maine, Longfellow proposed a literature that would carry poetry to the American masses, and he worked to that objective with considerable success, if not always with literal fact—for which one goes elsewhere, in any case. Longfellow's forte was feel and mood, for which he needed license. He had the master's touch.

More substantive are objections that he was not a profound, independent thinker and that he lacked passion—certainly that passion born of angry indignation over social injustice. Longfellow lived, for instance, during the nation's contentious slavery period, yet his *Poems on Slavery*, written in 1842 on a slow boat from Europe, were extraordinarily cool, for all their ideological correctness. Longfellow himself said that he was anxious to write "in a kindly— not a vindictive spirit." It was typical of the man. When the Civil War broke out, Longfellow's instinct—consistent, again, with the tone of the slavery poems—was to keep his sons out of it. He succeeded with Ernest. Charles ran away, enlisted, and suffered severe wounds from which he eventually recovered.

Limitations notwithstanding, Longfellow was a man of several parts (he was a translator and sometime novelist and playwright, as well as poet) and a more complex individual than is often realized. He was a gentle soul of strict, Puritan–New England morality, but never self-righteous. He prized serenity of mind and quiet of neighborhood. As a young boy he would place cotton in his ears against the Fourth of July din, just as in later years he would close the shutters of Craigie House against the crashing thunderstorm. (Significantly, his bookplate motto was *Non Clamor, sed Amor*.) Great grace and civility were his, and his eye searched until it found in person or theme an ennobling element. It invariably succeeded; as, indeed, in the instance of the Indian, so despised at the time in the American countryside. Accordingly, some would find Longfellow's poetry to be soft on Indian cruelty and partial to Indian culture—and Hiawatha to be too much the Christian gentleman.

Underpinning all of this were deep instincts of culture—not just for that of the Old World, not just for that of the indigenous American, but also for the prospectively enormous culture of developing America. Longfellow wrote with an eye towards the building of that culture, but he doubted that there would be a purity of triumph. "We are swallowed up in schemes for gain," he would write, "and engrossed with contrivances for bodily enjoyments, as if this particle of dust were immortal—as if the soul needed no aliment, and the mind no raiment." History authenticated the doubt.

Longfellow's life spanned most of the nineteenth century. He was born in Portland on February 27, 1807; he died in Cambridge, March 24, 1882.

In the tradition of the times, Longfellow's life had a strong European orientation. He lived abroad from 1826 to 1829 in preparation for a modern-languages professorship at Bowdoin, and, though not an inveterate traveler, he returned several times—as in 1868–69, when, full of years and esteem, he was awarded honorary degrees by both Cambridge and Oxford universities and was received by Queen Victoria at Windsor Castle. From Bowdoin, Longfellow moved on, at age twenty-eight, to Harvard, where he again taught languages, for which he possessed such a unique facility, and branched into belles-lettres. After nineteen years, he resigned his Harvard professorship to devote himself exclusively to literature. The year was 1854.

Henry Wadsworth Longfellow

By any measure, life was generous to Longfellow—despite frivolous complaints about surname and height. (Longfellow considered his name slightly preposterous, perhaps because it contrasted so with his lack of inches. He was a short fellow, of less than medium height.)

A genteel upbringing in Portland (he went off to school at age three, accompanied by a black servant); a home in Cambridge grand enough to have served as Washington's headquarters in 1775–76 (and to have received Martha, when she came north for their wedding anniversary); a summer place at fashionable Nahant on the Massachusetts North Shore—these were his. So were dear friends, among them Cornelius Felton, James Russell Lowell, Louis Agassiz, Massachusetts's abolitionist Senator Charles Sumner, and Charles Eliot Norton. So were ample funds: for useful and handsomely bound books, fine household appointments, choice wines for ceremonious dinners, and, finally, prudent benefactions. There was nothing of the poor, struggling poet about Longfellow. He oozed affluence, and his worth kept pace with his fame. "The Village Blacksmith" gained him $15 in 1840, but for "The Hanging of the Crane" he was paid $3,000 in 1874. He was a rich man, burdened only by some aggressive literary critics, the principal ones of whom he managed to outlive physically and survive intellectually.

The severest critic of all was unquestionably Edgar Allan Poe, for Poe passed beyond the standard accusations of derivativeness and borrowed imagery to accuse Longfellow of plagiarism for similarities that allegedly existed between Tennyson's "The Death of the Old Year" and Longfellow's "The Midnight Mass for the Dying Year," Poe's own "The Haunted Palace" and Longfellow's "The Beleaguered City." Today the charges are regarded as tendentious and lacking substance, and the similarities are understood to have been coincidental. The judgment of history perhaps helps to explain Longfellow's Olympian attitude. He refused to answer criticism or respond to attack, a tactic that infuriated critics all the more. When *Poems* appeared in 1845, Margaret Fuller resorted to satire in Horace Greeley's *New York Tribune*. "Mr. Longfellow has been accused of plagiarism," she wrote. "We have been surprised that anyone should have been anxious to fasten special charges of this kind upon him, when we had supposed it so obvious that the greater part of his mental stores were derived from the work of others. He has no style of his own, growing out of his own experiences and observation of nature. Nature with him, whether human or external, is always seen through the windows of literature."

Fanny Longfellow bristled over Margaret Fuller's attack, but not her husband, at least not publicly. He maintained his characteristic calm, the calm that had been his throughout the Poe attacks. (So free was Longfellow of vindictiveness that he is reported to have lectured enthusiastically in his Harvard classes on the merits of Poe's poetry during the very time that Poe was on the offensive against Longfellow's works.) Poe and Fuller died their tragic deaths in 1849 and 1850, respectively. Longfellow lived on for more than three decades. There would be critics still, but never again such dedicated detractors.

In 1835, Longfellow lost his first wife in Rotterdam to complications resulting from a miscarriage—the "beautiful and cultivated" Mary Storer Potter of Portland. They were wedded but four years. Eight years later he married Frances Elizabeth (Fanny) Appleton, a properly rich Beacon-Hill Bostonian, who produced Craigie House (it was a wedding present from her father) and six children. It was a beautifully serene period. In fact, so blessed was their fortune that fatalists troubled. Oliver Wendell Holmes passed Craigie House one day in 1861 and reportedly "trembled to look at it," sensing that "those who lived there had their happiness so perfect that no change . . . could fail to be for the worse."

Foreboding became reality that July 9. The Longfellows had delayed their departure to the Nahant shore because of the illness of Nathan Appleton, Fanny's father. It was a hot day, and Fanny was whiling it away by an open window, sealing locks of her daughters' hair in remembrance packets. Suddenly, either a match or hot sealing wax sent her summer dress up in flames. Panic-stricken, she dashed into her husband's study. Longfellow threw a rug around her and held her close to himself in an effort to smother the fire. Fanny Longfellow wasn't saved. She spent a reasonably restful night, but next day she lapsed into a coma and died. She was laid to rest in Mount Auburn Cemetery on their eighteenth wedding anniversary, her unmarked head carrying a wreath of orange blossoms. Longfellow was so badly burned about the face and hands that he was unable to attend the funeral.

Longfellow's grief was deep and lasting. His relationship with this wife had been rhapsodic, and during the years of their marriage he had produced some of his most successful work, including

Evangeline: A Tale of Acadie, The Golden Legend, Hiawatha, and *The Courtship of Miles Standish*. There is little evidence that Fanny Appleton Longfellow contributed intellectually to her husband's career. She seems, in a real sense, the epitome of the nineteenth-century wife of "station": totally feminine, complementary to spouse, opinionated but discreetly reserved, and slightly precious. At least Fanny is made to appear so in most of the recollections of her contemporaries and in the protective family record that Samuel Longfellow, the poet's brother and biographer, allowed to pass to history.

In 1956, the selected letters and journals of Fanny Appleton Longfellow were published, and though these are revelatory to a degree, Fanny still remains a woman worth knowing much more intimately than the glimpses allow, if only because behind that correct period facade lurked something of the feminist. In 1847 she became the first woman in the western world, so-called, to take ether during childbirth. When sharp tongues criticized her husband for permitting the risk, Fanny declared: "I feel proud to be the pioneer to less suffering for poor weak womankind." Similarly, she would be elated when news reached Boston of the acquittal in New York of a young woman charged with stabbing a seducer. "It is cheering that men begin to feel for women in these matters, and allow them a little justice," she commented, "but when will the law recognize the moral murder as great a crime as the physical?"

Fanny Longfellow's violent death had a predictably unnerving effect on her sensitive husband. There were days of delirium, then a period of outward calm during which Longfellow confided that he was "inwardly bleeding to death." To counter the grief, Longfellow immersed himself in the translating of Dante's *Divine Comedy*, a project long contemplated, once started, then put aside. He surrounded himself with male companions—Lowell, Sumner, the scholarly Norton—and clung the more tightly to his children. The daughter of the first ether delivery, Fanny, named for her mother, lived only a year, but five Longfellow children grew to adulthood in Craigie House, filling the father's days and, to an extent, the void in his heart. There were two sons, Ernest and Charles, but the girls seem to have been his special favorites—"Grave Alice, and laughing

Allegra, / And Edith with golden hair."

The Dante project provided the desired therapy, though the end product, for all its literal perfection, did little for Longfellow's reputation. His career was hardly in its twilight, however. Several verse stories, some previously published, were gathered into a Chaucer-type package and rolled from the presses in 1863 as *Tales of a Wayside Inn*. Later there came *The New England Tragedies, Christus, A Mystery, Three Books of Song, Aftermath, The Hanging of the Crane, The Masque of Pandora, Kéramos and other Poems, Ultima Thule* and more still.

Longfellow was a relatively young man of fifty-four when Fanny died. The bereavement and the whiskers he affected to conceal the scars from his burns added instant great age to his appearance. The impression projected, however, was not of a wearied and defeated man, but rather that of the patriarch, the poet laureate, the person in a world without end. This was, by common consensus, Longfellow's most handsome period, and he had many pursuers. He never again married, though. His joy and his consolations remained his family, his work—and the visitors who trooped to his door, the famous and the anonymous, to extend a greeting, to collect an autograph. Until his very last days, Longfellow was unsparing of his time. There was even a rule that any child who came to the door wanting to see the chair carved from the "spreading chestnut tree" was not to be denied entry. Theoretically, the chair was a gift to Longfellow from the children of Cambridge; in fact, the city fathers were anxious to assuage Longfellow's upset feelings over the cutting down of the tree to widen Brattle Street. Either way, Longfellow was tickled by the gift.

That chair is yet in its honored place in the Victorian clutter of Craigie House, a meticulously preserved shrine whose atmosphere suggests that Mr. Longfellow is merely out for a stroll and will return any minute. "The Old Clock on the Stairs" chimes the hours; the dining room table is set for guests; the curiously proportioned chair devised for the gangling Senator Sumner is by the fireplace, ready to receive friend and confidant; the family portraits (two Gilbert Stuarts among them) hang as hung in their honored places; the stand-up writing desk is, as ever it was, by the study window, the better to catch the last light of day and a view of children at play or going to and from school.

But, of course, Mr. Longfellow will not be back. He departed at

3:10 P.M. of a Friday afternoon in March of 1882, as quietly and gently almost as one of his poems. In the fall of 1881, the aging poet had suffered a severe attack of vertigo, followed by "nervous prostration." Still, poems flowed from his pen: "Mad River," "Possibilities," and, in February, one on Decoration Day. In late March he took a chill after a stroll on the veranda. That night peritonitis set in, and a few days later, he was dead. There was mourning throughout much of the world.

Two days later, as a light snow fell on Cambridge, Henry Wadsworth Longfellow was laid to rest in Mount Auburn Cemetery. His brother Samuel, a Unitarian clergyman, read from the Scriptures. Ralph Waldo Emerson, himself only a month for this world, came from Concord with his daughter Ellen to pay his respects. "I cannot recall the name of our friend," the Emerson of failing memory is reported to have remarked, "but he was a good man."

Apocryphal in part, perhaps, but accurate: Longfellow was a good man. And though his name apparently slipped Emerson's mind, posterity—happily—was to remember.

If You Travel . . .

. . .looking for Longfellow, the logical starting point is Craigie House in Cambridge, Massachusetts, Longfellow's home from 1837 to 1882, first as lodger and, after his marriage, as master. The house at 105 Brattle Street takes its name from the family that preceded the Longfellows as owners. It is a short half-mile walk from Harvard Square and the subway. By automobile, it is two blocks off Memorial Drive paralleling the Charles River, at the Hawthorne Street exit. Since December, 1973, Craigie House has been a preserve of the National Park Service, U.S. Department of the Interior. The house is open daily, except Christmas and New Year's, from 9:00 A.M. to 5:00 P.M. There is a modest admission charge.

Within a mile of Craigie House is Mount Auburn Cemetery, where Longfellow is buried, alongside other members of the family, including both his wives, son Charles, who was wounded in the Civil War, and "Grave" Alice of "The Children's Hour." Mount Auburn (q.v.) is the resting place for numerous literary figures, among them Francis Parkman, Oliver Wendell Holmes, Amy Lowell, James Russell Lowell, and Julia Ward Howe.

In downtown Boston, at 39 Beacon Street, is the Appleton home, where Longfellow and Frances Elizabeth Appleton were married, in the front parlor, before the fireplace. The home is kept by the Women's City Club of Boston and is open Wednesdays the year round, from 10:00 A.M. to 3:30 P.M. There is a modest admission fee. (During the Bicentennial period, the club experimented with Monday, Wednesday, and Friday openings during the summer season.)

Twenty miles west of Boston, on Route 20 in Sudbury, is the Wayside Inn immortalized by Longfellow in *Tales of a Wayside Inn*. The inn is under private management and functions yet as a guest house and eating place. It is open daily, except for Christmas Day, and is the scene of numerous meetings, wedding receptions and family reunions. The inn was built in 1686 and has undergone several restorations, including major ones following fires in 1955 and 1965. Dinner guests may tour the inn free. For others, there is a small charge. Lodging accommodations are limited (ten rooms) and in summertime must be made several weeks in advance.

Longfellow visited the Wayside Inn several times, seeming to prefer to go there in the fall, if a conclusion may be presumed from a diary entry for October 31, 1862: "October ends with a delicious Indian-summer day. Drive with Fields to the old Red-Horse Tavern in Sudbury—alas, no longer an inn! A lovely valley; the winding road shaded by grand old oaks before the House. A rambling, tumble-down old building, two hundred years old; and till now in the family of the Howes, who have kept an inn for one hundred and seventy-five years. In the old time, it was a house of call for all travellers from Boston westward."

Finally—in Portland, Maine—there is Wadsworth-Longfellow House at 487 Congress Street, where the poet spent his childhood. The house was built by Longfellow's grandfather, General Peleg Wadsworth, a Revolutionary War hero, and features documents, manuscripts, portraits, costumes, and household items associated with the Wadsworth and Longfellow families. The house is cared for by the Maine Historical Society and is open to the public Mondays through Fridays, from 9:30 A.M. to 4:30 P.M, from early June through September. There is a modest admission fee.

Chapter Ten

NATHANIEL HAWTHORNE

Novelist of New England's Bleakest Past

Nathaniel Hawthorne hated Salem.

He was a native son, having been born there July 4, 1804. But he was shamed by Salem's history—specifically that 1692 outbreak of medieval superstition which resulted in nineteen "witches" being hanged on Gallows Hill.

And the Salem of his own day irked him—the people who asked, "Who ever heard of the Hawthornes?"; the politicians and gossipers who managed his removal in 1849 from his Custom House post as surveyor of the port. Several times Hawthorne left Salem, hopeful of never returning; several times he was driven back by disappointed hopes and financial pinch. He escaped finally to Concord, Lenox, West Newton, Liverpool, Rome, Florence, and Concord, again, where he is buried in Sleepy Hollow Cemetery under a stone simply but poignantly inscribed, "Hawthorne." Still, it is in Salem that the Hawthorne memory lingers strongest, and where hundreds of thousands of the adulatory and the curious flock each year to savor the mystery of the man and his bewitching novels.

Salem is a captivating community, Hawthorne's antipathy notwithstanding. "New England's treasure house," it has been called, and not extravagantly. It is a city of monuments and museums, fine parks and drives, and glorious mansions dating from the period when Salem clipper ships dominated the seven seas. All about are weather-stained clapboard houses brimming with an eeriness that yet grips the imagination. Many of Hawthorne's characters walked the streets of Salem; the scenes and houses of his major novels are around one Salem corner or another; the supernatural influences that propel his plots—Matthew Maule's curse on the Pyncheon family in *The House of the Seven Gables*, for instance—are right out of Salem history. And the history of the Hawthornes, for that matter.

In the house at 54 Turner Street in Salem, one could be moving through the very pages of Hawthorne's famous **The House of the Seven Gables.** *A feature of the house is the secret chimney stairway, where one could hide from Indians or witch hunters, whichever may have happened to be the more dangerous at the moment.*

Family pride was strong among the Hawthornes, but in point of fact theirs was not a history to romance over for long. The family roots were planted in Salem by Major William Hathorne—as the family name was spelled until Nathaniel phoneticized it after his graduation from Bowdoin. (Or was he really anxious to assert an independence and establish a remove between himself and his ancestors?) William Hathorne emigrated from Wiltshire in 1637, settled first in Dorchester, then was enticed to Salem, where he served as magistrate. He once saved the Bay Colony from perdition at the hands of Quakers by having five Quaker women stripped to the waist, bound to the tails of carts, and lashed by a constable while being hauled through Salem, Boston, and Dedham. William's son John presided as a judge at the witchcraft trials, and one ungrateful victim—Rebecca Nurse—had the temerity before going off to the gallows to pronounce a curse on the Hawthornes into posterity. For years family misfortunes were blamed on Rebecca's ill-temper. Hawthorne, more sensibly, consigned the curse to his fiction.

Nathaniel Hawthorne's father came fifth in the generational line. He was a sea captain who died of yellow fever at Surinam while on a voyage from Salem. Nathaniel was five at the time. His mother donned widow's weeds, retreated to her room, and became a recluse in her own house, not even taking meals thereafter at the family table. Morbidness pervaded the place, casting its effects on Nathaniel and his two sisters. "We do not even *live* at our house!" he once exclaimed. He labeled the house "Castle Dismal," and as a young man apparently contemplated suicide. Hawthorne was to shake his personal ghosts as the years went by, yet there was a time when he too ate his meals behind his own shut door and when he ventured outdoors only under the privacy of night.

As a young man, Hawthorne's friends were few and his gambits fewer, though he obviously did enjoy going around to cousin Susan Ingersoll's marvelous seven-gabled house. Susan lived surrounded by family relics and a young man named Horace Conolly, reputed to be a nephew. Horace had pursued the ministry, law, and medicine, but quit each calling, one by one. Susan made him her heir and he, in gratitude no doubt, adopted her name. Horace was fond of cards and liquor, which helped endear him to Nathaniel—who was not a rake by any stretch of the imagination, but who did enjoy his minutes of relaxation, at least while a youth. They partied together in the kitchen of that fascinating 1668 house with its curious roof pitches and angles; with its low-slung ceilings from a period when women barely scaled five feet and men, on the average, were only a few inches taller; with its secret chimney stairway, where one could hide from whichever happened to be the more dangerous at the moment, Indians or witch hunters.

Hawthorne courted in Salem and wed his one and only love: Sophia Peabody, a sickly girl before marriage and a doting one after. Sophia was not without gifts, but seldom seems so interesting as her sister Mary, who married Horace Mann, the "father" of the American free public school system, or Elizabeth, the eldest and most intellectual of the Peabody sisters. Elizabeth was a student of Ralph Waldo Emerson (he helped her with her Greek), an admirer of Bronson Alcott, and a library assistant for a time to William Ellery Channing; she was an activist for abolition, a bookseller, one-woman publishing house, and founder of the American kindergarten. It was in Elizabeth's rooms in Boston that members of the Transcendentalist Club occasionally came together for their weighty discussions. With Margaret Fuller, the leading feminist of the age, Elizabeth Peabody was a moving spirit behind *The Dial*, the famed journal of New England transcendentalism. Later she became its publisher.

Hawthorne encountered transcendentalism primarily through Elizabeth and inevitably came into contact with George Ripley, organizer of the Brook Farm communal experiment in West Roxbury. Hawthorne was not an enthusiast for transcendentalism. Nevertheless, he joined the community and invested a precious $1,000 in its future, believing that Brook Farm promised that desired combination of work and leisure suited to his literary creativeness. He was hopeful, too, that life there might enable him to marry Sophia sooner rather than later. For one thing, small cottages for individual families were planned for Brook Farm.

On all counts the experiment disappointed Hawthorne. He was not cut out for Brook Farm's occupational tasks; indeed, his laboring talents were such that he speedily found himself assigned to duty on the manure pile—his "gold mine," as he wrote in letters to Sophia. There were other problems. The "conversations" of Brook Farm's distinguished clientele were, he found, sometimes brilliant and more often eccentric. More importantly, the "gold mine" and the almost endless visiting between quarters had not rendered Brook Farm conducive to writing. After two attempts at life there—the second as a boarder only—Hawthorne quit, a thousand dollars poorer and only a book of stories for children to show. But Brook Farm was not so total a waste of Hawthorne's time as he might have been tempted to think. Ten years later he drew on the experience for his novel, *The Blithedale Romance*, a loosely drawn *roman à clef* featuring an egotistical reformer, an innocent maiden under the sinister influence of a mesmerist, and a dark, queenly woman in love with the reformer. When the reformer reveals his love for the innocent maiden, the dark, queenly woman drowns herself. The dark, queenly woman was modeled in part on Margaret Fuller, who two years before the book's appearance had drowned in a shipwreck off New York's Fire Island.

Despite extensive exposure to movers and movements—at Brook Farm; at Concord, where he mixed with Alcott, Emerson, Channing, and Thoreau; at Lenox, where he was friendly with Herman Melville, then at work nearby on *Moby-Dick*—Hawthorne remained a singularly uninvolved individual, in his person and in his writing. He lived in one of the great periods of ferment in the history of the United States, but the currents of change and tides of debate flowed around him as if he were a pile driven into the bottoms of Salem harbor or Concord River. He was unmoved by issues large or small—from the reform of diet and attire on one level of concern, to the emancipation of slaves on another. Hawthorne's attitude toward slavery was vexing to friends and, most immediately, to Sophia's sisters. He felt no particular sympathy for slaves and in fact believed that "laboring whites . . . as a general thing, are ten times worse off than the Southern negroes." Sophia, sharing his sentiments, could become upset when a workman busy on the study tower being added to The Wayside, the Hawthorne home in Concord, went off to join Lincoln's army.

Hawthorne himself was not indifferent about the war with the South. He was anxious for a Northern victory, but not out of an anxiety for the preservation of the Union. He had long felt that the United States was too vast and multicultural for the country ever to achieve a satisfactory political homogeneity. War was worth supporting primarily in order that the North would have the say on the point "where our diseased members shall be lop't off." In point of fact Hawthorne would have been perfectly content to see New England as a separate nation and let the rest of the United States go as it would.

Hawthorne's attitudes towards the Civil War escaped from the parlors of Concord to the country at large in July, 1862, when he wrote in the *Atlantic Monthly* of a visit to Washington that had taken him to such nerve-centers of the conflict as Fort Ellsworth, McClellan's headquarters at Fairfax Seminary, Harper's Ferry, Manassas, Fort Monroe—and the White House itself. His unconcern for the issues flashed from his article, and the overall tone of dispassion clashed with popular sentiments. Inevitably this brought down on Hawthorne and the magazine an avalanche of protest. Negative as this was, it would have been even more intense had not an abrasive portrait of Lincoln been excised from the article at the insistence of James T. Fields, the *Atlantic*'s editor and the Fields of the publishing house, Ticknor and Fields, that handled Hawthorne's books. Hawthorne had sketched an "Uncle Abe" of coarse physiognomy and sly instincts, and, in the dead soberness of this moment of national history, had lapsed into humorous flippancy. He wondered, for instance, how Lincoln might "fold up his legs" when he sat down, an act, he observed, "which is said to be a most extraordinary spectacle." Fields elected to protect the magazine from public reaction and Hawthorne from himself. Hawthorne was unappreciative. He protested mightily, but Fields stood firm. Fields had the professional good sense, however, to preserve the disputed passage for posterity, and this he published after both Lincoln and Hawthorne were dead and Civil War emotions had ebbed.

There were religious jaundices as well—particularly, at one time, towards Catholicism, though these were to mitigate considerably during a two-year residency in Italy. Hawthorne managed a magnanimity when daughter Una leaned towards Anglicanism, but it is probably as well that he was not around when Rose, his youngest, "went to Rome." To Hawthorne, Catholicism had been that "old, corrupted faith" peopled by "torpid recluses" closed off in monasteries and convents. By twist of fate, Rose was to become one of those "recluses." After the death of her husband, George Parsons Lathrop, in 1898, she joined the Dominicans, and as Mother Alphonse established Saint Rose's Free Home for Cancer in New York

City. Later she moved her work to Hawthorne, New York, where Rosary Hill Hospital was opened and staffed by the Servants of Relief for Incurable Cancer, an order which Rose Hawthorne organized. She died there in 1926. Hawthorne himself had died decades before, something of a Unitarian or Trinitarian.

Of course, it is not Hawthorne's social views or religious predispositions that matter now. He is important as a novelist whose background and temperament enabled him to climb into history and recreate that bleak period of New England's past when a rigorous Puritanism gripped its soul. Hawthorne wrote many types of books: tales for boys and girls, children's histories, short stories, a campaign biography of Franklin Pierce, and a number of "romances." He also edited a magazine for a spell and shaped navy-man Horatio Bridge's impressions into the *Journal of an African Cruiser*. But it is in two "Salem" books that Hawthorne's reputation is generally considered to be anchored: *The Scarlet Letter*, the story of the young woman in Puritan Massachusetts who must wear the scarlet "A" on her breast for bearing a child out of wedlock; and *The House of the Seven Gables*, the story of a family living under the curse of a man sent to the gallows for witchcraft. The novels were published in 1850 and 1851, respectively. Since then few American children have left school without lingering memories of Hester Prynne, the long-suffering seamstress; the weak and cowardly minister who did her wrong, the Reverend Arthur Dimmesdale; the infamous Jeffrey Pyncheon; and the wronged Matthew Maule. In both books, Hawthorne probes deeply into the nature of sin and, in *The Scarlet Letter*, the sin of concealment particularly; in both books his genius flashes with unmistakable clarity.

The Scarlet Letter was written in Salem; *The House of the Seven Gables*, in Lenox—though everything in the novel rings of Salem, notably the house on Turner Street. There is some doubt that this multi-gabled house is actually the one that Hawthorne used as the setting of his novel. But there is no sensing this doubt from the appointments or the tour offered by guides. Hepzibah's little cent-shop; Clifford's chamber under the eaves; Judge Pyncheon's chair of death; the window beyond through which the butcher boy glimpsed his slumped figure—in the house at 54 Turner Street one could be moving through the pages of the novel itself. It is said that a great deal of imagination went into the restoration of the House of the Seven Gables before it was opened to the public in April, 1910. If so, it was an imagination that for visitors quickens the charm of the place and deepens the mystery of the novel.

The House of the Seven Gables sits in a cluster of historic Salem homes: the Retire Beckett House, built in 1655; the Hathaway House, dating from 1682; an old counting house; and Hawthorne's birthplace, a circa-1750 structure moved to the Seven Gables complex in the 1950s from its original site at 27 Union Street.

There is about the grouping an air of affluence and gentility, but these were hardly Nathaniel Hawthorne's blessings through most of his life. His career as a writer was constantly troubled by the necessity of finding appointments that would support him and his family through his periods of creativeness. Fortunately, he was adept at securing political posts (it especially helped knowing Franklin Pierce from student days at Bowdoin), and thus he served from 1839 to 1840 as measurer of salt, coal, and other commodities at Boston Custom House; as surveyor in Salem Custom House, from 1846 to 1849; and as American consul at Liverpool, from 1853 to 1857. The Liverpool post was one of the juiciest political plums at President Pierce's disposal, but a bad investment kept Hawthorne from capitalizing as much as he would have liked on Liverpool's financial opportunities.

Hawthorne was ambiguous about these political appointments, and in fact liked none of them except for the money each brought into his pockets. He reacted bitterly when a change in the national administration resulted in his ousting from his Salem appointment and responded selfishly when Congress voted changes that made the Liverpool post less lucrative than it had been. He never evened the score with Congress, but he did, it seems, with the person most responsible for his removal from the Salem surveyorship. This was Charles Wentworth Upham, clergyman, historian, and public official, who was married to the sister of Oliver Wendell Holmes. The sinister Judge Pyncheon in *The House of the Seven Gables* is reputed to be modeled on Upham.

Hawthorne's last years were less than personally satisfactory ones. He was writing regularly for the *Atlantic Monthly*, and at the top of the magazine's pay scale, receiving a then-generous $100 for an article of ten pages or less, and $10 per page additional for those that ran more than ten pages. (Longfellow was receiving $100 for two sonnets; Bayard Taylor, the poet, traveler, and man of popular letters, $60 for one article.) At the same time Hawthorne was busy with two romances, *Septimius Felton* and *Dr. Grimshawe's Secret*, a long sketch that is *The Ancestral Footstep*, and the fragmentary sections of *The Dolliver Romance*. He was busy and intellectually challenged, but he was sagging emotionally and psychologically. His daughter Una's precarious health weighed heavily on him, and his own health suddenly collapsed. He took to the woods when friends came to call, grew apathetic about his work, and headed into a deep, debilitating depression. However, Hawthorne showed "no positive malady," and Sophia thought—disastrously, it was to develop—that the best tonic would be a change of air and scene.

In March 1864, accordingly, Hawthorne was packed off to New York with William Davis Ticknor, Fields's partner and Hawthorne's devoted friend. Their intention was to catch a boat from New York for Havana. Prolonged bad weather, however, prevented a sailing, and after some restless days at the Astor House they decided to set out for Philadelphia. Ticknor was laboring under a worsening cold, and in Philadelphia this turned into pneumonia. In a few days' time, he was dead. It was a classic instance of role-reversal between the healthy and the infirm; the shock and necessary exertions did not help Hawthorne's condition.

Back in Concord, the decline became near-complete. It was thought that a carriage trip through the mountains of New Hampshire might snap him back. This time, ex-President Pierce was enlisted as companion and nurse. Hawthorne by now was suffering pain; he had indigestion, stomach distension, and other complaints. Hawthorne and Pierce met in Boston, where Hawthorne first consulted with Oliver Wendell Holmes, the essayist and physician. Holmes found his condition very unfavorable, but not immediately threatening of death. On May 12, accordingly, Hawthorne and Pierce boarded a train for Concord, New Hampshire. They were tied down for four days by rain, but finally on May 16 began the carriage trip that was supposed to be curative, moving leisurely to Franklin, Laconia, Centre Harbor, and reaching Plymouth, New Hampshire, the evening of May 18. They put up at Penigewasset House. That day Hawthorne had been virtually unable to walk or use his hands, and that night he died. Pierce discovered the dead body when he checked the bed between three and four o'clock in the morning. Dr. Holmes surmised that he died by fainting—"the gentlest of all modes of release." Four days later Hawthorne was laid to rest back in Concord. Longfellow, Holmes, Alcott, Fields, Emerson, and James Russell Lowell were among the pallbearers; Franklin Pierce accompanied Mrs. Hawthorne and the three Hawthorne children, daughters Una and Rose and son Julian. It was a glorious spring day. All was so bright and quiet, wrote Emerson, that pain or mourning was hardly suggested.

Sophia Hawthorne stayed on in Concord for four years, where she edited her husband's notebooks for publication in the *Atlantic*, taking what are said to have been great.liberties with the original manuscripts. Then, in 1868, she yanked up roots and children and left for Dresden, Germany, enticed partly by the romance of Europe, but impelled also by another decline in the Hawthorne family fortunes. Nathaniel Hawthorne's estate had been appraised at $26,000, and Civil War inflation was speedily eating into that. In addition, Sophia Hawthorne had come to the conclusion—"with very questionable justice," in the judgment of biographer Randall Stewart—that Fields had defrauded her and her husband of proper royalty income. Pierce had helped handsomely with Julian's education at Harvard, but Sophia found not a whole lot more to be grateful for. So she left.

Sophia Hawthorne was not in Dresden long. Within two years, uncongenial lodgings and continental wars forced her to London, where there were some friends and many invitations. Health problems, however, now compounded life's difficulties, and in the damp cold of the winter of 1871, Sophia Hawthorne, 61, died of "typhoid pneumonia" in her five-pounds-a-month home an ocean away from Salem and Concord.

It was sad, and almost as though Rebecca Nurse had had the last word.

If You Travel . . .

. . .in pursuit of Nathaniel Hawthorne, head first for Salem. The

House of the Seven Gables is at the foot of Turner Street, on the historic Salem Harbor waterfront. The house was built in 1668 by Captain John Turner and remained in the Turner family for more than a century, when it passed into the hands of the Ingersolls, relatives of the Hawthornes. Subsequently, the Emmerton family took possession, and Caroline O. Emmerton ensured its availability to the public in 1910. The House of the Seven Gables is the principal attraction in a grouping of old Salem structures that features the Hathaway House (1682), the Retire Beckett House (1655), and Nathaniel Hawthorne's Birthplace (ca. 1750). The complex is operated by an incorporated organization called the House of Seven Gables Settlement Association. Association membership dues and visitor admission receipts maintain the operation and, likewise, support social-work programs conducted by the Association.

The House of the Seven Gables is open the year round, including summer evenings, except for Thanksgiving, Christmas, and New Year's Day. The Retire Beckett House, and its gift shop, is open from April through November; the Hathaway House and Hawthorne's Birthplace, from July through Labor Day, as well as on spring and fall weekends. There is a modest admission fee. Daytime hours are from 10:00 A.M. to 5:00 P.M.

In Salem one may also visit the Custom House, where Hawthorne worked so discontentedly as surveyor of the port from 1846 to 1849. Admission is free. At the head of Salem's Hawthorne Boulevard is the Hawthorne Monument by Bela Pratt. Street markers guide the stranger to most of the landmarks.

Salem is an easy twenty-mile drive from Boston via Route 1 or 1A. Route 1A takes one along brief stretches of the scenic Massachusetts shoreline. Approaching Salem from the west on the Massachusetts Turnpike, drivers can avoid Boston entirely by connecting with Route 128 North and exiting at Salem. There is public transportation from Boston to Salem by both train and bus.

The Hawthorne pilgrimage continues at Concord, where Hawthorne first settled in 1842 with his young bride, Sophia Peabody. Their residence then was the Old Manse, which Hawthorne helped immortalize with his book, *Mosses from an Old Manse*. A dark gray, clapboard structure with a gambrel roof, the Old Manse was built in 1765 by the grandfather of Ralph Waldo Emerson. It is adjacent to the Concord Battleground and is open daily from June 1 through October 15, from 10:00 A.M. to 4:30 P.M., and Sundays from 1:00 to 4:30 P.M. The remainder of the year it is open only on weekends, except for April 19, Patriot's Day, when it is open all day. (Patriot's Day marks the anniversary of the battle of Lexington and is observed as a legal holiday in Massachusetts.) There is a small admission fee.

A short distance away on Lexington Road is The Wayside, the home which Hawthorne purchased when he returned to Concord in 1852, and to which he added the frame tower, reached by trap door, where he did much of his later writing. The Alcotts once lived in this house, and in the barn Louisa and her sisters staged their early plays. The Wayside suffered damage from fire, which required restoration, and has undergone a major piece of restyling, with a broad piazza added in the 1880s by Margaret Sidney (Mrs. Harriett Mulford Lothrop), author of the children's book series, The Five Little Peppers. Nevertheless, The Wayside is an authentic Hawthorne shrine and has on display considerable Hawthorne memorabilia, including furniture. The house is open from April 1 through October. Visiting hours are from 10:00 A.M. to 5:00 P.M., Thursdays through Mondays. (The house is closed Tuesdays and Wednesdays.) There is a modest admission charge for adults; children age fifteen or under are admitted free.

Concord is within fifteen miles of Boston, via Route 2 or 2A. Coming from the west over the Massachusetts Turnpike, drivers may take the 495 Exit and proceed north to Route 2 and Concord. There is public bus transportation from Harvard Square in Cambridge to Concord, by way of Lexington and Bedford Airport. There is also train service from Boston's North Station.

Across the state of Massachusetts from Concord, in the town of Lenox in the Berkshire Hills, is the little red cottage that was home for the Hawthornes in 1850–1851, when he was writing *The House of the Seven Gables*. It was here that Herman Melville would come to visit. The house is on a side road (West Hawthorne Street) leading to the east gate of the Tanglewood music-festival grounds, site of the famous summer concerts of the Boston Symphony Orchestra. The house, alas, is not open to the public.

Chapter
Eleven

HERMAN MELVILLE

A Stormy Passage over the Sea of Life

For Herman Melville, life was a rough passage. He was bedeviled by debts and disappointments. His masterpiece, *Moby-Dick: or The White Whale*, was a critical and financial failure. His books of poetry appeared mostly at his own expense. His final book, *Billy Budd*, was not published until more than thirty years after his death.

Melville craved literary recognition, but such that he knew in his lifetime was for lesser works. Even that wisped away, with the speed almost of an ocean wave-cap, twenty years before he was overtaken by death. He lived out his years mostly as a four-dollar-a-day deputy inspector in New York customs offices. The last decades were cushioned by legacies from both sides of his family. This was not, however, the comfort for which Melville yearned, nor the remembrance. He yearned for fame as a writer, but when he died in 1891, the obituaries were skimpy, and the *New York Times* mistakenly referred to him as Henry.

Of course, the recognition factor was to be rectified—but, alas, a generation after his death. In 1919, the centenary of Melville's birth sent scholars back to his books and, inevitably, *Moby-Dick*. Shrewder, more sophisticated minds discovered at last a talent that could stand shoulder to shoulder with Emerson, Hawthorne, Thoreau, Whitman; and a book that compared to any nineteenth-century literary classic, American, British, or European. The intellectual side of the Melville ledger was eventually righted.

On May 1, 1976—during the Bicentennial year of the nation's founding—there was a further redressing of Melville's memory with the opening to the public of Arrowhead—the farmhouse in Pittsfield, Massachusetts, that was home to Melville from 1850 to 1863. It was at Arrowhead, in the upstairs study facing the Greylock range, with its rolling form of a giant sperm whale, that Melville wrote *Moby-Dick*. It was here, to the north end of the house, that he added the piazza, where he puffed his pipe, paced up and down, and hammered out ideas for the six short stories that he would group together as *The Piazza Tales*. And here in Arrowhead is the stone and brick subject of "I and My Chimney," a delightful piece of introspection that outlived the magazine in which it appeared, the October 1855 *Putnam's*.

Arrowhead is hardly the same place it was when Melville's four children were romping about and the white frame house was often crowded with long-staying kin. Only 14.1 acres remain of the original 160-acre tract of farm land that Melville bought, house and outbuildings included, for $6,500. The piazza is gone from the house (or was, until its planned replacement), and inside considerable alteration has been done over the years by a series of owners. But the house, which dates from 1780, is sound, and the chimney is as the chimney was. Intact, too, are the chimney-stone and wall-panel inscriptions, freely adapted in text and spelling, from "I and My Chimney," and set in place by Melville's brother Allan, a later owner of Arrowhead:

The Root of the matter. "This is a most remarkable structure, Sir." "Yes," said I, "everyone says so." "The magnitude of this foundation, Sir! Twelve feet square; one hundred and forty-four square feet! Sir, this house would appear to have been built simply for the accommodation of your chimney." "Yes, my chimney and me."

* * *

I And My Chimney; as Cardinal Wolsey used to say, I and my King. Yet this egotistic way of speaking, wherein I take precedence of my chimney, is hardly borne out by the facts; in everything, except the above phrase, my chimney taking precedence of one. My chimney is grand signor here—the one great domineering object of the house, which is accommodated not to my wants but my chimney's.

He has the center of the house to himself, leaving but the odd holes and corners to me.

There is considerable work to be done around Arrowhead to return the house fully to what it was in Melville's time. Partitions must come down, fireplaces be unbricked, doors returned to old openings, and maybe a stairway redirected—although the latter project is uncertain. The present stairway is roomier and safer, while

From 1850 to 1863, Herman Melville lived in this farm house on "the
hither side of Pittsfield." In an upstairs room that looked towards the
Greylock range, with its rolling form of a giant sperm whale, he wrote
Moby Dick. Here, too he fused the ideas that he grouped as **The Piazza
Tales**. The piazza, which was to the right-side of the house, as sketched, is
being restored.

the original one might not conform to Massachusetts building codes. In any case, all this is less a problem of carpentry than it is a challenge of fund raising and of time. The restoration of Arrowhead represents a $250,000 commitment on the part of the Berkshire County Historical Society, Arrowhead's new proprietors. As a registered National Landmark, Arrowhead is eligible for matching government grants, but that still leaves the better part of $125,000 to be raised from other sources; $25,000 has already been pledged by the board of directors of the society.

How is the money being used? More than $16,000 is going for renewal of the chimney room and the northeast bedroom, the upstairs study where Melville built his fire and wrote with such intensity for such long stretches that his family feared for his health. Another $35,000 is required for restoration of the piazza, the front entrance, the barn, and a picket fence along what is now Holmes Road—Wendell Street in Melville's time. (The street was renamed years ago in honor of the then more celebrated Oliver Wendell Holmes, whose country place was a mile down the road from Melville's.)

The restoration process will extend over several years, according to Donald S. Smith, executive director of the Berkshire County Historical Society and curator in residence of the Arrowhead property. But this did not delay the opening of Arrowhead as a highlight of the nation's Bicentennial observance.

"The restoration is being arranged so that only one project will be worked on at a time," Smith declared, by way of reassuring early visitors that they will not find themselves competing with an army of carpenters. "We anticipate, actually, that many people will be greatly interested in seeing a restoration in progress."

Visitors to Arrowhead find five rooms available for viewing, including the chimney room, which was the original kitchen, and the upstairs room where Melville did his writing. On display are numerous Melville artifacts: his spectacles, books from his library, ironstone chinaware from the Melville dinner table, an unsigned gouache that brought a dash of color and a touch of Greylock indoors. Also, there are mementos of Melville's second daughter and fourth child, Frances, who was born at Arrowhead, such as her toy cupboard and tin utensils.

Two other rooms of Arrowhead are given over to period furniture and material relating to Berkshire County history. Another area is designed as the public room of an inn, in order to reflect the earliest, pre-Melville history of the house. No major section of Arrowhead or the grounds is expected to be off-limits during the extended restoration process. However, Smith does advise that groups larger than family size make reservations beforehand, either by writing to Arrowhead (780 Holmes Road, Pittsfield, Massachusetts, 01201) or by telephoning (413-442-1793). Guided tours are handled by volunteers of the Berkshire County Historical Society.

The historical society acquired Arrowhead on February 28, 1975, for $100,000. It was a purchase the society could not particularly afford, but one that it could not pass up. The society already owned three properties, and, as William H. Pierson, retired Williams College professor and a former society president, declared, "the very thought of adding another and even larger holding seemed to be nothing short of madness."

"At the same time," Pierson continued, "every reasonable indicator pointed to the fact that if the society was to flourish and grow, the acquisition of Melville's house offered the greatest promise of all the options it had or, indeed, that might ever come its way." The society took the plunge. It disposed of Headquarters House and Goodrich House, both in Pittsfield, and Citizens' Hall in nearby Stockbridge, and put the money towards Arrowhead. It was a gamble as safe as tomorrow's dawn.

When Herman Melville came to Arrowhead—on "the hither side of Pittsfield," as Hawthorne would have it—he enjoyed a notoriety as the man who had adventured in the Pacific, "had lived among the cannibals," and survived to tell his stories in *Typee* (1846) and *Omoo* (1847), books that fed popular reading tastes for the world beyond American horizons. The books grew out of Melville's amazing experiences, first as a teenage cabin-boy on the *Highlander* out of New York for Liverpool, then as a crew-hand on the whalers *Acushnet*, *Lucy Ann*, and *Charles and Henry* in the South Seas.

Melville, incidentally, was not the ship's hand that captains dream of. He jumped the *Acushnet* in the Marquesas Islands, and there fell into the company of his fortuitously friendly cannibals. He joined the crew of the *Lucy Ann*, but jumped it in Papeete, after being on the fringes of a near-mutiny. He made his way to Honolulu, where he clerked in a general store and developed further his essentially negative impressions about the Eastward flow of Christian civilization. The natives, Melville would one day write, "had been civilized into draft horses, and evangelized into beasts of burden."

Bored with bookkeeping and the measuring of calico cloth, and uncertain about his security—the captain of the *Acushnet* had recently sworn to his desertion before officials in the West Maui town of Lahaina—Melville abandoned another agreement. (He had entered a one-year contract with the merchandise firm and fulfilled ten weeks of it.) Seizing the shorter of two service options—three years' duty or the duration of the cruise—Melville enlisted in the navy and shipped out of Hawaii aboard the frigate *United States*. It was a masterstroke of planning or unbelievably good luck. The navy afforded protection to a fugitive, respectability to a deserter, and passage home over an exciting and, for Melville, new watery part of the world. Fifteen months after enlisting in the navy, Melville was mustered out, the behavioral slate wiped clean and the mind crammed with tales from four years of wandering that ached for the telling.

Not everyone believed those tales of *Typee* and *Omoo*, so exotic were the adventures. Reviewers debated the veracity of the writer and the credibility of his narratives. Publishers grappled with the problem of classification; was Melville writing fact or fiction, travelogue or novel? (Actually, there were elements of all.)

Nor were patriotic chauvinists entirely at ease. Taking shape were the sentiments that would burst full bloom in *Mardi*, Melville's third book—such as the unglamorous idea that Britain lost the Revolutionary War less at the hands of Americans than because of geography; such as, too, the notion that the United States was hardly the land of the free, while blacks were enslaved. In one episode of *Mardi*, a man with the red stripes of the lash across his back raises a correspondingly striped tapa standard in a so-called Temple of Freedom. The analogy was not so subtle as to be missed.

But the greater stir, by far, of Melville's early books was created by his observations about the missionaries who were fanning out into the Pacific, mainly from the American Board of Foreign Missions in Boston. They carried a shallow theology, Melville felt, and a shallower regard for the cultures they encountered. Accordingly, he saw their influence as spiritually and socially negative. Whig newspapers and religious journals excoriated him. But, as biographer Leon Howard has noted, Melville seemed less sensitive to allegations of prejudice than to charges that he had romanticized his adventures.

Melville settled in Pittsfield in 1850, anxious to recapture the contentedness that he knew from earlier stays in the community and that he sensed he needed to feel again as a serious writer. He was a city boy by birth, being born in New York City, at 6 Pearl Street, on August 1, 1819. But he grew up in Albany, not the city then that it is now, and Lansingburgh, now part of the city of Troy, New York. His was an unsettled bringing up. The heritage was proud, on both sides. (His mother was a Gansevoort, one of the noted Dutch families of early New York; Grandfather Melville, a Boston Tea Party veteran, was to be memorialized in Oliver Wendell Holmes's poem "The Last Leaf.") Fortunes had dwindled, however, and though there was much supportive visiting between family homesteads—in Boston, in Pittsfield—there was little assuming of respective financial burdens. There couldn't be. Herman Melville, accordingly, had no formal education after he reached fifteen. He went to sea at seventeen.

Melville was back in New York City after his marriage in 1847 to Elizabeth Knapp Shaw, a woman of standing as the daughter of Lemuel Shaw, chief justice of the Supreme Judicial Court of Massachusetts. They lived in a shared house at 103 Fourth Avenue, Melville turning out in rapid succession *Mardi*, *Redburn*, and *White-Jacket*. Neither Herman nor Elizabeth liked their living arrangement, and for a time they thought of securing a place of their own in the city. However, Elizabeth's New England preferences and Herman's nostalgia for some happier memories of youth led them to the Berkshires and Pittsfield. For Melville, Pittsfield represented tranquillity and stability, and for a time both were his. Moreover, Pittsfield would prove stimulating in ways that for him New York had never been. Nathaniel Hawthorne was six miles away, busy on *The House of the Seven Gables*, and the two began the friendship that was to mean so much to Melville until it formalized, to Melville's enduring disappointment. Holmes was back and forth from Boston to his Pittsfield home. Book editor and biographer Evert Duyckinck would drop by, as would others of New York's literary fraternity who were sojourning in the Berkshires.

It was, in sum, a good time to be in western Massachusetts. There were the inevitable farm chores to be done—planting and hoeing, harvesting and storing; crops ranging from potatoes to apples. But the writing went well. Under the shadow of Greylock and in the quiet of rural Pittsfield, Ahab, Starbuck, Queequeg, Ishmael, Father Mapple, and the rest of *Moby-Dick*'s immortal cast took on flesh. For Melville, *Moby-Dick* was a different kind of book. He had fished out the waters of autobiographical experiences and had launched out now to philosophical and psychological depths in order to probe the meaning of good and evil, of truth, and of life itself. His devices were his knowledge of whaling and an allegorical story involving a whale called Moby-Dick.

Moby-Dick, incidentally, was no figment of Melville's imagination. Monstrous sperm whales that could stove in a ship or crush a whaleboat with a snap of the jaws were for years the talk of the ports of the Atlantic; indeed, they were capturing the fascination of creative artists as late as the 1930s, when Gordon Grant was drawing of whalers and the sea. In 1820, the *Essex*, a Nantucket whaler, went down after being attacked by a huge sperm whale, and for twenty years, no less, tales were rampant of the ferocious white whale that Melville was to immortalize. The whale was Mocha Dick, and was in mid-terror when Melville completed *Moby-Dick* in 1851. Before he was finally killed in 1859, Mocha Dick had caused the deaths of more than thirty seamen.

Paradoxically, the great white whale was also to do Melville in, psychologically and professionally. *Moby-Dick* was an agony of effort—a book "broiled" in "hell-fire," by Melville's expression to Hawthorne. Melville had no idea that he had created a masterpiece, but he knew he had written a good book, and he had high hopes for its success, particularly after Hawthorne, to whom *Moby-Dick* was dedicated, reacted affirmatively. "A sense of unspeakable security is in me at this moment, on account of your having understood the book," Melville wrote back. "I have written a wicked book, and feel spotless as a lamb."

Hawthorne's perceptiveness was to prove the exception. Family was kind, as families usually are. But friends puzzled over the book; reviewers wrote inane critiques; and the public wondered why Melville could not stick with simpler reminiscences, such as those of

Typee and *Omoo*. Harper's, Melville's publisher, lost so much confidence in him that when Melville asked for a further advance against royalties on his next book, they said no, on the grounds that he had already been given $700. British publishers were similarly timid.

Harper's negativism fulfilled itself. Two years later its plant burned down, destroying the plates of Melville's books, along with bound copies and sheet stocks of his unsold books. The fire sent some Melville titles out of print for several years and left him $319.74 in debt to his publishers. To Melville the writer, it was the straw that broke the back. The five years of extraordinary output, that began with *Typee* and carried through *Moby-Dick*, that saw five thousand words a day flow from his pen, had netted him a meager $8,000—less than living expenses.

There was no upturn. The pre-Freudian times were not ready for Melville's next book, *Pierre*, a psychological novel that defied moral conventions by broaching the topic of brother-sister incest. The book virtually died on the shelf, only 283 volumes being sold in the first eight months after publication. Melville then took to travel (at in-law expense); then magazine stories, for as little as $5 a printed page; then lecturing, on the unlikely topic, "Statuary in Rome." Eventually, he reached to poetry to pour out the disappointment, the self-doubt, the utter desolation he experienced as a writer. It was an inconclusive, unsatisfying reach, artistically and emotionally. Nor was the effort helped by the fact that the reach had to be made almost in defiance of family, which forever preferred that Melville take care of health rather than pen. His was a family protectiveness that would lead to latter-day speculation that Melville the artist would have been better off had he unshackled himself of kin and let the spirit soar. Apparently, he never gave the idea a thought, a mildly surprising thing considering his restless energy and the maverick wanderlust of his early history.

As debts pressed in, Melville had looked to dispose of Arrowhead. In 1855 he offered the site to local authorities as the location for an insane asylum. When this deal fell through, he sold off eighty acres, "more or less," to George S. Wills for $5,500, completing the transaction in April 1856. That sum helped, but only for a time. Four years later Melville's in-laws intervened again, arranging for the purchase of Arrowhead from Herman and its transfer to his wife Elizabeth. This discharged Melville's substantial loan indebtedness to Judge Shaw, totaling almost $7,000, and provided Elizabeth an early advance against her family legacy. But it was not the end to their struggles. When a state department appointment to a foreign consulate fell through, the Melvilles closed up Arrowhead and moved initially into Pittsfield proper, then to New York City. Melville used some precious financial reserve to pay off his remaining $200 debt to Harper's, thus getting off his back and out of mind his "annual reminder," in one biographer's words, of his lack of success as a writer. Then he went to work in 1866 on his four-dollar-a-day job as deputy inspector of customs in offices at 207 West Street.

Melville got that appointment partially through acquaintanceship with the new collector of customs; partially, too, on the basis of his patriotic poetry. It was no plum of a job, but Melville kept at it for nineteen years, serving patiently as a minor public servant, while the world forgot him as an artist—this, despite the fact that his early books were creeping back into print.

The retirement years were not particularly golden. Melville wrote a little and brooded a lot. His second son died in faraway San Francisco in 1886. Stanwix had always been more worry than solace, and Melville apparently never referred to him in correspondence. Yet Stanwix was loved, and his death undoubtedly stirred anew other, older anguishes over Malcolm's death. Malcolm, the Melville's firstborn, died a suicide in 1867—perhaps, as the coroner's jury stated, while "suffering from a temporary aberration of the mind." But was that death triggered, quite literally, by a scolding delivered by Mrs. Melville for being out until three in the morning? Whatever, with Stanwix's death and that of several relatives and friends, Melville was left with a wife, two daughters, and grandchildren to outlive him—and apparently nothing of fame.

Death came to Herman Melville as unspectacularly as the life that family and critics had imposed upon him. He died just after midnight on September 28, 1891, of "Cardiac dilatation, Mitral regurgitation [and] Contributory Asthenia"—at home, 104 East Twenty-sixth Street, where his family would have him; and virtually anonymous, as his critics would have decreed as being meet and just. The funeral notices were brief, most agreeing that his popularity as a writer ended about 1853 and that his most famous book was

Typee. One paper observed that "even his own generation had long thought him dead, so quiet have been the later years of his life." There was no doubt of that fact.

The remains were consigned to Woodlawn Cemetery in the North Bronx, near Yonkers. A small piece of marble, decorated with scroll, quill pen, and vine, told what seemed to have been the whole story:

Herman Melville
Born August 1, 1819
Died September 28, 1891

History's verdict was more lavish.

If You Travel . . .

. . .to Arrowhead from New York City, plan on a three-hour drive and a distance of about 150 miles. Drivers should pick up Route 684 from the Hutchinson River Parkway and proceed to the Route 84 junction. There one has a choice of the Taconic State Parkway or Route 22 North. Route 22 is slower, but shorter. Drivers taking Route 22 should turn east on Route 23 at Hillsdale, New York, and connect with Route 7 in Massachusetts going north. Route 7 will mesh with Route 20 in Lenox and pass within a half-mile of Herman Melville's home. Watch for Holmes Road running off Routes 7 and 20 in Lenox. Arrowhead is at 780 Holmes Road, a short distance across the Lenox-Pittsfield line. It is an imposing white frame farmhouse with a granite marker out front identifying it as the residence for thirteen years of Herman Melville, "Mariner and Mystic."

Via the New York State Throughway/Massachusetts Turnpike— connecting as Route 90—drivers may exit at Lee and head towards Pittsfield and Arrowhead on Route 20.

From May 1 to October 31, Arrowhead is open Mondays through Saturdays, Tuesdays excepted, from 10:00 A.M. to 5:00 P.M. (Arrowhead is closed all day Tuesday during these months.) Sunday hours are from 1:00 to 5:00 P.M.

From November 1 to April 30, Arrowhead is open Tuesdays through Sundays from 2:00 to 5:00 P.M. During these months, Arrowhead is closed on Mondays. There is a modest admission fee.

A mile further down Holmes Road from Arrowhead, at number

497, is Holmesdale, the home in which Oliver Wendell Holmes spent several seasons and where he wrote "The Deacon's Masterpiece," "The New Eden," and "The Ploughman," featuring local themes. Holmesdale is cited on many road maps, but it is in private hands and is not open to the public. Several residences of more recent construction have cut off its view from the road. Holmesdale has likewise been remodeled considerably from Holmes's time.

In New York City, the grave of Herman Melville may be viewed at Woodlawn Cemetery in the Bronx from 9:00 A.M. to 4:30 P.M. daily, including Sundays and holidays. By automobile from downtown New York, the cemetery is reached via the Major Degan Parkway and East 233rd Street. Entrance to the cemetery is through gates on Jerome Avenue and Webster Avenue. By subway, one may take the Woodlawn train (#4) on the Lexington Avenue line. The cemetery is the last stop.

Chapter
Twelve

EMILY DICKINSON

From Rural Amherst, "Love Letters" to the World

In the intoxication of her early teens, Emily Dickinson enthused to a friend that she was growing "handsome" very fast indeed. "I expect," she declared, "I shall be the belle of Amherst when I reach my seventeenth birthday." There was a note of the facetious in the comment, and, two sentences further, she did indeed exclaim, "away with my nonsense." Yet Emily—she has ever been known familiarly—needn't have discounted. Life left her short of her expectation only in the type belle-beautiful she anticipated she would be.

Emily Dickinson's characteristics were engaging. "I . . . am small like the Wren," she wrote on another occasion, "and my Hair is bold, like the Chestnut Bur, and my eyes, like the Sherry in the Glass, that the Guest leaves." One ungallantly candid contemporary said hers was a face "without a single good feature." But whether she was good-looking or not is quite unimportant. What matters is that she possessed the substantive, enduring beauty of mind and spirit, of insight and expression—and these qualities did in time attract, for all time, the "perfect crowds of admirers" she looked forward to as a fourteen-year-old.

The admirers of her lifetime were few, however—or relatively so. Emily Dickinson was an exquisitely gifted poet, but the verse that was to crown her the "belle of Amherst," with title in the world beyond, was a private thing throughout her fifty-six years; or at least unpublic. Only seven of her 1,775 poems were published during her lifetime—1830–1886—and these anonymously. However, many more, into the hundreds actually, circulated among relatives and close friends, and they gathered to her a worshipful and steadily growing following. By the time of her death, her talent was a familiar Amherst tradition; five years after, her fame was national and leaping across oceans.

Amherst, Massachusetts: it was Emily Dickinson's experiential world. She was away from the community but briefly—to South Hadley for a year's study at the female seminary that was to evolve as Mount Holyoke College; to Washington for a few weeks in 1854, while her father was serving a term as a congressman, with a stop en route home in Philadelphia; to Boston twice, in 1864 and 1865, for medical care. She could not get back fast enough to the homestead, to Amherst's sunrises and flowers, its "lover" bees and "rowdy" bobolinks, to her bedroom retreat with its view of the Pelham Hills and Mount Holyoke Range. These were the inspiration and themes of her poetry:

> I'll tell you how the Sun rose—
> A Ribbon at a time—
> The Steeples swam in Amethyst—
> The news, like Squirrels, ran—
> ....;

these themes and the everyday dramas of loving and dying, with their overreaching questions about immortality.

Emily Dickinson set her thoughts down with a grace and skill that captivated all with whom she shared her art—with the crucial exception, of course, of the person she chose, quite by chance, as her "perceptor," Thomas Wentworth Higginson. His dubiousness about the absolute merits of her poetry—he thought the poems formless and spasmodic—was fateful. It sealed her obscurity as a poet during her lifetime just as surely as Emily's celebrated and puzzling reclusiveness sealed her obscurity as a person.

There were others whom Emily Dickinson might have approached for reassurance about her poetry—Longfellow, maybe, or William Cullen Bryant. Had she, her life might have been so different. But Higginson, a clergyman turned man of letters, had attracted attention with an essay in the April 1862 *Atlantic Monthly* offering advice to young writers, and Emily was emboldened to forward samples of her craft, with the inquiry: Is my verse alive? A long and earnest correspondence followed; many more poems moved by post between Emily in western Massachusetts and Higginson in eastern Massachusetts. Nothing convinced Higginson that here was a very special genius. Her poetry? *"Too delicate . . .* not strong enough to publish," he thought.

Amherst was Emily Dickinson's experiential world. She wrote in a house that is as intimidating in its twentieth-century literary eminence as it was in its nineteenth-century stateliness. A high hemlock hedge guards the privacy of the house as effectively as Emily Dickinson guarded her own privacy.

It was a notorious misjudgment, unredeemed by Higginson's coeditorship with Mabel Loomis Todd of the first and second series of *Poems by Emily Dickinson*, published in 1890 and 1891, respectively. It turns out even these editing tasks were assumed timidly by Higginson, he being never totally persuaded that the undertakings complemented his stature as literary critic. He lived long enough to learn otherwise, not dying until 1911. By then the first series of *Poems* had since passed into a seventeenth edition; the second series, a fifth; and Emily Dickinson was enshrined among poetry's immortals. Higginson was to rationalize his failure, but it did not gainsay the fact that his critical sense had played him history's fool. When the third series of *Poems* was published in 1896, his name was absent from the title page, and there appeared Mrs. Todd's.

Admittedly, Emily Dickinson never made understanding easy. Her poetry was new and different—in its images, its ideas, its sparseness, its unique punctuation. Then, too, her lifestyle, whether consciously chosen or psychologically induced, added elements of mystery—and fed conjecture. For beginning in her twenties, Emily Dickinson lived as a recluse, intensifyingly so: fleeing into the pantry passage when surprised by a visitor in the kitchen, conversing around corners, listening to parlor recitals from the "polar privacy" of her upstairs bedroom, lowering baskets of gingerbread from her bedroom window to children playing below. As the years passed, face-to-face contacts became more and more traumatic. She flitted about, virginal and ghostlike, in long, white dress and became so withdrawn that she would water the plants of porch and garden only under the protection of darkness.

Cultists and devotees maintain that Emily Dickinson was not shut in narrowly upon herself, and that the windows of home and mind opened broadly on the world through her quick wit and deep sensitivities. Besides, hadn't Emily herself said, "To shut our eyes is Travel"? True as this may be, the idiosyncrasies still have never been completely explained away. And just as they helped contribute to Higginson's befuddlement, so have they given rise to a flood of claptrap—pop psychology—about her life: parental resentments, disappointed romances, psychosexual problems of exotic sort. William Dean Howells of the *Atlantic* hinted that she was an American Sappho. To others she was a repressed Puritan heterosexual (actually there were several men in her life, all platonically so). To still more, she was a hopeless neurotic.

Recent scholarship has routed much of the psychological non-sense. Nevertheless, Emily Dickinson remains very much an enig-matic figure in the immortality that is hers. It seems but right. It would be a travesty if the sacred privacy she went to such lengths to construct and guard were to be stripped away now for no better purpose than to satisfy unrelated artistic curiosities about her life. Isn't it reward enough to have her art without her soul's being laid naked in the process?

By the same token, it seems right that the Dickinson homestead should be as private today as it was for Emily. The homestead is lived in and open to visitors—but not indiscriminately so. Just as one approached Emily by prearrangement, in the increasingly rare in-stances where that was possible, so does one visit the Dickinson homestead by appointment. The homestead is owned by Amherst College—has been since 1964—and is used essentially as a faculty residence. There are guided tours for the public from 3:00 to 5:00 P.M. on Tuesdays and Fridays, May 1 through October 1, and on Tues-days at the same hours during the rest of the year. But visits must be arranged through the office of the secretary at Amherst College (413-542-2321).

The Dickinson homestead sits behind a high hemlock hedge at 280 Main Street, just a few minutes' walk from the center of Amherst. It's a house as intimidating in its twentieth-century literary emi-nence as it was in its nineteenth-century stateliness. Then it was known as The Mansion. The Dickinsons were one of Amherst's distinguished families, and the house matched their prominence. Theirs was Amherst's first brick residence, and for years it was the site of what was once Amherst's grandest social occasion, the Com-mencement Tea—though, to be sure, it was not the house that brought the tea to the site, but the Dickinsons' connections to the college. Emily's grandfather, Samuel Fowler Dickinson, was a founder of the college; her father, Edward Dickinson, was college treasurer for thirty-eight years; on his resignation in 1873, he was succeeded by his son Austin.

In any case, one did not casually approach the Dickinson home-stead door then—and one does not now. Most especially, one does not intrude without that appointment. Julie Harris, the actress, once did, with embarrassing consequences.

This was several years ago, prior to Miss Harris's starring role in William Luce's smash Broadway play, *The Belle of Amherst*. Miss Harris arrived unannounced and learned that she could not be admitted to the house, but was free to wander about the grounds and through the garden that Emily tended with such loving care. It was fall, Miss Harris recalled in a note to me in 1976, and the big maple tree in the garden was scarlet. It must have been a mild day also, for a garden door was open, and Miss Harris slipped through it and up to Emily's bedroom while the then-resident curator of the homestead, Jean McClure Mudge, was occupied on the telephone.

Emily Dickinson

Of course Julie Harris was discovered, and of course there was a scene. Mrs. Mudge, not recognizing the "intruder," angrily demanded she leave. Miss Harris, too embarrassed, in her own phrase, to say who she was, quietly went off. Years later, when *The*

Belle of Amherst was on the boards, and Mrs. Mudge's own book on Emily Dickinson was published, there was a second meeting—and the revelation of the identity of the woman who came that fall day into Emily's bedroom. There were apologies all around, and generous forgivings—but others are advised not to go and do as Miss Harris did.

About one thousand visitors are shown through the Dickinson homestead each year by volunteer guides. There is a short acquaintanceship lecture on the family in the living room, with a picture portfolio as aid. Then visitors are ushered, almost solemnly, up the curved stairway, to the bedroom that was Emily's on the second floor's southeast corner. The homestead, incidentally, has been thoroughly modernized and, except for Emily's room, bears little resemblance to when the Dickinsons lived in it. The Dickinsons' marble fireplace dominates the living room still, but there similarities end. The room is bright and airy, and the bookcase is lined with volumes, many of which bear no relation to the Dickinsons or their period; at least such was the case when I visited in the spring of 1976. When Emily knew this living room, it was dark and forbidding, its windows shuttered against the heat of summer and draped against the cold of winter.

Even Emily's room is more a re-creation than an authentic shrine. There are some personal relics: her white dress, the red Civil War army blanket that she used as a kneeling pad in the garden, the room's Franklin stove; there are some family relics: a cradle, rush chair, kitchen clock, decanter and sherry glasses. But most of the original pieces have been dispersed, many escaping Amherst to Cambridge, where they are on display at the Houghton Library of Harvard University. In their place in the homestead are duplicate period pieces, selected and arranged according to Emily's own descriptions of the room and the later recollections of her niece, Martha Dickinson Bianchi. On the wall are portraits of George Eliot, Elizabeth Barrett, and Carlyle, as Emily would have them.

But re-created or not, the presence of the poet's spirit is overwhelming in the room, and particularly at the moment that Emily's white dress is lifted—reverently, as something holy—from the closet rack. (The dress, incidentally, is kept part of the year at the Amherst Historical Society Museum.)

Outside, a single pear tree remains of the fruit trees that once lined the flagstone walk. The hemlock and a white oak were contemporary with Emily Dickinson, but other trees planted by Edward and Austin Dickinson have tumbled before storms and removers. The barn—the Dickinsons had a hired man and kept cows, chickens, and horses—has been razed, but its weather vane and many of its timbers were used in the construction of the property's present garage.

Emily Dickinson wrote all but five of her poems in the house on Main Street, at writing tables set in various parts of the house. This house was a part of Emily, as much, in a way, as were family, friends, and poetry. The house was, in fact, a part of all the Dickinsons. It was built in 1813 by Emily's grandfather and lost by him twenty years later, partially because of an unstinting financial commitment to the survival of Amherst Academy, the educational institution which he helped to found and which grew into Amherst College. The grandfather's dedication was noble, but the loss of the house was a gnawing family humiliation, one not requited until Emily's father managed to buy it back in 1855.

Emily was born in this house, and, except for the "removal" years spent in a clapboard house on North Pleasant Street, she lived within its strong, protective walls. Next door another Dickinson house was built—for brother Austin and his wife, Susan Huntington Gilbert, Emily's dear friend of youth to whom she would send nearly three hundred poems, more than to anyone else. The house was "a hedge away" and linked by that "little path just wide enough for two who love." But the romance of its situating was to flee almost as fast as the romance that moved in with Austin and Susan.

That "little path" is posted now against trespassers, and thus becomes another symbolic extension of the history of the Dickinson family. The Dickinsons were close and interreliant. But all was not bliss—neither within the household, nor between the houses. Taking the second first, Austin and Susan's marriage was a disaster, and the old homestead evolved into a trysting place for Austin and Mabel Loomis Todd. "A hedge away," Susan fumed, warred with sister-in-law Lavinia—and endured her fecundity with the help of abortions. She had perhaps as many as four. Later, after Austin had transferred a strip of Dickinson property to Mrs. Todd in gratitude for her editorial work on Emily's poems, Lavinia sued to get it back—motivated, some say, by jealousy born of Mrs. Todd's success with Emily's poems. Lavinia got back the land, though at a price to the family's reputation and further delay to Emily's full entrance into the world of letters. Enraged and humiliated, Mrs. Todd quit her editing and slapped the lid tight on 665 as yet unpublished poems. It was not until 1914 that more Emily Dickinson poems reached the public, this time under the editorship of Martha Dickinson Bianchi, Susan's daughter, Emily's niece. All told, it took sixty-five years for Emily Dickinson's poetry to trickle out; no major poet has fared so poorly in publishing tempo.

Emily, of course, was spared many of these sordid tensions, having died in 1886. It is as well; beside the posthumous tensions, those of her lifetime pale—which is not to minimize them, either. Her father was an austere and dominating man, and, much as Emily loved him, she was intimidated by him, to such an extent, in fact, that while she was growing up she would conceal an inability to tell time. (She mastered the clock only by her mid-teens.) Daughter's dependency on father was such that his death was for her traumatic. Daughter also loved mother, but there was a distance emotionally and intellectually. Emily's mother, by daughter's own words, was a woman who "does not care for thought." It was a damning comment. Only in the mother's invalidism did the two grow intimate. Finally, there were brother Austin, ever close to Emily, and Lavinia, the youngest of the three Dickinson children.

Lavinia was Emily's shield from the world and, at the same time, a door to it. Lavinia traveled and she visited, and she returned with tales that would regale her favorite listener. As the years progressed, Lavinia evolved into an extremely difficult personality, battling with Susan, going to court against Mrs. Todd, and becoming quite unreliable as to her word—perjurious, in fact. Yet without Lavinia there might have been no legacy of poems. For it was Lavinia who discovered the astonishing cache, some eight or nine hundred poems, that Emily had threaded together into packets or dropped loosely into a bureau drawer; and it was Lavinia who decided that Emily's instructions to destroy her letters did not carry over to her poetry.

The loss of those letters is tragedy enough, as it involved Emily's long correspondence with many of the leading literary figures of the day; the letters contained clues, no doubt, to Emily's theories of poetry, something the world of scholarship knows now but barely. Yet matters might have been infinitely worse. Lavinia could have burned the poems also. Instead, while others dawdled, she pressed for publication, even after the first publisher approached, Houghton Mifflin of Boston, turned the initial selection down as "queer—the rhymes . . . all wrong." And she pressed through to publication even after the found publisher, Roberts Brothers of Boston, insisted that she pay for the plates, Emily's poems allegedly being a poor risk.

Emily Dickinson's last years were neither healthy nor productive. She died of Bright's disease, a malady characterized by albuminuria and high blood pressure. It was May when she breathed her last. They laid her in a white coffin covered with violets and ground pine. The memorial service was in the house—appropriately. Emily believed, but she held no creed, no formulated faith, and had never joined the local Congregational church, the only one of her family to hold back. There were prayers, and Higginson came from Cambridge to read a favorite poem of Emily's, Emily Brontë's "Last Lines": "No coward soul is mine." Then six "stalwart" men, all of whom had at one time or another worked the Dickinson farm and grounds, carried the coffin out the back door and to the cemetery three fields away on Triangle Street—West Cemetery. A small company followed.

Austin's wife Susan wrote a notice of her sister-in-law's death for the *Springfield Republican*: "She walked this life with the gentleness and reverence of old saints, with the firm step of martyrs who sing while they suffer." They are poignant words, and probably true, although Emily's martyr's cap, to the extent that she had one, might have been cocked; for all her reclusiveness, she possessed a gaiety and levity.

Susan added a note about Emily's quiet kindnesses, about the "treasures of fruit and flowers and ambrosial dishes" which were sent constantly to the sick and the well. Emily's gifts, she observed, made those many houses into which they arrived "mourn afresh that she screened herself from close acquaintance."

Later generations were to mourn still more, but to no particular point, really. Emily Dickinson is the immortal figure she is precisely because she was the Emily Dickinson of her pulse beat. One does not tamper with the temperaments of artists without tricking also with their art. Emily Dickinson's kin, for all their faults, knew this, much better than many of those who agitatedly poke about in the recesses she constructed so carefully and, seemingly, so permanently.

On the iron bars enclosing the gravesite are words that were Emily's, and might well be ours:

> On her divine majority
> Obtrude no more.

If You Travel . . .

. . .seeking the world of Emily Dickinson, you will find it in Amherst, Massachusetts. Amherst lies due north of Springfield in the western part of the state. It is about a 105-mile drive west from Boston, and 175 miles northeast from New York City.

From Boston at the one extremity of Massachusetts and from West Stockbridge at the other, Amherst is most conveniently approached via the Massachusetts Turnpike. Drivers should exit onto Route 91, running north-south to the Turnpike, in the Springfield-Holyoke area. They should proceed north on Route 91 a distance of about fifteen miles to the Hadley-Amherst exit (Route 9). Amherst will be less than ten miles east on Route 9.

From New York City, one may take the New England Throughway (Interstate 95), connect with Route 91 at New Haven, and drive north to Amherst. Or, one may take the Hutchinson River Parkway to Interstate 684 and travel north to Route 84; there one would drive east on Route 84 to Hartford, where the link would be made with Route 91 going north.

The Dickinson homestead is at 280 Main Street, behind a high hemlock hedge, just a few blocks from the center of Amherst. There is a marker outside the homestead.

A registered National Historical Landmark, the Dickinson homestead is available for interior viewing only by previous appointment through the Office of the Secretary, Amherst College, Amherst,

Massachusetts, 01002; telephone, 413-542-2321. Between May 1 and October 1, the house is open—stressing again, by appointment only—on Tuesdays and Fridays from 3:00 to 5:00 P.M.; the remainder of the year, on Tuesdays from 3:00 to 5:00 P.M. The homestead is owned by Amherst College and is used primarily as a faculty residence.

There is a modest admission fee for adults and a discount for students, while children under twelve are admitted free. There are also group rates, which vary according to the size and nature of the group. Income derived is used solely for the maintenance of the homestead.

Chapter
Thirteen

MARK TWAIN

Walt Disney Would Not Have So Dared in Hartford

Many communities lay claim to Mark Twain: Florida, Missouri, where he was born in 1835; Hannibal, Missouri, where he grew up and situated the classic adventures of Tom Sawyer and Huck Finn; Carson City and Virginia City, Nevada, where he lasted out the Civil War, prospected, and played at frontier journalism; Elmira, New York, where he married in 1870 and was buried in 1910. Wait—there were more places, including San Francisco at one end of the country and Redding, Connecticut, at the other. He worked as a newspaperman on the Coast; died back East in Redding.

Mark Twain—born Samuel Langhorne Clemens—lived just about everywhere in the United States and traveled the globe as writer, lecturer, humorist, personality quaint. He did not touch down long in any one spot—except, of course, Hartford, Connecticut, where he lived for twenty years, seventeen of them in a house as exotic as himself in the literary enclave known as Nook Farm. The Nook Farm years were 1873 to 1891, when Mark Twain was at the height of his fame and fortune, his powers and follies, his eccentricities, wit, extravagance . . . and pure genius. It was the Gilded Age, plutocratic and affluent, when everything seemed possible for the dreaming—with a lucky turn or two. Mark Twain-Sam Clemens, the pseudonym* and the man, was at once at war and at peace with this age, and he embodied the reality and the fantasy of it all; the preposterousness, too. The proof was in the pudding he called a house.

---

*The origin of the pseudonym "Mark Twain" is as well known almost as the pen name itself, being the Mississippi riverboat cry for checking two fathoms' depth. There were those out around Virginia City, however, who claimed the pseudonym had more to do with marking up drinks on the cuff.

Walt Disney might not have dared the house that Mark built in Hartford. It is a frenzy of gables and porches, staggered staircases, hallways the size of parlors, ornate rooms, and architectural surprises—like the kitchen built to the front of the house, "so the servants can see the circus go by without running into the street"; in reality this was done in order to reserve for Mark Twain and the family the scenic view, which lay to the rear. Hartford's first telephone was installed in the house, and the interior was brightened with Tiffany decorations. The whole was enclosed in slate and bricks of various hues, mostly—would you believe?—turkey red. The house in Hartford cost $100,000 to construct and almost that much for yearly maintenance in pre-pre-pre-inflation dollars. A tour guide recently described the house as one-third riverboat, one-third cathedral, one-third cuckoo clock. As such, the house was its owner: the one-time Mississippi River hand who married well, earned additional sums by his pen, lived in episcopal splendor, then let much of the good life slip away with schemes as nutty as the house and as quixotic as himself.

The house was and is a horror. But for Mark Twain, it "had a heart, and a soul, and eyes to see us with; and approvals, and solicitudes, and deep sympathies." The house in Hartford was "of us," he wrote—and the "us" included not only the twinned personalities Mark Twain and Samuel Langhorne Clemens, but wife Olivia Langdon Clemens, daughters Susy, Clara, and Jean, and son Langdon, who died before the house was built at 351 Farmington Avenue, but whose memory was carried within its walls.

A psychiatrist would have a picnic analyzing this fascinating horror. If it does not betray the folly of the man, then the machine in the basement museum of the house does. This is the Paige typesetter, a nine-foot, three-ton, two-thousand-part monster which Mark Twain-the-one-time-printer/Sam Clemens-the-perpetual-speculator thought would revolutionize the printing industry and make him wealthy beyond calculating. What would it take to buy all New York, he wondered, including the railroads, including the newspapers? The typesetter—named for its Rube Goldberg inventor, James W. Paige—brought Mark Twain/Sam Clemens nothing but bankruptcy. Because of it, and some other zanyisms, Mark Twain had to shut up the house in Hartford in 1891 and go abroad. The improvident side of himself being spared financial temptations,

For Mark Twain, his house in Hartford "had a heart, and a soul, and eyes to see us with." He and his family were happiest here, but not forever after. Daughter Susy died here, and Twain's wife would never step foot in the place again. Meanwhile, the house had become an impossible financial burden. Twain spent $100,000 to build the house, and almost that much in yearly maintenance. He sold it in 1903 for $28,000.

he could live more cheaply there. By 1891, his best books had been written. He should have been riding the crests of success and security; instead he was fleeing the consequences of prodigality.

Mark Twain the dreamer/Sam Clemens the father came back to the Hartford house only once after 1891. The house had long since been tenantless. Mark Twain actually found it "forlorn." Still the house was a "holy place," made holy by the death there of Susy, the eldest of the daughters and her father's favorite. Susy died August 18, 1896, just before she was to sail for London for what was to have been a happy family reunion climaxing a lecture tour that had extended for Mark Twain from Vancouver to Capetown. Twain had rented a house in Guildford and had planned an extended stay in England with the family. There was no happy reunion, however; only heartbreak. Shortly before she was to sail, Susy came down with spinal meningitis. Her condition slipped rapidly, and, sentimentally, she longed for the home of her birth and adolescence. At her request the house on Farmington Avenue was opened up, and a sickbed readied in the mahogany room. She was pleased, but there was no rally. Susy died in a matter of days, only twenty-four years old.

That Susy died "at *home*" was consolation to her father. "To us, our house was not unsentient matter," he remarked; "we were in its confidence, and lived in its grace and in the peace of its benediction."

It was in quest of that peace, some last benediction, that Mark Twain returned to the house. He did not find it. Susy's death left a void never to be filled, a sorrow never to be requited, either for him or for Olivia. Incidentally, Olivia did not go with her husband on that final visit to 351 Farmington Avenue. She had refused to enter the house again because of its crushing memories.

The house was put up for sale, but it hung on the family's back like some unlucky load. It was not until 1903, seven years after Susy's death, that the Clemenses managed to shake it off for the near giveaway price of $28,000. The house was picked up by the president of the Hartford Fire Insurance Company, Francis M. Bissell. He used it as a family residence until 1917. Then the house became, in turn, a private school for boys, a storage warehouse, an apartment building, a branch of the Hartford Public Library. Its future seemed less and less promising until 1929, when it was rescued from the City Coal Company by the then newly organized Mark Twain Memorial Committee. The property has been husbanded since as a unique and priceless piece of literary Americana. It has been exquisitely restored, and great pains have been taken to track down whatever might have strayed away or been discarded during the quarter-century of neglect. Some of the recoveries have been miraculous, such as the twelve-foot mantlepiece with its baronial arms, carved flowers and fruits, and bronze plate bearing the inscription: "The ornament of a house is the friends that frequent it."

Mark Twain had purchased the mantlepiece in Scotland, as salvage from an ancient castle. It was the central piece of his library and, in a way, of the house itself. But when the Mark Twain Memorial Committee took over ownership in 1929, the massive mantlepiece was gone, no one had any idea where. One day a man touring the home heard the story of the missing mantlepiece. By any chance, he wondered, could it be that dusty thing out among the hay and the harnesses of his father's barn in Redding? Sure enough, it was, and the mantlepiece was returned triumphantly to Hartford. It was a turn of events that gives hope to this day that the Tiffany glass panel will be found which was set as a divider between the front hall and the drawing room. Tour guides give detailed descriptions of the panel in case miracles still happen.

As for Mark Twain, there was no Hartford in his plans after Susy's death. He returned from Europe in 1900, ending a stay abroad of almost ten years, and took a furnished house at 14 West Tenth Street in New York City. Characteristically, he did not stay there for long. He moved to Riverdale, then Tarrytown, then back to the city and a house at 21 Fifth Avenue, at Ninth Street, with a summer retreat at Tuxedo Park. Finally, it was out to Connecticut again, but nowhere near Hartford! Twain built an Italianate estate at Redding in the state's westernmost area, Fairfield County, and moved in in June of 1908. He called the house Stormfield, and there at seventy-five he died, April 21, 1910. Stormfield itself burned down fifteen years later.

Restless, restless, restless. The nineteenth century was a restless age, and if anyone epitomized its restlessness it was Mark Twain. He lived more places than a half-dozen of his most restless contemporaries. But in Hartford the wandering spirit was at rest. Here the family was happiest, and here Mark Twain was at top productive form. *The Adventures of Tom Sawyer* and *The Adventures of Huckleberry Finn* were issued from Hartford. So, too, *A Tramp Abroad*, *The Prince and the Pauper*, *Life on the Mississippi*, and *A Connecticut Yankee in King Arthur's Court*. The writing was done, or at least roughed out, in the third-floor billiard room, on a small desk turned away from the window so Twain would not be disturbed by movements beyond the windowpane. Like his expatriate contemporary Henry James, who wrote against the view of a London brick wall, Mark Twain needed his own vast convenient neutrality. So he faced across a billiard table to a bookcase—although neither was so neutral as James's brick wall, nor so undistracting—particularly the billiard table. Twain was a passionate billiards player and could shoot billiard balls by the hour. Yet the writing got done, then it was off to the quiet of Quarry Farm, above Elmira. Quarry Farm was his sister-in-law's place and a favorite work spot for Twain. He polished his manuscripts there.

Meanwhile, the Hartford writer had become a Hartford publisher. It seemed the most logical of enterprises for Twain, given his creative skills, the demand for his books, and the imminent success— he thought—of the Paige typesetter. *Huckleberry Finn* was about ready for production, and Twain had ideas for more books, written by himself and others. Dollar signs danced in his head, and Charles L. Webster and Company came into existence. Charles Webster was a nephew, and although the firm bore his name, the dominant influence was Mark Twain's. Charles functioned as surrogate, and as errand boy—forever at Aunt Livia's beck and Uncle Sam's call.

The beginnings of the publishing house were promising. Ulysses S. Grant managed, with great effort, to finish *Personal Memoirs* before dying, and the book rolled from the presses of Mark Twain's company with great hoopla and acclaim. As a first royalty, Twain paid $200,000 to Grant's widow. The book was a fateful success for Twain, however, for it lured him into a string of celebrity books: memoirs of more Civil War generals; books about General George Armstrong Custer, the Indian fighter; about General Winfield Scott Hancock, a hero of Gettysburg; something by King Kalakaua on Hawaiian legends. It was steadily downhill to the "authorized" biography of Pope Leo XIII by one Father Bernard O'Reilly, a book which Twain thought would sell at least 100,000 copies, as he naively believed it would be bought by Catholics as a religious duty. It wasn't. The book bombed.

All the while there was that infernal typesetter. By 1885 the machine had already cost Twain $150,000, but he refused to give up on it. In 1889 he bought Paige's interest out and became sole owner of the machine. Twain paid $160,000, and Paige would get $25,000 a year more for seventeen years. It was sheer madness. His back to the financial wall, Twain was soon draining off money from the publishing house to finance the machine, was borrowing from Olivia's mother and wherever else he could. When a bookkeeper of the publishing house made off with $25,000, the sum could be dismissed as a mere pittance, nothing to fret about. Mark Twain was accustomed to far more spectacular losses.

Inevitably, the publishing house began to totter, and, inevitably, Mark Twain was bitter. He found a convenient scapegoat in his nephew and heaped on him abuse that is an embarrassment to read from the distance of almost a century. The abuse was excessive and at least partially unwarranted. For the facts are that Mark Twain was to blame in no small part for the collapse of Charles L. Webster and Company. He was an imperious director. He ignored advice, overrode decisions; and though he had access to the name writers of the day, his vanity would not let him share the billing of his own firm with any of them. As a result, he saddled the firm with limp ideas and second-rate authors. In 1892, the company did publish two books by Walt Whitman—*Selected Poems* and *Autobiographia*—but by then Twain was off in Europe and was an absentee partner.

Of course Mark Twain made it back from his financial failures, thanks to royalties from his books and a Standard Oil tycoon named Henry Huttleston Rogers. Rogers became Twain's benefactor and mentor in the ways of investment capitalism. The student was an erratic learner. Twain made profits, large profits. But if there was a bum scheme around, it and Twain could still find one another and he would lose back thousands. Still, to the end, he remained the inveterate gambler, the grubby prospector after the big bonanza. All this is counter to the popular image that made of Twain a national hero. He was never so devil-may-care as he posed. Nor was he the social reformer many thought him to be. He was actually an avaricious cuss. The irony is that Twain saw through the national greed and excoriated the malefactors of great wealth. The paradox is that he saw no application of his social insights to himself. He was quite at home with the ultra-profit system and with its most successful practitioners. In fact, he and Andrew Carnegie were "Saint Andrew" and "Saint Mark" to one another.

The fixation with money carried to the deathbed. When Clara, the last of the family, arrived at Redding for the final days, she found her father "pathetically anxious to inform me about the financial state of affairs, expressing regret that there was less then he hoped there would be." If regrets were to be shared, then Clara was the person to share them with; she lived deep in the father's treasury. Actually, Twain was quite well situated at his leave-taking. The estate—including cash, security, house and land in Redding, two horses, a cow, and several vehicles—was valued at close to $200,000, a not inconsiderable sum in 1910, although, to be sure, only a fraction of what would accrue to the estate as the years went by from royalties from Mark Twain's books.

This Mark Twain—living gloriously, lusting to get rich quickly, consorting with the very personifications of inordinate wealth—is in decided contrast to the homespun and unaffected Mark Twain, the social critic who hated pretense and hypocrisy, the lovable public figure who swigged scotch, puffed cigars (forty a day), identified with the humble, and had a wise and witty comment for everything. ("If you don't like the weather in New England, just wait a few minutes.") In his old age this Mark Twain was grown cynical and pessimistic. He saw swindlers under the bed, robbers in the closet, and, with the help of Clara, became convinced that associates closest to him were the most dishonest of all. He was cantankerous, vindictive, and on top of all, guilt-ridden, holding himself responsible (not unwarrantedly, some believe) for illnesses that had beset his wife and children. The public got to know this Mark Twain only in recent years, when long-suppressed papers came to light.

But then there always was more than one Mark Twain. He was as complex and as unpredictable as a person with two names and several careers might be expected to be. It was only the less pleasant Mark Twain who died in Redding.

What of the glamorous Mark Twain—the Mark Twain who adventured about Hannibal, piloted riverboats, prospected, lectured, and wrote books? He lives on library shelves and in the memory of anyone who has ever opened a book. It is the better of the twinned selves.

This Mark Twain lives in the house in Hartford. The Hartford image there may be idealized, but for anyone who has read a word of the adventures of Huck Finn and Tom Sawyer, to name but two of Twain's books, it is the image that is most agreeable.

If You Travel . . .

. . .to the house that Mark built in Hartford and your starting point is New York City, plan on a drive of over two hours. The Mark Twain Memorial is about 125 miles from New York via the Hutchinson River Parkway east to Route 684, then to Route 84 into Hartford. Drivers should take the 46-Sisson Avenue exit, which bears off to the driver's left, and proceed on Sisson to Farmington Avenue; turn right there, and a short distance ahead, at 351 Farmington, will be Twain's house. Approaching from Boston and the east, drivers should exit at Sigourney Street, turn left on Hawthorne Street, right on Imlay, and left on Farmington. From Route 84 to the house is less than a mile, from whichever approach.

From June to August 31, the Mark Twain Memorial is open daily to visitors. The remainder of the year, it is open Tuesdays through Sundays, being closed Mondays—as well as on Easter, Thanksgiving, Christmas, and New Year's Day. It is closed on Labor Day. Weekday hours are from 10:00 A.M. to 5:00 P.M.; Sundays from 2:00 to 5:00 P.M. There is a modest admission charge, slightly higher if one also visits the Harriet Beecher Stowe Cottage nearby.

In Fairfield County in western Connecticut is the town of Redding, where Mark Twain died in 1910 in an Italianate mansion of his designing. The mansion burned down in 1925, but memories of Mark Twain linger about Redding in the Mark Twain Memorial Library on Redding Road (Route 53) and in its Jean L. Clemens Memorial Building, named for Twain's daughter and constructed with proceeds from the sale of her farmhouse and forty acres of land. The library has books from Mark Twain's shelves, some letters, and personal items, such as a letter box and clock. These are viewable. Library hours are from 10:00 A.M. to 5:00 P.M. weekdays, and 10:00 A.M. to 1:00 P.M. on Saturdays. Thursday evenings the library is open until 8:30 P.M. Routes into Redding are 53, 58, and 107. The most convenient approach is Route 107 off Route 7 at Georgetown. Route 7 runs northward from the New England Throughway, east of Stamford. From Stamford, the distance to Redding is about twenty-five miles.

Though Mark Twain died in Redding, he is buried in Elmira, New York—in the Langdon family plot of Woodlawn Cemetery (his wife was a Langdon). Elmira is fifty-eight miles west of Binghamton, New York, on Route 17. One should take the Church Street exit to Walnut and turn right on Walnut. Woodlawn Cemetery—not to be confused with adjacent Woodlawn National Cemetery, where 2,982 Confederate soldiers who died here as prisoners of war are buried—is at the end of Walnut. Mark Twain's grave is not advertised as a tourist attraction; the Langdon family, in fact, is reported to be reserved about publicity. However, the cemetery is open every day until dusk, and people are free to enter.

On the campus of Elmira College, nearby, is the small octagonal study that Mark Twain found so congenial as a writing studio when in the area, and where he polished *The Adventures of Tom Sawyer* and other stories. The study is viewable daily, by appointment. Incidentally, Elmira College was founded in 1855 and, until it became coeducational in 1969, was the oldest women's college in the nation granting degrees that were the equal of those from men's colleges.

Chapter
Fourteen

HARRIET BEECHER STOWE

The Gentle New England Lady Who Rocked a Nation

There's a Down-East theory that the Civil War began in Brunswick, Maine. It's not so barmy as at first might seem the case. For it was in Brunswick, in an elm-shaded house at 63 Federal Street, that Harriet Beecher Stowe wrote the book which was sufficient catalyst for President Lincoln to exclaim upon meeting the diminutive Mrs. Stowe: "So this is the little lady who made this big war?" Hers, of course, was *Uncle Tom's Cabin*, the novel which synthesized the moral and social issues of slavery on both sides of the Mason-Dixon line and which achieved an international renown as people around the world read it as a mirror on the dark side of the American soul.

It was, of course, much more than Harriet Beecher Stowe had anticipated, or ever intended. Quite accurately, she saw hers as an American story. Quite naively, she had considered it a message of peace and suasion that Southerners might respond to by voluntarily manumitting their slaves. After all, hadn't she portrayed Southerners, with few exceptions, as kind and philanthropic? And wasn't her arch-villain a Northerner, from Vermont? Simon Legree—hiss.

The New England touches—Simon Legree being only one among several—were strategic to Mrs. Stowe's innocent hopes of placating the South. But they were also characteristic. It was New England and New Englanders that Harriet Beecher Stowe knew best, and her better books—there were sixteen in all—were those that drew on the area and its people. Mrs. Stowe lived for eighteen years in Cincinnati. She traveled widely, captivated Europe, and was captivated in turn by European culture. There was even a late-blooming love affair with the state of Florida. But nothing of all this diluted Harriet Beecher Stowe's essential New England identification. New England has returned the compliment, with love:

—in Litchfield, Connecticut, where Harriet Beecher Stowe was

Harriet Beecher Stowe lived less than two years in this house in
Brunswick, Maine, but the house will forever be associated with her name.
Here she wrote Uncle Tom's Cabin, and became to Abraham Lincoln and
the rest of the world "the little lady who made this big war" between North
and South in the United States.

born June 14, 1811. On the town green is a granite memorial and tondo of bronze honoring her, her distinguished father, Lyman Beecher, and her famed, if eventually notorious, brother, Henry Ward Beecher. A marker erected in 1908 by the Litchfield County University Club reads: "Here stood the Church in which / Lyman Beecher preached 1810–1826 / One half mile north stood the house / where were born / Harriet Beecher Stowe 1811 / Henry Ward Beecher 1813." Remnants of the house are incorporated as part of the Forman School buildings on Norfolk Road;

—in Hartford, Connecticut, where the twelve-room "cottage" in which Mrs. Stowe lived from 1873 until her death in 1896 is preserved as a museum, crammed with relics: Mrs. Stowe's furniture, souvenirs from foreign travels, china, oils, including many done by herself—a facet of Harriet Beecher Stowe's talent not generally known;

—in Brunswick, Maine, where the house in which the Stowes lived, and where Harriet wrote *Uncle Tom's Cabin*, survives as an inn and restaurant. Since 1963 it has been a designated National Historical Landmark of the Department of the Interior;

—in Brunswick, still, where the church is located in which Mrs. Stowe had the "vision" that inspired the book. First Parish Church is revered as a holy place as well as literary shrine. In pew 23 of the Broad Aisle is a bronze plaque set in place in 1928 by the Topsham-Brunswick chapter of the Daughters of the American Revolution: "Here she saw as in a vision the death of Uncle Tom."

The rest is history. Mrs. Stowe went home to 63 Federal Street and poured out the vision, exhausting the paper supply at hand and having to reach for brown grocery wrapping paper to complete the writing. After dinner, she gathered the children into the sitting room—husband Calvin was away in Cincinnati—and read aloud the tale of Uncle Tom's death. Tears flowed. So did Calvin's, when, upon returning to Brunswick, he came across the manuscript in a bedroom drawer—where Mrs. Stowe had tucked the sheets away in the suspicion that they were too violent for publication. Reassured by Calvin's reaction, Mrs. Stowe approached the *National Era*, an abolitionist weekly published in Washington, with the idea for a serial that would "hold up in the most lifelike and graphic manner possible Slavery, its reverses, changes, and the negro character." The suggestion was accepted, and an envisioned three or four installments grew into one of the seminal works of American history: a two-volume book that would coalesce sentiments of mind, heart, and politics on the inequities of that "patriarchal institution"—Mrs. Stowe's words—slavery.

In many respects, Hartford, Connecticut, is the obvious visiting place for communicating with the memory of Harriet Beecher Stowe. The Stowe cottage is exquisitely preserved and authentically furnished. Next door is Day House, in which are collected manuscripts, books, and papers of Mrs. Stowe, together with others of Hartford's celebrated nineteenth-century Nook Farm community, including Mark Twain, Charles Dudley Warner, and Isabella Beecher Hooker, Harriet's half-sister and a leader in feminist causes.

In Hartford, though, one is encountering the Harriet Beecher Stowe of fame—and dotage. Her last three books were written here, but that fact, as most other remembrances about Nook Farm, is overwhelmed by the shade of Mark Twain, the architectural monstrosity that he erected across the greensward from the Stowe cottage, and the fact of the physical deterioration of Mrs. Stowe. In the Twain-dominated setting, Harriet Beecher Stowe reduces in history, as in her own time, to sweet old lady of secondary importance, wandering in her senility into Mark Twain's house to pick the prize flower in his conservatory, or into Charles Dudley Warner's place to sit at the piano and sing "Love Divine" in cracking voice.

Hartford, in other words, is not where one ecounters the Harriet Beecher Stowe of energetic youth and electric mind—to say nothing of the Harriet Beecher Stowe of such immediate financial need that, like it or not, she had to write in order for the family to make ends meet.

To find this Harriet Beecher Stowe, one best goes to Brunswick. The Stowes lived there but a relatively brief period of time—from spring, 1850, to fall, 1852. The vibrations, however, are real, particularly about the house on Federal Street, which Mrs. Stowe thought cold and plain and which she complained about with some bitterness. "Sunday night I rather watched than slept," she wrote on December 29, 1850. "The wind howled and the house rocked just as our old Litchfield house used to. The cold has been so intense that the children kept begging to get up from the table at meal-times to warm feet and fingers. Our air-tight stoves warm all but the floor—

heat your head and keep your feet freezing."

That's the half of it. She was also in something of a dither about money and fretted about husband Calvin's meager salary as Collins Professor of Natural and Revealed Religion at Bowdoin College: $1,000 a year, subsequently increased by $500. "There is no doubt in my mind that our expenses this year will come two hundred dollars, if not three, beyond our salary," she also wrote that December 29. "We shall be able to come through, notwithstanding, but I don't want to feel obligated to work as hard every year as I have this. I can earn four hundred dollars a year by writing; but I don't want to feel that I must, and when weary with teaching the children, and tending the baby, and buying provisions, and mending dresses, and darning stockings, sit down and write a piece for some paper."

Harriet's complaint is mounted in typed, photographic blowup in the foyer of Brunswick's Stowe House, which advertises itself—not inexactly—as "Maine's most historic inn." The inn is carefully preserved and antiqued, with a taproom colorfully got up in stained glass, church pews, oak doors from Boston's old South Station— and named (what else?) Harriet's Place. Mrs. Stowe, from a temperance background and troubled in later life by alcoholism in the family, would probably not have approved the name, but there is no demurrer locally. Harriet's Place is a favorite oasis with Bowdoin students.

For all of Stowe House's quaintness, however, there is less of Harriet Beecher Stowe about the place than Robert Wallace Mathews, who holds controlling interest in Stowe House, would prefer. "We hope some day to restore part of the upstairs, furnish it with period pieces and memorabilia, and perhaps have it available for tours," said Mr. Mathews, "but that's a couple of years off at the outside. Until we get a bit further on our feet, we have no choice but to operate as a commercial establishment more than a historical landmark." (Stowe House, Brunswick, dates from 1807 and has been run as an inn since 1946. In 1957, a public corporation was formed for purposes of insuring its continuance as a quality inn and restaurant. Stowe House came under Mr. Mathews's direction in October, 1972.)

A dining room and fifty-four-room motel have been appended to the original structure. Yet the commercial aspects of Stowe House do not subvert its character. The elm trees of Mrs. Stowe's day are mostly gone, swept away by wind, age, and disease. But the exterior of Stowe House closest to Federal Street is precisely as it was when Mrs. Stowe lived there. Inside, the historical feel is quickened by framed passages from *The Life and Letters of Harriet Beecher Stowe*, photographs, and an old poster advertising a stage dramatization of *Uncle Tom's Cabin*. Incidentally, overnight visitors to Stowe House sleep in the adjoining motor lodge. Guest rooms in Stowe House proper are occupied by permanent residents and students from Bowdoin College—the latter an old tradition. Henry Wadsworth Longfellow and his brother Stephen roomed in the house when they were students at Bowdoin, only three blocks away. An upperclassman named Franklin Pierce, later fourteenth president of the United States, stopped in often, as probably did another student contemporary, Nathaniel Hawthorne.

Between house and campus is First Parish Church, where Mrs. Stowe had her "vision." A thriving place of worship still, First Parish Church is a fascinating example of mid-nineteenth-century Gothic frame architecture, with hand-hewn timber beams, student gallery (from the days when church attendance was mandatory for Bowdoin students), and sounding-board pulpit. President William Howard Taft spoke from this pulpit, and so did poet laureate John Masefield, Eleanor Roosevelt, and Dr. Martin Luther King. It was from this pulpit on July 8, 1875, that Longfellow read the poem written for the fiftieth anniversary of his graduation from Bowdoin, "Morituri Salutamus." Longfellow, always reluctant to speak in public, was enticed into the pulpit by the explanation that the arched sounding board would partly cover him. "Let me cover myself as much as possible," responded Longfellow; "I wish it might be entirely."

The Stowes worshiped in First Parish Church in company with pillars of the Brunswick community: Pennells, Skolfields, Merrymans, Dunnings, Otises, Minots. Many she grew to know well, and some evolved into characters for *The Pearl of Orr's Island*, Mrs. Stowe's "Maine story," which John Greenleaf Whittier thought "the most charming New England idyl ever written." In 1851 and 1852, the book was still a decade away but its ideas were seeding themselves, however unconsciously. Evolving too were Orr's-Island impressions from Stowe family outings to that fingerlike strip of sea-land near Brunswick so perfect for sunning, swimming, fishing, picnicking. Developing, too, were Maine appreciations—for lobsters, chowders—as well as the Maine proclivity for a vocabulary laced with sea terms.

Harriet Beecher Stowe—daughter of a preacher; sister of five preachers; wife of a preacher—was where she would be expected to have been that Communion Sunday of March 2, 1851: in church. Rev. George E. Adams was minister, and when he spoke the words, "Inasmuch as ye have done it unto one of the least of these my brethren, ye have done it unto me," the "vision" was upon Mrs. Stowe. Charles Edward Stowe, her son and biographer, provides the details: "Suddenly, like the unrolling of a picture, the scene of the death of Uncle Tom passed before her mind. So strongly was she affected that it was with difficulty she could keep from weeping aloud. Immediately, on returning home she took pen and paper and wrote out the vision which had been as it were blown into her mind as by the rushing of a mighty wind." A quarter-century later, she herself would recall: "My heart was bursting with the anguish excited by the cruelty and injustice our nation was showing to the slave, and praying God to let me do a little and to cause my cry for them to be heard." Mrs. Stowe knew her prayer was answered; eventually she came to believe that God was the author of *Uncle Tom's Cabin*, she but his instrument—his amanuensis.

Curiously enough, Harriet Beecher Stowe was not an early-on "declared abolitionist," as most of her family were, notably her father and her brother, Henry Ward Beecher of Plymouth Church in Brooklyn. Slavery was the consuming moral and political issue of the day, and Mrs. Stowe was undeluded about its evilness. But it took a combination of slowly maturing forces—some personal, like a visit to a Kentucky slave plantation; some political, like the Fugitive Slave Act of 1850—to jar feelings into passion, until at last, under the influence of her "vision," she would do as "sister Katey" had urged: put pen to paper "to make this whole nation feel what an accursed thing slavery is."

Henry Ward Beecher had promised Harriet that if she wrote about slavery, "I myself will scatter it thick as the leaves of Vallombrosa." There was no need. *Uncle Tom's Cabin* needed nothing except, perhaps, higher-speed presses. Ten thousand copies were sold the first week of publication; 305,000, the first year. In Mrs. Stowe's lifetime, sales would climb to the 3 million mark, and the book would be circulating in thirty-seven languages. Only the Bible knew more versions. Controversies surrounding the book would be so fierce that Mrs. Stowe would write *A Key to Uncle Tom's Cabin* in defense against charges that her novel distorted the nature of Southern slavery and exaggerated its evils and abuses.

Meanwhile, there was the paradox that the book which should have made Mrs. Stowe rich beyond financial cares never did. She had the option of putting up half the initial production costs and sharing half the profits, or taking a straight 10 percent royalty on sales; cautious Calvin decided on the royalty arrangement. Furthermore, most of the foreign editions were pirated, so that Mrs. Stowe received very little from tens of thousands of copies that were printed abroad. Nor did she receive anything from the scores of dramatic productions that played year upon year before millions of people. The Uncle Tom plays exploited her intellectually as well, taking so many liberties with the story line that the plays eventually shared little in substance with the book beyond title. What money Mrs. Stowe did make from *Uncle Tom's Cabin*—not insubstantial, nevertheless—was heavily depleted by an ostentatious "dream-house" in Hartford, which she lost to expenses (and history, to urban decay), and by bad investments in Florida real estate. She settled, accordingly, for comfort, not wealth.

There were other paradoxes; as of concept—that this book, which Mrs. Stowe once believed "too mild" for abolitionist tastes because of its solicitousness for Southern feelings, should become far and away the most potent piece of nineteenth-century antislavery propaganda.

And finally, the paradox of fate—that so many of the characters over whom half a world agonized should be debased by the dramas, then caricatured by history. Uncle Tom, his wife Aunt Chloe, little Topsy, who *'spected* she just growed, and others of Mrs. Stowe's story were first burlesqued in song and dance. Then they devolved into stereotypes, particularly as sociology and new sensibilities exposed the popular misconceptions of even the good of heart, including Mrs. Stowe herself. Unwittingly, Mrs. Stowe had helped cast Aunt Chloe as an Aunt Jemima; Topsy as a comic-relief black youngster. But no one fared worse than Uncle Tom, the pious, long-suffering slave, who was transformed in time from object of

compassion to symbol of contempt, his name becoming synonymous with that of an abjectly servile black. As J. C. Furnas sums up
in *Goodbye to Uncle Tom* (New York, 1956): "Mrs. Stowe's book was
obviously decent and Christian, obviously warm with hopes of
helping poor people with dark skins. Nevertheless, it became a
principal occasion for Negroes to say, 'God deliver us from our
friends.' "

This was not as Harriet Beecher Stowe would have had things.
But, then, so much in life ran counter to her hopes and preferences.
Of her six children, she lost one to cholera, another to drowning, a
third to alcoholism, a fourth to drug addiction. Meanwhile, a close
friendship with Lady Byron induced her to explode the Lord
Byron-Augusta Leigh incest story in the august *Atlantic Monthly*—
and almost overnight the Stowe image among thousands on both
sides of the ocean changed from lovable lady to malicious gossip.
(Mrs. Stowe's exposé almost sank the *Atlantic*, losing it fifteen
thousand subscribers.) Then, alas, there was the scandal of her
adored brother's life. Henry Ward Beecher may have been the most
famous preacher of his day, but he was also something of a roué. A
celebrated adultery trial in which he was a principal divided the
Beecher clan and added to the weight of years on frail Harriet's
shoulders.

Harriet Beecher Stowe was long gone from Brunswick by the time
these problems beset her. Calvin had accepted a professorship at
Andover Theological Seminary, and the family lived in Andover,
Massachusetts, from 1852 until his retirement in 1864. (The Stowes
closed their house in Brunswick in September of 1852.) After that it
was Hartford, a city Harriet had known in her youth and remembered fondly. The family settled initially in the dream-house that
was the symbol of her triumph over early poverty and wintered in
Florida, where Mrs. Stowe had bought a house at Mandarin on the
St. Johns River near Jacksonville—and where she also invested in
cotton land and orange groves, placing son Fred in charge with
hopes that the responsibility would wean him from the bottle. It
didn't. She had overreached herself maternally and financially.
After a practical reassessment of powers and assets, she bought the
house at Nook Farm which enabled her to live serenely and within
the family's means. Here she wrote the last of her books, including

Poganuc People, based on her childhood in Litchfield, a book which critic Edmund Wilson in another day would find, along with *Old Town Folks*, "a kind of encyclopedia of old New England institutions, characters, customs and points of view." Calvin preceded Harriet in death, dying in 1886. He was taken to Andover for burial alongside Henry, the son who had died almost thirty years before while attempting to swim the Connecticut River during an outing with chums from Dartmouth College.

Mrs. Stowe had gone to Andover from Brunswick somewhat reluctantly. She had come to love the community that she initially regarded as backwoods. The suns of summer, the snows of winter (Federal Street was perfect for sledding), the people—everything about Brunswick had won her heart. "For my part," she told Calvin in 1852, "if I *must* leave Brunswick, I would rather leave at once. I can tear away with a sudden pull more easily than to linger . . . knowing that I am to leave at last. I shall never find people whom I shall like better than those of Brunswick."

Harriet Beecher Stowe revisited Brunswick, but never made it back for a permanent stay, only Andover. On July 1, 1896—eighty-five years after birth; six years after senility had set in—she closed her eyes in sleep in her Hartford cottage and was gone. Mourning was widespread. Brunswick sent a representative to the funeral services: Mr. G. F. Dunning, whose family had built the sailing ships that had helped spread Brunswick's name across the seas. Mrs. Stowe's casket was decorated with a wreath sent by blacks of Boston; the card read, "The Children of Uncle Tom."

Harriet Beecher Stowe was laid in the ground between Henry and Calvin in the Andover Chapel Cemetery. Her three surviving children put over her grave a cross of Scottish granite. It endures, as impervious to time as *Uncle Tom's Cabin*.

If You Travel . . .

. . .seeking the Harriet Beecher Stowe of the *Uncle Tom's Cabin* period, head towards Brunswick, Maine. Brunswick is thirty miles above Portland via Interstate 95. Stowe House, where the book was written, is at 63 Federal Street and is open the year round as an inn and restaurant. There is a gift shop, and there are Stowe exhibits in the foyer of the inn. No admission fee is required. Federal Street is in central Brunswick, running parallel to Maine Street, the second-widest main street in New England, after that of Keene, New Hampshire's. Number 63 is at the crest of the hill.

First Parish Church, where Mrs. Stowe had the "vision" that inspired the book, is two blocks away, adjacent to the Bowdoin College campus. The Stowe pew—number 23 in the Broad Aisle—is marked with a bronze plaque. The church is open every day, though not necessarily the front door. Community activities are held in the church's various meeting rooms, with entrance via side or rear doors. The main church is accessible through these entrances—or by calling at Pilgrim House, the parish center diagonally across from the church on the corner of Cleveland Street.

A scenic half-hour's drive from central Brunswick, along State Route 24, is Orr's Island, the setting for Mrs. Stowe's "Maine story," *The Pearl of Orr's Island*. Orr's is a picturesque fishing, lobstering, and resort ridge of land, connecting by bridge with Bailey's Island, thence trailing off at the edge of open ocean. Directional signs to the two islands pick up at First Parish Church.

The post–*Uncle Tom's Cabin* Mrs. Stowe is met most intimately at Nook Farm in Hartford, Connecticut, in the cottage in which Mrs. Stowe lived from 1873 until her death in 1896. Nook Farm is a 125-mile drive from New York City, via the Hutchinson River Parkway east, to Route 684, to Route 84 into Hartford. One should take the 46-Sisson Avenue exit, which bears off to the driver's left, and proceed on Sisson to Farmington Avenue; turn right and a short distance ahead at 351 Farmington Avenue will be Nook Farm. (From Boston and the east, drivers should exit at Sigourney Street, turn left on Hawthorne Street, right on Imlay, left on Farmington.) The distance from Route 84 to Nook Farm is less than a mile.

From June to August 31, Nook Farm is open daily. The rest of the year, it is closed on Mondays, in addition to Easter, Thanksgiving Day, Christmas, New Year's, and Labor Day itself. Weekday hours are from 10:00 A.M. to 5:00 P.M.; Sunday, from 2:00 to 5:00 P.M. There is a modest admission charge, and a discount for children under sixteen.

Day House, in the Nook Farm complex, contains a collection of 12,000 volumes, 80,000 manuscripts, and numerous photographs, drawings, and other materials relating to the lives, work, art, and architecture of Nook Farm and its people. The collection is of special interest to researchers, scholars, and students.

Twenty miles due west of Hartford is the town of Litchfield, where Harriet Beecher Stowe was born in 1811. On the town green, at the junction of Routes 63 and 202, is the Stowe monument, fashioned by A. Bertam Pegram Scott. The Litchfield County Historical Society maintains a collection of Beecher material and manuscripts, which are available for study. The society's hours are from 11:00 A.M. to 4:30 P.M., or by appointment, Tuesday through Saturday (P.O. Box 385, Litchfield, Connecticut, 06759; telephone, 203-567-5862).

The Harriet Beecher Stowe grave is at Andover, Massachusetts, in Andover Chapel Cemetery, twenty-five miles from Boston on State Route 28. She lies between her husband Calvin, who left the Bowdoin College faculty for a professorship at Andover Theological Seminary, and her son Henry, who died in 1857 in a swimming accident.

Chapter
Fifteen

When You're in the Vicinity of . . .

CONCORD, Massachusetts

Louisa May Alcott

One of the most popular of New England's literary visiting places is Orchard House, the house that was home for twenty years to Louisa May Alcott and the place where she wrote her classic, high-spirited novel of a family's love and four daughters' growing up, *Little Women*. In 1975, some 43,300 visitors toured Orchard House, more than four times the number that visited the same year at Emerson's house, a short distance away on Lexington Road. Not one, I would say, went away from Orchard House without the roots of romance stimulated in some way.

Orchard House, in a definite sense, is *Little Women* itself. Louisa used the house as the setting for the book, and the book's principal characters were, of course, the Alcotts, under easily recognized pseudonyms. In *Little Women*, the family name becomes March. Anna, the oldest of the Alcott daughters, appears as Meg; Louisa, as Jo; Abigail May (just May, if you please), as Amy. Only Beth, who died at twenty-two, just two months before the Alcotts moved into Orchard House, was not assigned a pseudonym. A perfected personality, in Louisa's eyes, she needed no name but her own.

Before settling here, the Alcotts had lived twenty-two places in twenty-one years. Bronson Alcott paid $1,000 for twelve acres of land and two old buildings, which were then attached and renovated. Thus the kitchen portion of Orchard House dates from 1650, and the main house from 1730. Out back, tucked into the hillside, is the late nineteenth-century "chapel" that was the center of the Concord School of Philosophy, Bronson Alcott's realization of a lifelong educational dream. The School of Philosophy was for adults and functioned as one of the first summer schools in the nation.

Orchard House, Concord, Massachusetts, Louisa May Alcott wrote **Little Women** *on a semicircular shelf-desk set between the second-floor windows, upper-right.*

More than 10,000 persons flocked to Concord for its lectures over ten years' time before the meetings were discontinued in 1888. The Hillside Chapel was reopened for lectures in the summer of 1976.

Fascinating as the Hillside Chapel is, the main attraction for visitors to the property remains Orchard House. The visitor's tour begins in the kitchen, with its iron stove, its hot-water heater of Bronson Alcott's designing, and its "luxurious" soapstone sink provided by Louisa in the affluence born of her writings. The tour then moves into the dining room, scene of the wedding of Meg and John Brooke in the book—Anna and John Pratt in real life. This room was the scene, too, for the dramas that the Alcott girls liked so much to stage for company seated in the adjoining parlor. (The guide on my visit reminded that Louisa was a "tall, manly type" and that she usually "preferred the part of a boy.") Downstairs also are a small studio and Bronson Alcott's study, crammed with books, many of them handled by himself, and mementos, such as the small bust of Socrates that Alcott carried around in his pocket, then set on the mantle on his return as a sign that he was home.

Upstairs are the bedrooms: the master bedroom, where Mrs. Alcott knitted, met with the girls, and kept her cherished chess pieces; May's room, with her sketches decorating the walls still, signaling the accomplished artist she was to become (unfortunately, she submerged individuality to specialize as a copyist of Turner); and, most interesting of all, Louisa's bedroom, which she shared with Anna and where she did her writing on a semicircular shelf-desk built to the wall between the two front windows. It was at this desk that *Little Women* was written. Looking out the window, Louisa might see her father sitting by the road, lying in wait for a passerby to engage in conversation.

Louisa May Alcott (1832–1888) was an astonishingly productive author. She would write from twelve to fourteen hours a day, nonstop, and had trained herself to write with her left hand as well as her right, as protection against writer's cramp. Before her death at age fifty-five, Louisa May Alcott had signed her name to thirty-six books and produced in addition a number of thrillers, under the pseudonym A. M. Barnard, that are just now being directly credited to her. The thrillers are an intriguing adjunct to a talent that was considerably more cosmopolitan than many might think, as indeed her own life-story is much more exciting than that of your average nineteenth-century New England woman. Louisa May Alcott was a Civil War nurse, for one thing. She was also a wise and witty feminist, and her account of Concord's male-dominated Centennial observance in 1876 makes relevant reading in our feminist-conscious post-Bicentennial period. Naturally, Louisa knew Emerson well, and he gave her access to his library, where she feasted on Shakespeare, Dante, Goethe, Carlyle. Similarly, she was a friend of Thoreau, and she and her sisters enjoyed long walks with him through Concord's fields and woods, studying birds and the wide variety of flowers and shrubs to be found in the area. May Alcott's flower paintings in Orchard House reflect these walks with Thoreau.

Incidentally, sixty percent of the furnishings in Orchard House belonged to the Alcotts. They range from the water pitcher that was Emerson's wedding present to Anna, to Louisa's "mood pillow" on the parlor settee. If the pillow was set on end, pointed upwards, Louisa was in a good mood; if laid flat, tread carefully.

Orchard House is operated by the Louisa May Alcott Memorial Association. It is open from April to mid-November, Monday to Saturday from 10:00 A.M. to 5:00 P.M., and Sunday from 1:00 to 5:00 P.M. (The last tour starts at 4:30 P.M.) There is a modest admission fee, with a discount for children. The house, at 399 Lexington Road, is well marked. It is within a few miles of Route 128, a primary state road, via Route 2 or 2A.

At 20 Pinckney Street on Boston's Beacon Hill is a three-story red-brick house with a marker outside announcing that Louisa May Alcott once lived there. It was actually only one of several residences that she bought or rented in her last years. For instance, there were also the cottage at Nonquit, the apartment on Boylston Street, and the house at 10 Louisburg Square. It was in this house on Boston's finest square that Bronson Alcott died on March 4, 1888. Louisa, unwell herself, had gone to visit him, knowing the end was close. Little did she realize that her own life would end two days later. Sensitiveness to strangers sent her fleeing by a side door, after a knock came to the front. In her haste she left behind her fur wrap, and thus caught the chill that killed her.

Henry David Thoreau

No trip to Concord is complete without a pilgrimage to Walden Pond, site of Henry David Thoreau's celebrated experiment in independent living, where he tested the proposition that as man simplifies his life, the laws of the universe will appear less complex; solitude will not be solitude; nor poverty, poverty; nor weakness, weakness. The cabin that Thoreau built for $28.12½ cents—ten feet wide by fifteen feet long—has long since been reduced to a lumber pile. But the spot where the cabin and adjoining woodshed stood is marked with stone pillars linked by chain. Set in the ground over Thoreau's chimney foundation is a stone carrying his prophetic words, "Go thou my incense upward from this hearth."

The precise location of the cabin, where Thoreau lived from July 4, 1845, to September 6, 1847, was not established until 1945, when foundation pieces were found in the roots of a white pine tree that had blown down in the 1938 hurricane and had been lying around since. The cabin site is on a rise above a cove at the far end of the pond from today's public beach. It is from a parking lot above the beach that the trek begins for the Thoreau pilgrim. It is not an easy walk, nor a particularly short one. The foot paths are rugged and unpaved; the distance, a half-mile or so. But the effort is rewarded. The scenery is spectacular, and on the right day the mood can be as sacred as it must have been when Thoreau lived here. This would hardly be the summertime, however, when shouts rise up from swimmers and the surrounding hills echo to the snap of picnickers' beer-can tops.

By the way, the cabin spot is not easily found. I have talked to people who have been going to Walden Pond for years and who have never seen the site. The best approach is down the right-hand side of the pond, with the public beach at one's back. After a short distance, the walker will notice trees marked with a circled *T* in white paint. Follow the circled *T*'s, and they will lead to the site.

Since January of 1975, Walden Pond has been a preserve of the Massachusetts Department of Natural Resources. The department's restoration program has included repair of the steep banks, which were threatening to slide into the basinlike pond, an information center, new bathhouse and toilet facilities, and a rerouting of the road (State Route 126) that rims the area. This has given the woods that tower over the pond a chance to restore themselves. Somehow the department manages to keep litter to a minimum, although the walker inevitably comes upon the ubiquitous beer can and disposable bottle.

Back near the center of Concord, at 156 Belknap Street, is the Thoreau Lyceum, headquarters of the Thoreau Foundation, a nonprofit public organization concerned with books and ideas relating to Thoreau. The Lyceum is not a museum, although its building features much Thoreau memorabilia, such as his town desk, three original survey maps by Thoreau, lead pencils from the family business, and mortar chips, glass, nails, etc., from the cabin at Walden Pond.

But probably the most interesting item is the cabin replica built behind the Lyceum close by the Boston-Fitchburg railroad tracks along which Thoreau used to hike. The replica is exact, down to caned bed and writing desk (originals of which are in the Concord Antiquarian Society Museum on Lexington Road). There is even the trapdoor leading down to the cellar, six feet square by seven deep, where at Walden Thoreau found his potatoes were protected against freezing in the fine sand of its depth. The replica of the cabin is at the Thoreau Lyceum rather than Walden Pond because of souvenir hunters, who would probably strip it bare in a short time. As it is, someone made off with Thoreau's gravestone from Concord's Sleepy Hollow Cemetery. The "HENRY" marker now there is a replacement.

Henry David Thoreau (1817–1862) lived in seven houses around town. Lyceum headquarters is not one of them, although it is next door to the lot on which the family's Texas House once stood. The house in which Thoreau was born is on Virginia Road; the house in which he died is on Main Street; the house in which he lived during his Harvard years is now the east end of the Colonial Inn. None is a formal public shrine.

Thoreau's spirit permeates Concord, partially because he is memorialized in street and park; partially also because there are people in Concord living still on land he surveyed for their ancestors. More particularly, his spirit permeates the place because of all Concord's great literary figures, he and his books have the greatest

The original cabin that Henry David Thoreau built at Walden Pond for $28.12½ is long gone. This replica stands behind The Thoreau Lyceum in Concord.

currency—beginning with *Walden*, of course, but extending to *Cape Cod*, *The Maine Woods*, other books of observation and reflection, and his pamphlet-length essays, such as "On the Duty of Civil Disobedience." Emerson, Hawthorne, Bronson Alcott, for all their greatness, were people of the nineteenth century. Thoreau is a man of the twentieth: as philosophical ecologist ("Thank God they can't cut down the clouds," he once said in rebuke of those depleting woods and forest); as champion of blacks and of Indians (he was an intense abolitionist, and his interest in the Indian had grown to eleven notebooks before he died, prematurely); as witness to principle (thus his willingness to go to jail for not paying his poll tax, as protest against the Mexican War).

Incidentally, it would be nice to be able to certify as authentic the exchange that reportedly took place on the occasion of the jailing, the exchange in which Emerson is said to have called upon the imprisoned Thoreau and remarked, "What are you doing here?"; whereupon Thoreau is said to have responded, "What are you not doing here?" Alas, the story is apocryphal. Henry was "sprung" by his Aunt Maria, who produced the $1.75 that was unpaid over several years by Thoreau. Thoreau was in jail only overnight, and likely was free by the time Emerson had even heard of the incident. Thoreau withheld his poll tax—a tax assessed, it seems, for no other reason than that the person was drawing breath—because it was the closest he could come to directing his protest against the national government and national policy; naturally, there was then no such thing as an income tax that one could withhold. So he chose the poll tax and, interestingly enough, continued to pay his local taxes, including the school tax and the road tax. These taxes were not "the specific imposition of the political state."

Walden Pond is reached from downtown Concord either by Walden Street or by Thoreau Street, which connects with Walden Street as Route 126. Route 126 crosses Route 2 and leads to the parking areas for Walden Pond. Parking areas, like footpaths, are unpaved, thus helping to preserve the rustic atmosphere.

Belknap Street, location of the Thoreau Lyceum, is near the railway station. After crossing the tracks going west, the Lyceum is found a couple of hundred yards down the street, on one's right. There is a green mailbox out front. The Thoreau Lyceum is a membership organization. It publishes a quarterly newsletter, *The Con-*

The Thoreau cabin site at Walden Pond sits on a rise at the far end of the water from the public beach. The spot was not pinpointed until 1945, when foundation pieces were found in the roots of a blown-down tree.

cord Saunterer, runs a gift shop, and operates a bookshop specializing in Thoreau-related material. Membership applications may be had by writing the Curator, The Thoreau Lyceum, 156 Belknap Street, Concord, Massachusetts, 01742. The Lyceum is open weekdays, Monday to Saturday, from 10:00 A.M. to 5:00 P.M., and Sundays from 2:00 to 5:00 P.M. It is closed on national holidays and on April 19, anniversary date of the Battle of Concord in 1775. There is a modest admission fee, with a discount for children grades 1–12. Members of the Lyceum enter free, with guests. Group rates for high school and college students may be had by writing the Curator or by telephoning 617-369-5912.

CUMMINGTON, Massachusetts; New York City

William Cullen Bryant

William Cullen Bryant (1794–1878) was a certifiable child prodigy. He could read at sixteen months. At eighteen months he was handling the New Testament in Greek. At fifteen years of age he entered Williams College, as a sophomore. At seventeen, he wrote "Thanatopsis," a poem so distinguished that Richard Henry Dana of the *North American Review* hesitated to publish it, fearful of a hoax. Dana doubted that there was anyone this side of the Atlantic who could produce such fine verse. "Thanatopsis" languished almost six years in Bryant's desk. It was published in 1817; the fame of the author was virtually instant.

Bryant had a varied career. After a year at Williams, he read law and in 1815 was admitted to the bar in Plainfield, Massachusetts, not far from his home town of Cummington. He disliked law as a profession, however, and was happy to escape to publishing. He served for a time as coeditor of the *New York Review and Athenaeum Magazine*, and in 1826 became an editor—and subsequently an owner—of the *New York Evening Post*, a paper in existence to this day. He remained with the *Post* for the rest of his life.

When Bryant came to the *Post*, it was primarily a commercial paper: one sheet, folded so as to make four pages, with all but the second given over to legal notices, advertising, and similar fare. Bryant gave the *Post* a literary tone and a liberal bend. He supported Lincoln, was solidly behind John Brown, backed Andrew Johnson's policy of reconciliation, and spoke out eloquently for free speech and labor unions.

He earned the reputation as being "the American Wordsworth," but the fact was that his newspaper preoccupations cut deeply into his production of poetry. His output was relatively small when compared with that of some of his contemporaries. The quality, however, was high, and gained for Bryant a place in poetic history. His favorite themes were the seasons and objects of nature, which he had come to know and to love during his growing up in western Massachusetts, and which he was to draw upon all his life.

In Cummington, midway between Pittsfield and Northampton, is the William Cullen Bryant Homestead—a rambling, white clapboard house nestled in the gentle hills of Hampshire County. Here Bryant wrote "Thanatopsis" and many more notable poems. The homestead had been sold by the Bryants in 1835, but the poet/editor bought it back in 1866 and spent summers there the last twelve years of his life. The atmosphere is reminiscent yet of his lines from "A Summer Ramble":

> Rest here beneath the unmoving shade,
> And on the silent valleys gaze,
> Winding and widening, till they fade
> In yon soft ring of summer haze.

The Bryant homestead is a National Historic Landmark. It was acquired by the Trustees of Reservations in 1929, through a bequest from Bryant's granddaughter, Minna Godwin Goddard, and is now open to the public. The home dates from 1783, and in it are considerable Bryant memorabilia. The home is open Fridays, Saturdays, Sundays, and holidays, from mid-June to mid-October. Hours are from 1:00 to 5:00 P.M. There is a modest admission fee, with a reduction for children. The homestead is just off State Routes 112 and 9 at Cummington. Pittsfield is twenty miles to the west; Northampton, twenty miles to the east.

In New York City, the park behind the New York Public Library, at Forty-second Street between Fifth Avenue and the Avenue of the Americas, is named for William Cullen Bryant. At the east end of the park is a handsome, but graffiti-stained, monument to Bryant; it features a bronze statue in a colonnade setting. Reproduced on the base of the statue are these lines of the poet:

> Yet let no empty gust
> Of passion find an utterance in thy lay;
>   A blast that whirls the dust
> Along the howling street and dies away;
>   But feelings of calm power and mighty sweep,
> Like currents journeying through the windless deep.

The lines comprise the final stanza of Bryant's poem, "The Poet," wherein he spelled out his counsel to those "who wouldst wear the name / of poet midst thy brethren of mankind / And clothe, in words of flame / thoughts that shall live within the general mind." It is advice that stands the test of time.

HAVERHILL, Massachusetts

John Greenleaf Whittier

There was a time when several thousands of visitors flocked annually to the home in Haverhill where the poet John Greenleaf Whittier was born and where he lived for twenty-nine years. But that was when State Route 110 was a main artery between Worcester, Lowell, and Lawrence to the southwest, and Portsmouth, Newburyport, and Portland to the north. Today, superhighways speed motorists wide of the Whittier birthplace, and only about fifteen hundred persons call over a year's time, many of them schoolchildren. But for those who do go out of their way to stop, the experience is infinitely rewarding. For to pause here is to step not only into New England's past, but almost into the very lines of Whittier's immortal poem *Snow-Bound*. Here in the countryside of the east end of Haverhill lie the scenes of *Snow-Bound*, all very much as they were at the time of

John Greenleaf Whittier was born here in 1807. The pastoral charm of this section of Haverhill, Massachusetts, has so perfectly endured that Whittier could return today and be no stranger to the surroundings.

the poem's writing in 1847, including the barn across the road from the homestead. It was to the barn, we remember, that the boys of *Snow-Bound* tunneled "with merry din / And roused the prisoned brutes within." The present barn is not, however, the one built by Whittier's father and by Uncle Moses in 1821. That barn burned down in 1970. A replacement was found in the town of Bradford and, at a cost of $30,000, brought to Haverhill. The replacement is of the period, so there is no disjointing of antiquities.

Five generations of Whittiers lived in this Haverhill homestead. The site—148 acres originally; 75 now—was acquired by Whittier's great-great-grandfather, Thomas, who came to this country from England in 1637. The house was eight years in the building, Thomas facing it southeast in order to get maximum sun by season. The construction was done by the Whittiers themselves, and evidences their Yankee practicality. The hearth, for instance, was built with ballast bricks from sailing ships that carried supplies from England. And, notice, the downstairs bedroom is raised two steps above first-floor level. Underneath is a boulder that it was too inconvenient to move.

The downstairs rooms of the Whittier homestead are open to visitors. Everything in them belonged to the Whittiers—the candle-maker, the foot-warmer, the desk—or is intimately associated with their memory. One enters through what is actually a side door, passes through a tiny hallway containing a desk from the schoolhouse that Whittier attended, then steps into the kitchen immortalized in *Snow-Bound*. It is as though Whittier had only momentarily left the room. The dress boots are by the chair next to the hearth, his dress coats hang on the door to "mother's room" (father died in 1830), and atop the family desk is Whittier's dress hat, one no doubt from his latter years. There is a wonderful story that after Whittier achieved fame, he answered knocks to his door with his hat on, thus to convey the message to pesky visitors that he was on his way out.

Off the kitchen in one direction is the buttery, or pantry, with its dry sink and now-antique cooking utensils. In another direction is the step-up bedroom with its short poster-bed from that era when people did not grow nearly so tall as they do today. (Whittier was enormously tall for his time at 5-foot 10½-inches.) A third door from the kitchen leads to the borning room, where Whittier came into this world. This was the parlor, or "best room," when not used for births. In still another direction is the dining room-sitting room. Here one sees the red cloak of Phoebe, the "niece" for whom he wrote the poem "Red Riding Hood." Here, too—would you have guessed?—are photos of Whittier College in California. The college may be widely known today as the alma mater of Richard Nixon. But it was named for John Greenleaf Whittier, as is the town of its location.

John Greenleaf Whittier (1807–1892) was one of the towering figures of his day, not only as poet, but also as religious mystic (more than one hundred of his poems grew into hymns) and as dedicated abolitionist in the Quaker tradition. In 1833, he was a delegate to the first antislavery convention at Philadelphia, was one of its secretaries, and signed its Declaration. He edited antislavery journals, endured numerous threats of violence for his antislavery activities, and on one occasion—while editor of the *Pennsylvania Freeman* in Philadelphia—had his office sacked and burned by a mob. Recognizing "the necessity of separate political action on the part of Abolitionists," Whittier helped found the Liberty Party, in his word the "germ" of the Republican Party of Abraham Lincoln. His activities cost him dearly as a poet and writer, and he tells us in an autobiographical letter dated 1882 that his "pronounced views on slavery made my name too unpopular for a publisher's uses."

With time came vindication, of course, and wide respect. He had moved by now to Amesbury, a town just up the road from Haverhill, and people were constantly at his door to consult and to pay homage. Opportunities for "public stations" were numerous. He declined most, though he did serve a term in the Massachusetts legislature and was an influential political element in its deliberations for years thereafter. Harvard College named Whittier to its board of overseers, and he became a trustee of Brown University. Both posts must have seemed deliciously lofty to the one-time farm boy whose highest formal education had been two terms at Haverhill Academy.

John Greenleaf Whittier never married. There were romances, but the principal ones were with non-Quakers, and Whittier's commitment to Quakerism would not let him marry "outside of society." He stayed a bachelor, acquiring at the same time the reputation of being something of a philanderer. Van Wyck Brooks tells amusingly of the "pilgrims" who threatened to engulf his later years, notably "the lady poets who sent him snips of their dresses, begged him for intimate souvenirs, proposed to marry him."

Whittier, though frail of health, lived to the grand old age of eighty-five. He died of a stroke while visiting friends in Hampton Falls, New Hampshire. The first generations of Whittiers are buried in an upland meadow of the old farm, but later generations, including John Greenleaf Whittier, rest in the Quaker section of Union Cemetery in Amesbury. Each member of the family commemorated in *Snow-Bound*, and the niece who was part of the household for twenty years, is buried here. They lie side by side under a row of nine small marble stones, with the poet's stone slightly larger.

Haverhill is some forty miles north of Boston and is reached from Boston and the west via Routes 128-95-97, or Routes 128-93-125. Also, one may take Route 495 from the Massachusetts Turnpike to Exit 40 in Haverhill. The homestead is one mile north on Route 110; near the homestead Route 110 becomes the John Greenleaf Whittier Highway. The homestead is set back about one hundred yards and is not visible from the highway. However, the approach is well marked with both stone memorial and wooden sign. Within walking distances are the scenes of "Kenoza Lake," "Suicide Pond," "In School-Days," "The Countess," "The Sycamores," "The Old Burying Ground," and "The Homecoming of the Bride." If it is summertime, "Fernside Brook" may be dry, but if you look quickly you may catch a glimpse of "The Barefoot Boy."

Whittier's birthplace is open year round, Tuesdays through Saturdays, from 10:00 A.M. to 5:00 P.M., and Sundays from 1:00 to 5:00 P.M. There is a small admission charge. It is operated by trustees of the John Greenleaf Whittier Homestead.

Available from the Haverhill Historic Trails Committee is a pamphlet that guides travelers to area landmarks connected with Whittier's poetry. Snippets are included from the pertinent poems.

Seven miles further north on Route 110 is Amesbury, the town to which Whittier moved in 1836 with his mother, his Aunt Mercy, and his youngest sister, in order to be nearer the Friends' meeting house. He took a house on what is now called Friend Street. The meeting house was located nearly opposite the house. (In 1851, a new meeting house was built a few blocks away, with Whittier having a major share in its designing.) It was in the Amesbury home that *Snow-*

Bound was written, on a desk in the present "manuscript room" that contains still, in its glassed upper portion, many of Whittier's own books and early editions of his poems. The house was a small, four-room cottage when the Whittiers moved in, and was greatly expanded by them over the years. Yet it has not been altered since the death of the poet, and the garden room, where he did his writing for some forty years, is precisely as Whittier left it. The house has been a Whittier memorial since 1918.

The Amesbury home, at 86 Friend Street, is open the year round, Tuesdays through Saturdays, from 10:00 A.M. to 5:00 P.M., except for Thanksgiving and Christmas Days. There is a small admission charge. To reach the Amesbury home of John Greenleaf Whittier from Haverhill, one continues on Route 110, turns left on Main Street in Amesbury, and proceeds several blocks to the intersection of Friend Street, where one should again turn left. The home will then be on the driver's left.

Whittier spent long portions of the last fifteen years of his life with cousins in Danvers, Massachusetts, where he had his own study in an estate known as Oak Knoll. It was here that his fancy was engaged by little Phoebe, the adopted daughter of cousin Abby Johnson Woodman, and from his pen flowed "Red Riding Hood." To Phoebe, the poet was "Uncle Greenleaf." Whittier wrote about one hundred poems at Danvers, but Oak Knoll is no memorial. It was razed some years ago to make way for a housing development.

LENOX, Massachusetts

Edith Wharton

Edith Wharton (1862–1937) filters down through literary history as the diarist of a dying American aristocracy. She was of wealth, and had considerable experience of its claim on privilege and standing. Her novels, however, came to reflect a critical attitude toward the elitist view that money and breeding were the best of desirable combinations; social conformism, a golden rule of the small world that had everything. But there were ambiguities still. In *The Age of*

Innocence, the novel for which she won a Pulitzer Prize in 1921, Wharton's heroine, Countess Olenska, discovers that her family (of purest Old New York pedigree) would rather see her return to an impossible marriage and her brutish, degenerate husband than experience themselves the scandal that would be attendant upon her divorce.

Yet, if the social view of the world in which she moved and wrote was limited, Edith Wharton's talent was not, and she is survived by a number of memorable books, among them *The Valley of Decision* (1902), *The House of Mirth* (1905), *Ethan Frome* (1911), *A Son at the Front* (1923), *Hudson River Bracketed* (1929), *Certain People* (1930). Her greatest, of course, is *The Age of Innocence*.

Ironically, Edith Wharton was born a Jones. Unlike most Joneses, however, she passed her earliest years with governesses and language tutors, and in travel between New York, fashionable Newport, and the pleasantest places of Europe. In 1885 she married a Boston banker of a Virginia family, Edward Wharton, and continued to move genteelly between the United States and Europe. Her "cottage" at Newport—Land's End along the cliff walk—was a showplace of elegance. Around the turn of the century, Edith Wharton settled into a twenty-nine-room mansion on the shore of Laurel Lake in Lenox. She called it The Mount and considered it her first "real" home. She was happiest here in this "spacious and dignified house." Mornings were spent writing; afternoons, gardening; evenings, entertaining—often on "that dear wide terrace." Henry James was a visitor, and he titled her "the Lady of Lenox" presiding over "a delicate French chateau mirrored in a Massachusetts pond."

Edith Wharton stayed several years in Lenox, but eventually spent most of her time in France, where she had moved to spare "Teddy"—Mr. Wharton—the rigors of American winters. They were divorced in the second decade of the century.

With the outbreak of World War I, Edith Wharton devoted herself to Red Cross work, raising funds, visiting the front lines, helping to provide care for the sick and the homeless. Edith Wharton Committees sprang up in a number of American cities, and the governments of both France and Belgium awarded her high decorations for her services. She stayed on in France following the war, and after 1926 her residency there was permanent. Books kept pouring from her pen—she wrote forty, in all—and she remained an avid gardener. She died at her residence near St. Brice sous Forêt on August 11,

1937, and was buried in the American cemetery at Versailles.

Edith Wharton's home in Lenox is not a formal literary visiting place. For years The Mount was the dominant building of Foxhollow School, a private boarding school. Foxhollow School closed in October, 1976, and the following January the property was purchased by Donald I. Altshuler, attorney, developer, and entrepreneur. He put The Mount up for sale for $300,000, fifteen acres of land included. Several months later the offering was withdrawn, however, and Mr. Altshuler was contemplating the possibility of making The Mount the focal point of a resort and conference center of Foxhollow. As of December 7, 1977, when I talked with him, he did not rule out the possibility of The Mount serving also as a literary visiting place. There are no Edith Wharton memorabilia left at The Mount, only some original blueprints of the house. But Mr. Altshuler said that an effort could be made to collect some Wharton-associated items. The National Park Service is sufficiently interested in seeing The Mount preserved to have made a recent $10,130 grant for certain renovations. Though the future of The Mount is thus uncertain, just to drive by and look is to get a meaningful glimpse into the world, now long gone, of Edith Wharton and her novels. The Mount is on U.S. Route 7 in Lenox, just south of Pittsfield in the western part of Massachusetts.

CAMBRIDGE, Massachusetts

Mount Auburn Cemetery

Mount Auburn Cemetery has been called, for reason of its size, the "City of the Dead" (at one time its cemetery population was larger than the living population of the biggest cities in several states); the cemetery might better be called, for reason of its departed, the "City of the Distinguished Dead." There is no cemetery in the United States to rival it in terms of the numbers of the literary famous who are buried in one place. The cemetery is open daily, from 8:00 A.M. to sunset in the wintertime season, and from 8:00 A.M. to 7:00 P.M. in the longer days of summertime. The cemetery office at the north entrance, on Mount Auburn Street near Brattle, will furnish a guide to the locations of the graves of noted persons—together with a list of rules and regulations for the parklike cemetery (no bicycles or motorcycles; no picnicking, sunbathing, or lolling on the grass; automobile speed limit of fifteen miles per hour; etc.). Among the famous who are buried here:

—Oliver Wendell Holmes (1809–1894), poet, essayist, lecturer, physician, professor, and, of course, autocrat of the breakfast table.

—Julia Ward Howe (1819–1910), poet, author, social reformer, abolitionist. She wrote the new words for the army marching song about John Brown's body, titled them "The Battle Hymn of the Republic," and was paid four dollars upon their appearance in the *Atlantic Monthly*.

—Elizabeth Cabot Cary Agassiz (1822–1907). She kept the records of her husband Louis's expeditions to Brazil and around Cape Horn and published *Louis Agassiz: His Life and Correspondence*. She was a founder and the first president of Radcliffe College. Louis Agassiz is also buried here.

—Thomas Bailey Aldrich (1836–1907), author, poet, essayist, and for nine years editor of the *Atlantic Monthly*.

—Felix O. C. Darley (1822–1888). Darley is best known as illustrator for the leading authors of the time: Irving, Cooper, Dickens, Hawthorne, Longfellow. He also wrote and illustrated books of his own: *Sketches Abroad with Pen and Pencil*; *Pen and Pencil Sketches in Europe*.

—Henry Wadsworth Longfellow (1807–1882), poet and professor, perhaps the most widely known of all American poets.

—William Ellery Channing (1780–1842), Unitarian clergyman, social reformer, and author, whose six-volume *Works* passed through at least seventeen editions.

—James Russell Lowell (1819–1891), poet, critic, essayist, professor, diplomat, and first editor of the *Atlantic Monthly*. Lowell was one of the great shapers and deciders of literary values in nineteenth-century America and was himself a brilliant all-around man of letters. He served as minister to Spain and later to England under President Hayes. Elmwood, his birthplace and home in Cambridge, is now the official residence of the presidents of Harvard University.

—Amy Lowell (1874–1925), critic, lecturer, and author of eleven volumes of poetry. She belonged to the modern, impressionistic school and was one of the great controversialists of her day, as literary artist and as person. Before women were smoking cigarettes in public, she was puffing cigars.

—Francis Parkman (1823–1893), historian and author of *The Oregon Trail*, among more than twenty other books. He focused particularly on the struggle for power in America between the French and the British civilizations.

—Mary Baker Eddy (1821–1910), founder of the Church of Christ, Scientist, of which her book *Science and Health with Key to the Scriptures* is the cornerstone. Her tomb, near the shores of Lake Halcyon, is considered one of Mount Auburn's noted memorials.

There are additional interesting literary figures buried in Mount Auburn Cemetery—Gamaliel Bradford, for instance; Octavius Brooks Frothingham, James Thomas Fields, William Davis Ticknor. There is also an artist's grave of particular note: Winslow Homer's.

* * *

What of the celebrated James brothers—William (1842–1910), psychologist and philosopher; Henry (1843–1916), novelist and critic? William James died at his country home at Chocorua, New Hampshire, near Conway, and his remains were brought back to Harvard, where he had begun teaching twenty-seven years before. There was a memorial service at Appleton Chapel, followed by cremation at Mount Auburn Cemetery. His ashes were carried to Chocorua and scattered on the mountain stream where he used to swim in the warm weather.

Henry James died in England and was cremated in London. His sister-in-law, the widowed Mrs. William James, brought his ashes to the United States, literally smuggling them into the country. It was wartime and she was anxious that there be no possible interference by customs. The urn was buried beside the graves of his mother and sister in the Cambridge cemetery that Henry James had visited a dozen years before, and about which he had placed these memorable words in his notebook:

Isn't the highest deepest note of the whole thing the never-to-be-lost memory of that evening hour at Mount Auburn—at the Cambridge Cemetery when I took my way alone—after much waiting for the favouring hour—to that unspeakable group of graves. . . . The moon was there, early, white and young, and seemed reflected in the white face of the great empty

Stadium, forming one of the boundaries of Soldiers' Field, that looked over at me, stared over at me, through the clear twilight, from across the Charles. Everything was there, everything *came*; the recognition, stillness, the strangeness, the pity and the sanctity and the terror, the breath-catching passion and the divine relief of tears. . . . But why do I write of the all unutterable and the all abysmal? Why does my pen not drop from my hand on approaching the infinite pity and tragedy of all the past? It does, poor helpless pen, with what it meets of the ineffable, what it meets of the cold Medusa-face of life, of all the life *lived*, on every side. *Basta, Basta!*

The burial ground of Henry James's reflection sounds for all the world like Mount Auburn Cemetery, and it is not surprising therefore that some guide books actually locate Henry James's remains in Mount Auburn—the 1937 Federal Writers' Project book, *Massachusetts, A Guide to its Places and People*, for one. In point of fact they are in Cambridge Cemetery, operated by the city of Cambridge and adjacent to Mount Auburn Cemetery. The entrance to Cambridge Cemetery is on Coolidge Avenue, which runs off Mount Auburn Street and alongside the eastern end of Mount Auburn Cemetery. The cemetery gate is at 76 Coolidge. There are directional signs in the cemetery to the family plot of the Jameses. Cambridge Cemetery is open from 7:00 A.M. to 5:30 P.M. during wintertime, and from 7:00 A.M. to 7:30 P.M. in summertime.

CAPE COD, Massachusetts

Henry Beston; Joseph C. Lincoln

For writers, Cape Cod has ever been a favored working place, maybe even an inspirational one. Henry Thoreau walked Cape Cod's dunes and beaches and produced his memorable book on this "bared and bended arm of Massachusetts." Kurt Vonnegut, Jr., lived here for some twenty years. Conrad Aiken kept a home here, and, of course, the name of Eugene O'Neill will forever be associated with Provincetown. No two names are more synonymous with Cape Cod, however, than those of Henry Beston and Joseph C. Lincoln. Beston, a naturalist, wrote perhaps the most notable book about Cape Cod since Thoreau. Lincoln, a novelist, made a veritable business out of Cape Cod yarns. For both Beston and Lincoln, the Cape is grateful.

* * *

In 1927, Henry Beston (1888–1968) contracted for the building of a tiny, two-room cottage on a sand dune near the end of Nauset Beach in Eastham. Late in the season, Beston, thirty-nine years old and single, moved in for what he expected would be a few weeks. Caught up in the spell of the Cape as September lengthened into autumn, Beston stayed on for a year in the cottage he called the Fo'castle. He observed, he meditated, and he wrote the book wherein "he sought the Great Truth and found it in the Nature of Man." The book was *The Outermost House*, subtitled *A Year of Life on the Great Beach of Cape Cod*, and was published in 1928.

The following year, Henry Beston married Elizabeth Coatsworth, the poet and writer, and settled in Nobleboro, Maine. There, on Chimney Farm, he raised a family and did much more writing: *Herbs and the Earth* (1935), *American Memory* (1937), *The St. Lawrence River* (1941), a book in the Rivers of America series, *Northern Farm, A Chronicle of Maine* (1948). He also wrote children's stories and in 1950 edited a regional reader of the state of Maine, *White Pine and Blue Water*. There were other volumes, but *The Outermost House* would remain the book with which Henry Beston's name would be preeminently connected. Incidentally, "Henry Beston" was originally a pseudonym, but was eventually taken as the writer's legal name. Beston was born a Sheahan in Quincy, Massachusetts.

In time Henry Beston's Fo'castle was neither "the outermost house" on the back side of Eastham nor the only house south of Nauset Light. A few other houses were built braving wind and tide out on that peninsula of sand about a mile's distance from the public entrance to Coast Guard Beach. Indeed, Fo'castle was not to stay on its original location. Twice it had to be hauled back from the tide's reach, and several years ago, for conservation's sake, it was moved to the protected side of the dunes. Meanwhile, the cottage was designated a National Historic Landmark of the Department of the Interior. Though Fo'castle was not open to the general public, it did occasionally provide shelter for researchers, thanks to the courtesy of its owners, the Massachusetts Audubon Society, and the people were free to walk the beach from the Coast Guard station for a close exterior view and to read the memorial plaque set in place October 11, 1964. A distant view was possible from a lookout point just past the Captain Penniman House on Fort Hill Road. Beston's "outermost house" was the second on the dunes from the right.

Was! In the wild blizzard of February 6–7, 1978, Fo'castle was washed out to sea by rampaging tides. Salvagers recovered bits and pieces, but not enough to reconstruct the cottage. "It's gone," said Wallace Bailey of the Audubon Society, "and the land is under water." The sentimental can still visit and from Fort Hill Road see where Fo'castle once stood. At low tide they may catch a glimpse of the cottage's pilings. A couple were left after the storm. But in mid-February, 1978, that was all that remained from Henry Beston's solitary stay of 1927. That, and a classic book.

* * *

Joseph C. Lincoln (1870–1944) was a Cape Codder born and bred. His birthplace was a small, one-and-a-half-story white clapboard house near the center of Brewster; his home in later years, a stunning shingle residence overlooking the water at Chatham. The Lincoln family had been on the Cape since the mid-1600s and had produced a long line of sea captains. Joe Lincoln's grandfather, his father, and several uncles were of the sea, and their experiences no doubt flavored the novels that flowed so facilely from his pen, beginning with *Cap'n Eri* in 1904 and continuing until the year before his death, when *The Bradshaws of Harniss* was issued (Harwich is generally regarded as the Harniss of Lincoln's novels). In all, some fifty books were written by Joseph C. Lincoln, including *Cape Cod Ballads* (1902), a collector's item, and a few books of his later years done in collaboration with his son, Freeman Lincoln.

Joseph C. Lincoln's novels are easily faulted for their repetitiousness, their easy moralizing, their elementary style. Yet they possessed the salt of old Cape Cod and neatly mirrored its characters. Joe Lincoln books were extremely popular in their day, and it is said that not one ever failed the test of financial return. Some titles ran to editions of 100,000 copies, and second-hand bookdealers will tell you that his books are still being asked for by readers and collectors.

Lincoln had a winter home in Hackensack, New Jersey, and later in Villanova, Pennsylvania. He also had an apartment in Winter Park, Florida. But when the sun was high in the sky and the wind warm off the water, you could count on Joe Lincoln's being at Chatham. His home, a familiar postcard picture, is a short way past the Chatham Bars Inn, east of the center of town. The house is in private hands and not open to the public.

Joseph C. Lincoln died in Winter Park, but is buried in Chatham. In Chatham's Atwood House (1752) is a wing dedicated to his memory. Atwood House, once the home of a pre-Revolutionary War deepwater sea captain, is the headquarters and museum of the Chatham Historical Society. It is located on State Harbor Road, a mile from the center of town, and is open to the public from late spring to early fall on Mondays, Wednesdays, and Fridays. The hours are from 2:00 to 5:00 P.M. There is a small admission charge.

NEW LONDON AND WATERFORD, Connecticut

Eugene O'Neill

When I visited 325 Pequod Avenue in New London in September of 1976, the place was alive with carpenters busy about the restoration of a unique theatrical, and national, landmark. Number 325 Pequod is Monte Cristo Cottage, boyhood home of Eugene O'Neill (1888–1953), playwright and 1936 Nobel Prize winner. This same cottage was the setting for *Long Day's Journey into Night* and for *Ah, Wilderness!* It had been lately acquired by the Eugene O'Neill Memorial Theater Center in adjacent Waterford, and workmen were readying the cottage as a museum dedicated to the memory of the playwright and the history of the American theater.

The restoration will have been completed by the time this book is published, and the cottage should now be open on a permanent basis (target date for completion of the renovation was Summer of 1978). The schedule of hours and days when the cottage is open will have to be checked, as the information was not available at press time.

What was available when I visited were detailed plans for this cottage with its twin parlors, fourteen-foot ceilings, and open veranda facing the Thames River across Pequod Avenue. On the veranda, rocking chairs will be grouped, no doubt according to the well-known 1900 photograph taken there of Eugene, his brother, and their father, James. O'Neill's father was, of course, a famous matinee idol, and there were those who thought his name would one day be synonymous with that of Edwin Booth. Alas, he is more famous as a figure in his son's dramas. The name of the cottage, incidentally, comes from the play in which James O'Neill achieved his greatest fame, *The Count of Monte Cristo*.

Inside the cottage, the milieu will be 1890. The front parlor will feature the setting for *Long Day's Journey into Night*, and the wicker table will be that from the original Broadway set. The dark back parlor of O'Neill's memory will be arranged according to the dining room setting of *Ah, Wilderness!* Some years ago, windows were placed in the back parlor wall; they will be left there for purposes of light.

The remainder of the cottage's downstairs will be given over to changing exhibits and a reading room (the old kitchen) for students and researchers into O'Neill and the American theater. Upstairs will be stored the sizable collection of O'Neill and theater memorabilia that has been gathered together by the Eugene O'Neill Memorial Theater Center in Waterford. The Center, on Town of Waterford land, is about three miles away from Monte Cristo Cottage. It functions not only as a custodian of the O'Neill heritage, but also as a live development organization dedicated to encouraging new uses, forms, and methods of theater work. This includes theater as it relates to recreation and education, as well as to the continuing development of professional theater. Among other things, the Center is the home for the National Theater of the Deaf, the National Playwright's Conference, and the National Critics Institute. There are several theaters, indoors and outdoors, and a fine O'Neill-theater library.

Ironically, Center headquarters is the imposing farmhouse of Edward Crowninshield Hammond, a wealthy squire-type, whom O'Neill was to satirize unmercifully in *Long Day's Journey into Night* and in *A Moon for the Misbegotten*. Remember Hogan's pigs in Harder's ice pond in the latter play? The pond is still there, but it's a saltwater pond now, the waters of Fishers Island Sound having changed the contour of the land during the 1938 New England hurricane, bringing in the sea.

Eugene O'Neill used to walk this strand, of course, but the memories were not happy ones. Nor were they of New London. "It wasn't a friendly town," he once remarked to a newspaperman. Yet the area obviously had a powerful, lasting effect on O'Neill. One O'Neill scholar—Timo Tiusanen—concluded that no less than ten O'Neill plays reflect the area in some way.

The O'Neill Theater Center is open Mondays to Fridays, from 9:00 A.M. to 5:00 P.M., the year round, or by appointment. It is about 130 miles from New York City, via the New England Throughway-Connecticut Turnpike (Interstate 95). Drivers should take Exit 75 off the Connecticut Turnpike onto Route 1A towards Waterford. After a little more than four miles on 1A, drivers should take a right turn onto Avery Lane; proceed straight at the traffic light onto Great Neck Road (Route 213), and follow 213 past Harkness Memorial Park to the entrance to the Center. The route is circuitous, but clearly marked with O'Neill Theater roadsigns. Other approaches:

From Hartford and the north: Take Route 2 out of Hartford and follow Norwich-New London signs to Colchester. Take Route 85 to New London (Route 2 goes to Norwich) and stay on Route 85 to Waterford. Shortly after passing the Speed Bowl on the right and Oakdale Motel on the left, turn right onto Cross Road. Follow Cross Road to the end and turn left at the traffic light onto Route 1A. Follow Route 1A and turn right onto Avery Lane at Silva's Package Store. Continue to the traffic light. At the light, go straight ahead onto Great Neck Road and Route 213. Follow 213 past Harkness Memorial Park to the entrance of the Center.

From Boston and Providence: Get onto Route 195 out of Providence and follow it onto the Connecticut Turnpike after crossing the Thames River Bridge at Groton. Take Exit 75 and follow Waterford signs back over the turnpike onto Route 1A and follow Route 1A for about four miles, then turn right onto Avery Lane at Silva's Package Store. At the traffic light go straight ahead onto Great Neck Road and Route 213. Follow 213 past Harkness Memorial Park to the entrance to the Center.

To reach Monte Cristo Cottage, drivers should continue on Interstate 95 to the Downtown New London exit (#83). The cottage is on the west bank of the Thames River.

Incidentally, the restoration of Monte Cristo Cottage was figured as a $175,000 project. Initial funding came through the City of New London Community Development Fund ($60,000), the Frank Loomis Palmer Fund ($10,000), the National Parks Service through the Connecticut Historical Commission ($5,000), and the National Endowment of the Arts ($12,000). Additional funds were being raised at the time of my visit.

PORTSMOUTH, New Hampshire

Thomas Bailey Aldrich

At 386 Court Street in this charming New England port city is the boyhood home of Thomas Bailey Aldrich (1836–1907), poet, novelist, editor. It is the home depicted in Aldrich's most famous work, *The Story of a Bad Boy* (1870), and it is preserved almost to the letter of the book. Built about 1790, the structure is a modest, square colonial of frame construction: four rooms down, four up, central stairway, double chimney. On the second floor, over the front door, is the hall bedroom from which the mischievous Tom Bailey—the predecessor of Tom Sawyer, Huck Finn, and similar fictional types—lowered himself out on the Fourth of July of the novel. The rooms of the house brim with memories of Tom Bailey; of the grandfather, Captain Nutter; of Miss Abigail, the captain's prim, tobacco-hating sister; of Kitty Collins, the Irish maid; and of Sailor Ben, who showed Tom and his pals how to fire the Trefethen cannon (eccentric Silas Trefethen had bought cannon for a war with England that never materialized). The setting, of course, was "Rivermouth," the Portsmouth of the story.

In a memorial building to the rear of the house are Thomas Bailey Aldrich artifacts: manuscripts, autographs, first editions of his books, pictures, and other items, such as the table on which he wrote *The Story of a Bad Boy*.

Thomas Bailey Aldrich died after a career in New York and Boston that carried through to the editor's chair of the *Atlantic Monthly*. The boyhood home was dedicated as a public memorial on June 30, 1908. Attending were William Dean Howells, whom Aldrich succeeded at

This house in Portsmouth, New Hampshire, was the boyhood home of Thomas Bailey Aldrich. Here "Tom Bailey" cavorted, the same "Tom Bailey" who was a literary precursor of the Huck Finn and Tom Sawyer types.

the *Atlantic*, Mark Twain, Thomas Wentworth Higginson, and other notables of the day. The home is open weekdays, June through September, from 10:00 A.M. to 5:00 P.M. There is a modest admission charge, with a discount for children. Portsmouth is fifty-five miles north of Boston via Route 1, Interstate 95, and the New Hampshire Turnpike.

JAFFREY, New Hampshire; New York City

Willa Cather

One thinks of Willa Cather (1876–1947) and one thinks of Nebraska, of Red Cloud, and of Czech and Danish girls of pioneer plains' life—like little Antonia, fighting the elements, working the fields, driving the cattle home. Tableland America was, of course, Willa Cather's milieu. But it is in Jaffrey, New Hampshire, in the shadow of Mount Monadnock, that she is buried.

Jaffrey was a favorite visiting place for Willa Cather. For twenty years she came to the old Shattuck Inn, now private, on Dublin Road, arriving in the fall, entering by the back door, and climbing three flights of stairs to rooms reserved for her facing the mountain. She used as a studio a tent pitched in the woods, and there she worked, oblivious to the autumn chill. Here parts of *My Antonia* and *One of Ours*, the novel that won a Pulitzer Prize, were written. The New England hurricane of 1938 wiped out the fir trees that sheltered her hillside retreat, and after that she did not return—except to be buried in the Old Town Burial Ground, after services in New York.

Why Jaffrey? It is said that Willa Cather once attended the funeral there of a child of friends and was struck by the quiet and serenity of the fern-covered burial ground. There, she decided, she too should one day be put to rest.

Or was it, as one biographer has suggested, that she wished to meet Death on a hilltop, like Myra Henshawe in *My Mortal Enemy*?

In any case, Willa Cather lies in Jaffrey under a marker that reads: "The truth and charity of her great spirit will live on in the work which is her enduring gift to her country and all its people." There is also a quote from *My Antonia*: "That is happiness, to be dissolved into something complete and great."

Jaffrey is about eight miles north of the Massachusetts line on Route 202 out of Winchendon, Massachusetts.

On Bank Street in New York City's Greenwich Village is a plaque marking the site of her home from 1913 to 1927. Another plaque is at the northeast corner of Fifth Avenue and Tenth Street. It commemorates the residency of Willa Cather in the Grosvenor Hotel, which once stood at 35 Fifth Avenue. From 1932 until her death, she lived at 570 Park Avenue, just above Sixty-second Street.

RIPTON, Vermont, and
FRANCONIA, New Hampshire

Robert Frost

Ordinarily one would not think of a nature trail as a literary visiting place. But Mamaroneck, New York, has its Leatherstocking Trail memorializing James Fenimore Cooper; no less appropriately, Ripton, Vermont, has its Robert Frost Memorial Nature Trail. Frost spent the last twenty-five summers of his life in these middle Vermont hills, and he knew their paths as well as the meter of a good poem. Nature served many themes of Robert Frost—nature and nature's complements: the fences that make for good neighbors; the country roads that diverge; the miles to go; the promises to keep. Many of Robert Frost's ideas were born of his walks through nature.

Robert Frost (1874–1963) was not a native Vermonter, of course. He was born in California; spent his boyhood there and in Lawrence, Massachusetts; wandered the Carolinas, the West, to Dartmouth, Harvard, and England, before settling in Vermont in 1915 to a life of farming and poetry. His was a career that budded late and bloomed gorgeously. Oxford and Cambridge honored him with degrees, and he was a prize of the John F. Kennedy White House. Engraved in the memory of almost all Americans alive in 1960 is the picture of Robert Frost reading a poem at the Kennedy inaugural, his white hair and manuscript pages whipped by the icy winds that foreboded the tragic end of that administration.

Robert Frost would approve of this nature trail in the Green Mountain National Forest. It is discreetly short, being only three-quarters of a mile long, and tastefully planned. At points along the trail, poems of Robert Frost appear in steel etchings on wooden posts. The effect on the visitor during foliage season is especially moving. It is almost as though one were in a grand outdoor cathedral, with the changing leaves giving off the colors of magnificent stained glass windows. The nature trail is not far from the site of the Bread Loaf Writers' Conference, which Frost founded. And only a half-mile away is the summer cabin where Frost stayed, its interior of spare, make-do furnishings virtually unchanged from the summers of his occupancy.

The Robert Frost Nature Trail was dedicated April 28, 1976. Thirteen years went into its planning, with much more ambitious schemes being tabled before the decision was made on the side of simplicity. It was thought that this was as Frost would have preferred. As was noted at the dedication, Robert Frost would have been embarrassed by something lavish and the hawking of postcards, souvenirs, and books of poetry.

Ripton, Vermont, is located on Route 125, east of Middlebury. It is a two-hundred-mile drive from Boston and more than three hundred miles from New York City. A particularly scenic drive is along U.S. Route 7, which runs north through Bennington, Manchester, Rutland, and Brandon. To reach the nature trail, drivers should bear east on Route 125 at East Middlebury. Ripton is the next town on 125.

* * *

Across the Green Mountains, across the New Hampshire state line and into the White Mountains is another Frost memorial. It is the Robert Frost Place in Franconia, where the poet lived from 1915 to 1920. House, barn, and eight acres of land were acquired in 1976 as a public trust for the town of Franconia and as a literary landmark for the nation. Beginning in 1877, a summer program of concerts, lectures, and readings was introduced in the barn where Frost kept a horse and a cow. The summer program is conducted with the assistance of a poet in residence, selected by the *Atlantic Monthly*.

The Franconia period was one of the most productive for Frost. Here, in a simple, eight-room, white frame farmhouse, on a hillside overlooking the mountains, he wrote his third book of poems, *Mountain Interval*, and most of his fourth collection, *New Hampshire*, which won a Pulitzer Prize. Three of Frost's most celebrated poems appeared in these books: "The Road Not Taken," "Birches," and "Stopping by Woods on a Snowy Evening."

The Frost Place is located on Ridge Road in Franconia. Drivers on Interstate 93 should depart at Exit 38 and take Route 116 approximately one mile to Bickford Hill Road, turn right over the bridge, and take the left fork onto Ridge Road. The Frost Place is a quarter-mile further on the right.

The property is open to the public during July and August, Tuesdays through Saturdays, from 10:00 A.M. to 12:00 noon and from 1:00 to 4:00 P.M. Through September and into October until Columbus Day, the property is open on Saturdays, Sundays, and Mondays for the same hours. The house is then closed for the season. There is a modest admission charge, with a discount for students, and children under ten are admitted free. Visitors are admitted to two museum rooms of the house; the barn, where one hears recordings of Frost reading his poetry; and Poetry Trail, which winds through the woods and displays Frost poems in related locations.

Concerts and poetry readings are featured during the summer months, on Fridays at 8:00 P.M. There is an admission fee, with, again, a discount for students and children.

When Robert Frost bought his Franconia property, it sat on an expanse of fifty acres. The price tag was $1,000. To purchase the Frost Place and just eight of the acres in 1976 cost $66,500. Restoration and development costs have run another $35,000, bringing the investment in a Franconia memorial to the poet to over $100,000. As of April, 1977, individuals, organizations, the town of Franconia, and the New Hampshire Bicentennial Commission had reduced that debt by nearly one-half. Additional funds were being sought as this book went to press. Tax-deductible gifts may be made to the Robert Frost Fund of the Town of Franconia. Mailing address is The Robert Frost Place, Box F, Franconia, New Hampshire, 03580.

SOUTH BERWICK, Maine

Sarah Orne Jewett

Twelve miles north of Portsmouth, New Hampshire, on Route 236 in South Berwick, Maine, is the Sarah Orne Jewett Memorial honoring one of the major women writers of her time. Sarah Orne Jewett (1849–1909) wrote of a Maine whose clipper ships were being overtaken by steamships, and whose small farms were being forsaken by the special types that sacrificed to keep them solvent—a Maine, in a word, that regretfully was passing from existence, to be replaced by the Maine of the twentieth century.

Sarah Orne Jewett's medium was fiction, the novel and the short story, and her emphasis was on local color and Maine's marvelous assemblage of characters. Van Wyck Brooks commented that most of the people of her books "were like the trees that grew in the cracks of the rocks and kept their tops green in the driest summer." She knew them as a woman who made a point of traveling with a doctor on his rounds should. The doctor was Sarah Orne Jewett's father. He was local historian and gifted storyteller, and Miss Jewett's talent with words was first his with the tongue.

The Country of the Pointed Firs (1896) is considered Miss Jewett's best book. Other notable works include *Deephaven* (1877), *A Country Doctor* (1884), *A Marsh Island* (1885), *A White Heron and Other Stories* (1886), and *The Tory Lover* (1901), reissued in 1975 as *Yankee Ranger*. Bowdoin College in 1901 conferred on Miss Jewett its first honorary degree given to a woman.

Sarah Orne Jewett was born in this house at 101 Portland Street and did most of her writing here. She had a bedroom-study that is preserved precisely as she had it arranged. The Jewett House is maintained by the Society for the Preservation of New England Antiquities. Built in 1780, it stands two-and-a-half stories and features a handsome Doric portico and raised-panel door. The central hall is said to be one of the most beautiful in New England. Throughout the house are books, old glass and silver, willowware, carved ivory, antique furniture, and cooking utensils.

The Jewett House is open from 1:00 to 5:00 P.M. on Tuesdays, Thursdays, and Sundays, June through September. There is a small admission charge.

CAMDEN, Maine

Edna St. Vincent Millay

Maine has produced a number of outstanding poets: Edwin Arlington Robinson, Robert Tristam Coffin, Henry Wadsworth Longfellow. Or was Longfellow of Massachusetts, Maine being still a part of that state when he was born in Portland in 1807? Whatever, Edna St. Vincent Millay fits comfortably into Maine's imposing company of poets.

Edna St. Vincent Millay (1892–1950) was born in the town of Rockland, in Knox County, and grew up in Camden. Though her career took her away from Maine, Maine—its bayberry and seaweed, eelgrass and meadow hay—was forever a part of her poetry.

In Camden is the Whitehall Inn and the parlor room where in the summer of 1912 "Vincent" Millay recited for guests the poem "Renascence," which she wrote at nineteen as a contest entry, and which drew wide attention when it subsequently appeared in the anthology, *Lyric Year*. Caroline B. Dow, head of the National Training School of the YWCA, was among the guests that summer night in Camden, and she became instrumental in shaping Edna St. Vincent Millay's career, inviting her to come to New York and encouraging her to enter Vassar and to write more poetry.

The room in the Whitehall Inn (once the home of a nineteenth-century sea captain) is set aside as a memorial to the poet. Decorating it are her school diploma from Camden High, photographs, and various of her writings. In nearby Camden Hills State Park is an Edna St. Vincent Millay Monument overlooking the scene that inspired "Renascence." A bronze plaque recalls the poem's opening lines:

> All I could see from where I stood
> Was three long mountains and a wood;
> I turned and looked the other way,
> And saw three islands in a bay.

Edna St. Vincent Millay went on to be one of the notable figures of the so-called Lost Generation, that group of writers who came of age during or immediately following World War I, and who evolved life-styles and interests which for the times were startling and unique. "Vincent," for her part, was social rebel and ardent feminist. She solidified her fame, and her standing in the Lost Generation, by winning a Pulitzer Prize in 1923 for *The Harp-Weaver and Other Poems*.

Camden is on U.S. Route 1, and Maine Routes 52, 105, and 173. It is about seventy miles north of Boston.

A plaque once marked the house at 200 Broadway in Rockland, where she was born and where she lived until 1904. Recently it was removed at the request of new owners and placed in the public library, where it is kept in a safe.

In New York City, Edna St. Vincent Millay lived on the top floor of 25 Charlton Street, and in a narrow, 9½-foot town house at 75½ Bedford Street. Both are private, but on the pilgrimage sight-list for devotees.

At Austerlitz, New York, off Route 22, is Steepletop, the white frame farmhouse and seven-hundred-acre tract, where Edna St. Vincent Millay lived from 1925 until her death. She wrote in an upstairs room under a sign that called out: SILENCE. A quarter-century after her death, Steepletop became a colony for writers, composers, and artists under the aegis of her sister and brother-in-law, Norma Millay and Charles Ellis. Mr. Ellis is now deceased, but Steepletop continues as a creative center and as a National Historic Landmark in which the memory of the poet is enshrined. Norma Millay is one of its directors. The Millay Colony for the Arts, as the center is called, considers as its first responsibility the maintenance of privacy for its working artists and writers, and after that, accessibility to the public. Its "future" plans call for the admission of visitors on a limited basis, according to a letter from a Millay Colony official dated September 13, 1976.

GARDINER, Maine

Edwin Arlington Robinson

Gardiner, Maine, was "Tilbury Town" of Edwin Arlington Robinson's poetry, and much of his poetry is evocative of this town on the

Kennebec and its people. Here he came as a young boy, and here he lived until going off in his mid-twenties to New York, where, among other things, he worked on construction of the underground railroad system and became known as the "poet in the subway." He never removed New England from his poetry, however, and eventually he returned to the region to write some of his very best verse.

Edwin Arlington Robinson (1869–1935) won three Pulitzer Prizes: in 1922 for *Collected Poems*, in 1925 for *The Man Who Died Twice*, and in 1928 for *Tristram*. At one corner of the Gardiner Green is a granite monument to his memory. Gardiner is situated along Interstate 95, U.S. Route 201, and State Route 126, just below Augusta.

Across the Kennebec and fifteen miles towards the ocean on State Route 194 is the tiny community of Alna. Robinson was born here—or, more specifically, in the village called Head Tide, which lies to either side of the bridge that crosses the Sheepscot River. Robinson's birthplace, private, is the second house beyond the village store.

PART THREE

SOME FOREIGN WRITERS
REMEMBERED

Chapter
Sixteen

TEILHARD DE CHARDIN

In New York City, a Sad, Sad Ending

From Grant's Tomb on Morningside Heights, to the plaques commemorating tree plantings along Forty-second Street, New York is a city of landmarks and monuments to its famous. It is inevitable that a few worthies have been overlooked. But not many. New Yorkers have been as conscientious about remembering their notables, as innkeepers were about chronicling the beds in which George Washington slept. They've missed few . . . and given the benefit of the doubt to many. There are people commemorated around New York that it would take a day's hunt in the Public Library in order to identify.

Marie Joseph Pierre Teilhard de Chardin—geologist, paleontologist, philosopher, evolutionist, Jesuit priest, writer—is among the overlooked. The New York Public Library card file on Teilhard is almost three inches thick, but the traces of him along the streets outside are as scarce as the fossils he tracked across several continents in search of the links between man and ape: a few cultists; a shrinking number of old associates; a few enduring enemies; and the American Teilhard de Chardin Association, a small but purposeful organization dedicated to extending knowledge and understanding of his thought—still sadly twisted, be it said. Recently one right-wing group petitioned the New York Archdiocese to declare Teilhard a "heretic" and correct the "unfortunate error by which he was given a Catholic burial."

Jesuit Father Pierre Teilhard de Chardin lived his last years in New York, and died there on an Easter Sunday afternoon over twenty years ago. In New York he endured his last anguishes, a paradox to the end: genius and obedient servant; man of science and of belief; honored in the world, but still an enigma in the church he served more loyally and trustingly than it served him.

Teilhard lived in New York from 1951 to 1955—a celebrity, of course, but not so celebrated as to be spared his tiny rectory room when the Jesuit community at Eighty-third Street needed the space. Nor so celebrated that after his death people rushed about erecting memorials to his memory or renaming halls in his honor. Some have spoken of him in the same breath as Aristotle and Aquinas; very many regard him as a giant of the twentieth century. But around New York there are no public Teilhard reminders; no Bloomsdaylike walks to the scenes of his activities; no Teilhard trails; no annual pilgrimages to the Jesuit cemetery upstate, where he is buried. Teilhard de Chardin lived and died an outsider, and he remains a stranger. When the *New York Times*, December 3, 1973, noted the seventy-fifth anniversary of St. Ignatius Loyola Church, its story recalled the rich and distinguished who had worshipped there: McDonnells, Murrays, Cuddihys, Graces, Farleys, Roskobs, Bouviers, Wagners. No one thought to tell *Times*woman Laurie Johnston: "Teilhard de Chardin also lived here, prayed here, helped out occasionally with a parish Mass."

Yet this may be as it should be. Teilhard did not embrace New York any more fervently than New York embraced him. He liked the city, including the heavy snows and crisp winter days; they reminded him of Peking. He was even hopeful that New York could be his "second Peking." "In 1925 Peking was the chance of my life," Teilhard wrote just before Christmas, 1952. But the enthusiasm was quickly tempered by the reflection: "I'm no longer forty years old."

In fact, Teilhard was past seventy when he settled in New York, and the city was in some respects more a place of exile than it was a spot which Teilhard, given his background, would seek out for its great personal challenges. He came to New York to assume the post of research associate at the Wenner-Gren Foundation for Anthropological Research in uptown Manhattan, and to research the fossil collections of New York's Museum of Natural History. As events developed, he also came to wind down a life that had begun inauspiciously in Auvergne in 1881, and built to controversial summits, particularly among churchmen, as, out of his findings, Teilhard spun an evolutionary philosophy about God and man . . . in a complex and often mystifying new vocabulary, featuring words like Christogenesis, complexification, noosphere, and anthropocentrism, and concepts like Hominization and Omega Point. Teilhard's thought hardly conformed to Jesuit or Roman orthodoxy, and he had long since been forbidden to teach and to publish.

When Teilhard made his decision to come to New York, his standing with church authorities was at a low ebb. Ostensibly that decision was Teilhard's own. However, subtle ecclesiastical pressures were also at work, including Pius XII's 1950 encyclical *Humani Generis*, a document which Teilhard, with reason, suspected was aimed at his theories. Teilhard concluded that he had become "an embarrassment" to ecclesiastical officialdom, and decided that a "shelter out of France" might be best for all concerned. And where was a sensitive septuagenarian with a serious heart condition to take himself to be out of the way? To the scenes of happy memories and large triumphs of earlier years? Not when these are in the remote parts of China, central Asia, the East Indies, Burma, Java, and the sub-Sahara. Teilhard opted for New York.

Many European friends resented his New York "assignment." They figured Teilhard was being hustled, and felt that it was hypocritical for his superiors to allow him to go to New York, "on the pretext that this would best forward his scientific work," when at the same time they were holding a blanket of censorship over the results of most of that work. (Shortly before, a German translation of some Teilhard articles in *Etudes*, a Jesuit monthly, had been barred from publication by church officials, and there was no guarantee that his writings in the United States would fare any better.) Before departing from Paris, Teilhard heeded the advice of friends and established a private agency for the preservation of his letters and manuscripts. A canonist was consulted on whether a person who had taken the vow of poverty was free to dispose of his own papers, and he found ecclesiastical law of two views on the matter. With some friendly clerical nudging, Teilhard chose the more favorable of the interpretations, and appointed his devoted secretary Mlle. Jeanne Mortier as his literary executrix. That wisdom was to insure the eventual publication of the immense body of Teilhard's work. His bibliography grew to some five hundred titles within a decade or so after his death.

Whatever ideas Teilhard managed about the purity of the New York "permission" faded as an expected one year in the city grew to several, then were wiped out in summer, 1954, after Teilhard had returned to France to lecture and for some sentimental journeying. It was not a successful trip. The publicity was extravagant and upset his essentially modest nature. He was visibly tired and under considerable strain. The principal lecture of his itinerary—a talk on Africa and the origins of man—did not go well, and when Teilhard went to superiors to ask permission to respond to a critic, they seized the opportunity to order him back to New York. Ironically, the order reached him on the feast day of St. Ignatius, his Order's patron, July 31. Five days later, Teilhard left Paris for London. After another five days, he sailed for New York. It was to be his last sea voyage. A depression set in, of the type that had once impelled him to say to a Canadian friend: "Pray for me, that I may not die embittered."

Teilhard had every reason to die embittered. Rome had kept a wary eye on him since 1922, when some speculations of his on possible new interpretations of Original Sin had sent orthodoxies fluttering. The Jesuits provided some protection (possibly out of the practical consideration, as Martin Jarrett-Kerr has argued, that any condemnation of Teilhard would also have constituted a condemnation of the Society). But the protection was not foolproof. By and large, Teilhard's life as a religious was a constant struggle with censorship and repression. The substance of his work—including *The Phenomenon of Man*, completed in the early 1940s—was of course not published until after his death; he was forbidden to participate in major intellectual conferences, including one in New York in 1940 involving Albert Einstein and Jacques Maritain; when a professorship became open at the Sorbonne in 1948, a post that he dearly wanted, he was prohibited from standing for it. Church officials admired his spirituality and, of course, were gratified by his respect for authority, remarkable even for a day of great clerical deference to officialdom. But obviously they preferred him away from the center of things—off in China somewhere, or in New York. Teilhard sensed as much and was given to "fits of weeping" and states of near-despair. "What distresses me," he once commented, "is not that I am shackled by Christianity, but that Christianity should at the moment be shackled by those who are its official guardians: The same problem that Jesus had to face 2,000 years ago." Nor did Teilhard find bliss in New York. "My life is running along more or less smoothly," he wrote a friend in January, 1952, "with just a slight undertone of disquiet from not feeling completely at home here in my Order. Everyone is as kind as possible to me, but even so I can't help appearing rather a bird of passage, or something of a parasite."

Except for passing complaints in his correspondence, Teilhard's feelings over the way he was handled by the church were extraordinarily controlled. (A fellow Jesuit once remarked: "If you met the devil, I expect you'd say, 'You know, he's not as bad as all that.' ") Biographer Claude Cuénot has written that Teilhard "was no reformer in the sense of the sixteenth-century reformers," and he is correct, of course. There was never a strong possibility of a breach between Teilhard and his Order, though Teilhard often discussed "in the abstract" the idea of leaving the Society of Jesus and was encouraged to make the break by several of his associates; reportedly, he was held back by "an instinct of military honor" and "respect for the *grande dame*." Still less was there a possibility of a break with Rome, in spite of very real grievances. Teilhard was able even to live with censorship and the *Index of Prohibited Books*, though he found them revolting and absurd and was penalized mightily by the rationale that infused both.

When it was nearly all over, Teilhard would look back on the occasion of his golden jubilee as a Jesuit and comment that he would do the same thing again, if he were able to turn the clock back. He would say something of the same four months before he died to Father Joseph Donceel, S.J., of the Fordham faculty, when Donceel inquired whether he was not sorry he had become a Jesuit because so many of his ideas had been suppressed. "But if I had not been a Jesuit I would not have had these ideas," Teilhard responded. "I picked them up in the Society."

"He was the most marvelously benevolent man I've ever known," Teilhard's good friend Roger W. Straus, Jr., president of the New York publishing house of Farrar, Straus & Giroux, commented recently. "He took the long view, and felt that his ideas would be accepted in time."

Teilhard settled in New York on November 26, 1951, securing "billet" (his word) in St. Ignatius rectory, "thanks to the good offices of Father [John] LaFarge," then of *America* magazine. Teilhard had hoped to move in with the editors of *America* at their residence on

108th Street—a hope apparently entertained also by Father LaFarge. The arrangement adopted, however, was a fourth-floor room in the rectory at 980 Park Avenue, near Eighty-third Street. The space was tight but the neighborhood suited Teilhard fine. It reminded him of Paris' rue de Grenelle, and had the advantage, Teilhard wrote, of putting him "in the center of the city, a quarter of an hour from the Natural History Museum, and, more important still, from the Wenner-Gren Foundation."

Then, as now, St. Ignatius was a composite religious community, made up of the teachers at Regis High School, the fathers of St. Ignatius Loyola parish, the staff of the Jesuit Seminary and Mission Bureau, and several Jesuits assigned to individual apostolates. The community numbered about seventy, overall, many of them lodged in a series of brownstone flats running along Eighty-third Street. Later (early March, 1954), when it was decided to raze these flats and erect a new residence, bedrooms became scarce, and "guests" or "extras" in the community—about seven in all—were required to find rooms elsewhere. Out went Teilhard. In characteristic good grace, he sympathized with the person who had to give the order.

He moved in briefly at the Lotus Club, courtesy of Roger Straus, and finally into a small bedroom-sitting room of the Fourteen Hotel on East Sixtieth Street. This he shared with Father Emmanuel de Breuvery, S.J., an economic specialist at the United Nations also displaced by the construction at St. Ignatius. In his new location, Teilhard shifted to saying Mass at the Dominican church of St. Vincent Ferrer on Lexington Avenue at Sixty-sixth.

Meanwhile, Teilhard's room at St. Ignatius was assigned to a young Jesuit just out of tertianship teaching at Regis High, Martin J. Neylon. Neylon, now Bishop of the Caroline and Marshall Islands, recalled its dimensions in a letter sent in 1974 from the American trust territory: "The room was very narrow, with one window— chest high, almost neck high for a tall man. [The window] looked down on Park Avenue and a small market, Florence Market, sandwiched between two large apartment houses. Behind the door, there was a single straight-backed chair, a washstand, in that order, from door to window. I kept the room just as Father Teilhard had it. Being so narrow, you could do nothing else with it." (During Teilhard's occupancy, a visitor remarked that the room no doubt had been designed as a servant's bedroom—which Teilhard jestfully agreed was an anachronism proving the fact of social progress.)

One Sunday morning, while he was correcting papers, a knock came to Father Neylon's door. It was Teilhard looking for an umbrella that he had left behind. Teilhard sat down on the edge of the bed, and for two hours they chatted away. The conversation is lost to posterity. "I do not remember now what we talked about," Bishop Neylon wrote.

Other memories are stronger. Father Robert I. Gannon, late of Fordham and Teilhard's New York superior as rector at St. Ignatius, lauded him as an exemplary Jesuit, "amiable, gracious and humble," a man who "never missed the customary monthly chat with the superior." Father Charles E. F. Hoefner, who arrived at St. Ignatius in 1929 and became its prefect, remembered him as "most gentle and very easy to get along with—never moody or sad." For Father William R. Walsh, S.J., parish priest at St. Ignatius and librarian for the community, Teilhard was an "unassuming, modest, pleasant" man. Father Walsh occasionally served Teilhard's daily Mass, in the community tradition of one priest serving the priest who followed him to the altar. He recalled Teilhard's Mass as "devout, simple, correct—rubrical in the old-fashioned way." (Years earlier Mme. Charles Arsène-Henry, wife of the French ambassador to Japan, had said: "Whoever has not seen Teilhard say Mass has seen nothing.")

Yet, though respect was obviously present in the relationship between Teilhard and his New York confreres, there seems to have been a marked formality about it. Mrs. Rachel H. Nichols of the Wenner-Gren Foundation has recorded how Teilhard would help with the dishes after Foundation parties, "gaily" wiping glasses while she washed, and how "he was as delighted as a child" when she took him to see "the bright lights of Broadway." No kindred warmth brightens recollections at St. Ignatius. Teilhard is remembered as an alert man and one who was always welcome at recreation because of "his sense of humor" and his "cultivated and charming" ways. However, to the disappointment of some, he "did not talk shop" and, most disappointingly, he "was not a raconteur." Nor would the cerebral Teilhard plop down in a chair to enjoy that new novelty gadget, the television. "He was a good companion," one Jesuit sums up, "but not striking in any way." (Which is not to say that Teilhard was aloof. Father Donald R. Campion, S.J., former editor of *America*, cites young Jesuits meeting Teilhard in Washington and finding him "very direct, very democratic and very much fraternally interested in their own scientific inclinations.")

The Jesuit in New York who probably encountered Teilhard's ideas most immediately was his superior, Father Gannon. Twenty years after Teilhard's death, Father Gannon, now deceased, carried the theological misgivings that imbued ecclesiastical authorities of the 1950s. "The general impression he made . . . was that of a poet and a scientist who did not worry too much about the implications of Catholic theology," Father Gannon said in a 1973 letter to me. "It did not seem to bother him that some of his poetic ideas created difficulties with regard to Original Sin, Grace and the Redemption. When such matters came up in conversation, he would laugh and change the subject. He was dreaming up interesting theories, not denying his faith."

In New York Teilhard enjoyed a special renown. He neither gloried in it, nor used it to gain favor for himself. He went about his affairs quietly and inconspicuously, making no special requests and expecting no more than the next person. He felt, as Claude Cuénot notes, that he had a prophetic gift. But that feeling he carefully modulated. "His modesty was such that he never seemed to realize the genius he possessed, thinking that he was no better, or more important than anyone else."

Teilhard gave the bulk of his New York time to Wenner-Gren, though he came and went on his own terms and was not involved in general hours and procedures of the foundation, except to advise the late director, Dr. Paul Fejos, from time to time. He was pleased when the foundation agreed to sponsor a return field trip for him to Africa in 1953, enabling him to set down on paper some last thoughts on the origins of man. He would also write about being "preoccupied . . . with the urgency of bringing about a reform of anthropology." Between January 30, 1951, and January 14, 1955, Wenner-Gren provided grants-in-aid totaling $22,500 to Teilhard to do research on human evolution and to help finance the African trip. Yet the fact is that he appears to have been occupationally dissatisfied much of the time in New York. "I find plenty to do from day to day," he commented in May, 1952, "but I do wish that some main objective would present itself." Four months before his death, he complained in a letter: "Time goes by, and for six months there has been nothing of real importance in my existence." For a person who had been a physical and intellectual dynamo all his life, no complaint could be more significant.

With considerable time on his hands, Teilhard read a lot (Greene to Dostoievski; Blondel to Spengler); played the tourist (Central Park, the Bronx Zoo); called on friends (Childs Frick, the wealthy amateur palaeontologist, in Roslyn, Long Island). He especially welcomed opportunities to be with French people and old associates, and here New York was generous. Romain Gary, the novelist-diplomat, was at the United Nations. André Malraux occasionally passed through town. So, too, Georges Salles of the Louvre. Claire Taschdjian, his secretary at Peking Union Medical College in the early 1940s, was over in Brooklyn with her husband Edgar. (Teilhard had married them in Peking.) Jacques Maritain was nearby at Princeton University. He seldom lacked for company.

A born traveler, Teilhard frequently got away from New York to discover the wider United States. By train and bus, he visited Montana, New Mexico, California, the Midwest, Maine—being thoroughly impressed with the natural wonders of the country, but puzzled why phenomena like "the granitization of America" had never been probed. The wonder of his American odyssey seems to have been the cyclotrons at Berkeley. Teilhard viewed these as one of the "extraordinary products of the 'noosphere' "—his word for the collective memory and intelligence, the milieu in which individuals think, love, create and feel together as integral members of one organism, Humanity.

The 1950s were Eisenhower years, and though Teilhard "shed a tear" for Adlai Stevenson, he came to find Ike "more and more likeable." The appointment of John Foster Dulles as secretary of state disappointed him, however, as he saw this translating into a hard line with Moscow. Eisenhower's choice for the vice-presidency likewise caused distress, and set Teilhard thinking about the anomalies of the American political system, particularly that by which "a second-rate stop-gap . . . may at a moment's notice" be raised by some accident to the highest office in the land. Enter, Richard Nixon.

Such opinions notwithstanding, Teilhard was essentially an apolitical person. Nor were the politics of religion his. On occasion he was offended by political American Catholicism, but he maintained a strict discretion—even in 1937 when he showed up at Boston College to receive an honorary degree only to be told the award had been withdrawn. Apparently Boston's William Cardinal O'Connell had given the Jesuit institution a choice between His Eminence's presence on stage and that of Teilhard. Boston College caved in. Teilhard quietly took a place in the commencement crowd.

The immaturity of American Catholicism frequently amazed Teilhard, and he was once especially struck by some comments of Redemptorist Father Francis J. Connell, late dean of Catholic University's School of Sacred Theology, on the possibilities of flying saucers and of inhabited worlds other than earth. *Time*'s issue for August 18, 1952, had Father Connell speculating that "if these supposed rational beings should possess the immortality of body once enjoyed by Adam and Eve, it would be foolish for our superjet or rocket pilots to try to shoot them. They would be unkillable." One can imagine Teilhard's further bemusement when he read Father Connell's listing of the four principal classes into which outer-space dwellers might fall: (1) they might have received, like earth men, a supernatural destiny from God . . . might even have lost it and been redeemed; (2) God could have created them with a natural but eternal destiny . . . i.e., like infants who die unbaptized they could live a life of natural happiness after death, without beholding God face to face; (3) they might be rational beings who sinned against God but were never given the chance to regain grace, like evil angels of the Fall; (4) they might have received supernatural gifts and kept them, leading the paradisaical existence of Adam and Eve before they ate the forbidden fruit.

Its inanities notwithstanding, Teilhard was flattered to be honored by American Catholicism—although honors became noticeably less official after he received the Gregor Mendel Medal from Villanova University in 1937 and startled traditionalists with some "dangerously Darwinian" propositions. In Philadelphia, Teilhard also addressed the Academy of National Sciences and gave press interviews which had him affirming a conviction that "man was born from the animal kingdom," and speculating that the "missing link" would one day be found in a lower stratum from the one in which Peking Man was found, in 1925. (Later he came to regard South Africa as a better possibility.) His comments were widely reported, and when Teilhard sought to correct certain misrepresentations, the results were "only slightly less sensational." Catholic authorities took note—most immediately, it seems, in Boston; it was the Philadelphia incident that most likely led to the rescinding of the degree at Boston College.

Institutional nervousness over Teilhard's orthodoxy quickened with the years, so that after he settled in New York in 1952, any honoring of him took on, if not clandestine, then certainly uncharacteristic features: A cocktail party at Catholic University; dinner with the priest-editors of *America*; a closed meeting at Fordham. Sometimes these events assumed exaggerated significance with biographers. The Fordham meeting, for instance, is depicted by Robert Speaight as a "symposium," and by Cuénot as "an officially organized discussion." In fact, nothing official appears to have taken place at Fordham until well into the 1960s, when Teilhard was dead and Vatican Council II had made it possible to sponsor on Catholic campuses events that would have been proscribed in the 1950s. Father Donceel recalls a private Fordham gathering in the early '50s, at which four or five carefully chosen persons were invited to discuss evolution and scientific theories with Teilhard. However, Father Laurence J. McGinley, S.J., Fordham president at the time, has no recollection of it—a detail which would make any gathering that might have taken place very unofficial, indeed. Fordham's official Teilhardian events took place mainly between 1965 and 1969, when Father Christopher F. Mooney, S.J., was head of the theology department and organizing an annual Teilhardian seminar. (The world was beginning to change. When Mooney was working on his doctorate between 1961 and 1964 at the Institut Catholique in Paris, he guarded his topic, lest he be yanked off it by superiors. The doctorate: *Teilhard de Chardin and the Mystery of Christ*, subsequently published by Harper & Row and in Doubleday's Image series.)

Death came to Teilhard swiftly and mercifully—and on the day that he had frequently prayed to be "delivered"—Easter Sunday. He appears to have been ready—even anxious—for his "escape." The last months had been marred by the deaths of several close friends; by news of the suppression of the priest-worker movement in France; and by the exposure of Piltdown Man as a forgery. (The last was the hypothetical early man whose existence had been inferred from skull fragments found at Piltdown, England, in 1912. The "discoverer," Charles Dawson, had been a friend of Teilhard's, and Teilhard himself seems to have been set up to "find" an eyetooth of the specimen.) Teilhard had his suspicions about Piltdown Man, however, and so was not overly unsettled by that news. He was less prepared for the suppression of the priest-worker movement, an experiment he had followed with considerable interest. The suppression made him virtually despair of Rome. "The sin of Rome (for all its casual benedictions on technique and science) is not to believe in a future, and an achievement (for heaven) upon earth," Teilhard commented. "I know because I have been stifled for fifty years in this sub-human atmosphere." At the time he wrote those words Teilhard was speaking more and more of death, confiding to many, including his diplomat-cousin Jean de Legarde, that he would like "to die on the day of the Resurrection." On Saturday, April 9, he went to confession to Father de Breuvery.

Easter morning—April 10, 1955—Teilhard rose early and celebrated Mass as usual. Originally he had planned to have dinner with Roger Straus at Straus's country home in Purchase, but in a telephone conversation that morning Teilhard called the date off, saying he "felt a little tired." Reorganizing his Easter, Teilhard headed for St. Patrick's Cathedral and the Pontifical High Mass. Teilhard, as Speaight notes, was "no lover of ecclesiastical pomp, but it seemed as if he could not have enough of the Resurrection." In the afternoon, Teilhard strolled through Central Park, then enjoyed a twin production of *Pagliacci* and *Cavalleria Rusticana* by the New York City Opera. Afterwards he stopped for tea at the apartment of Mrs. R. Hoff de Terra at 39 East Seventy-second Street.

It had been an exceedingly pleasant day, in spite of the tiredness, and what better way to cap it than with a visit to a friend from the exhilarating field days when each new fossil discovery might unlock some mystery? Teilhard had known the de Terra family from expeditions to the East Indies (1935), Burma (1937–38), and Java (1938), and the bond was close; he and Helmut de Terra "understand each other like a couple of brothers," Teilhard once wrote.

Teilhard was in excellent spirits and was congratulating himself on this "magnificent day," when suddenly everything came apart. Teilhard placed a paper on the windowsill and was about to take a cup of tea, when he toppled full length on the floor "like a stricken tree." Father Pierre Leroy, Teilhard's friend from his second Peking period, recorded that "it was thought at first that he had fainted and a cushion was placed under his head." After a few minutes Teilhard opened his eyes and said, "Where am I? What's happened?" "You're with us, don't you recognize me?" said his hostess. "Yes, but what's happened?" "You've had a heart attack," he was told. "I can't remember anything," remarked Teilhard. "This time I feel it's terrible." Teilhard had actually suffered a rupture of the coronary artery.

Teilhard's doctor was called; he was out; another was summoned. His advice was to send for a priest. Father de Breuvery was phoned; he too was out. A call then went to St. Ignatius. Father Gannon took the news and rang on the intercom the priest on door-duty, Father Martin T. Geraghty, now in retirement at Seven Springs, a Jesuit house in Monroe, New York. "Father de Chardin has just died," Father Gannon said. "Please go and anoint him." It was about four or four-thirty in the afternoon, according to Geraghty; six o'clock, according to another source. Father Geraghty continues the narrative in a letter to the author dated December 15, 1973*:

"He gave me the address . . . I dressed quickly in my street-clothes, took the Holy Oils, hailed a cab, and arrived at the town-house, while thinking all the time since having received the call about Father de Chardin's death: What a beautiful day to die . . . Easter Sunday, the day of Christ's glorious victory over sin and death, the day when Christ made death no longer a transition from the land of the living to the land of the dead, but a passing from the land of the dying to the land of the living.

"The town-house had been converted into apartments. On either the second or third floor (I think it was probably the second) was the apartment that I wanted. At the door two middle-aged ladies met me, and led me into the kitchen, which was the first room one entered. I had never met Father de Chardin in life. Thus, my first meeting was to encounter him lying still in death just beyond the doorway that led from the kitchen to the living room that fronted on

---

*Father Geraghty's letter to me covered eight typewritten pages. In long-hand was the following postscript: "You are the only one to whom I have ever detailed this information. No one ever asked!!"

the north side of the street. In death he had dignity. He was dressed in his clerical street-clothes, but his Roman-collar and rabat had been removed in an attempt to help him breathe. His body was lying in an east-west position, with his feet facing the east and his head facing west, the direction where the sun goes down, where a luminary like Father de Chardin subsides. It was an ascetic, aristocratic head, looking very calm and peaceful, even joyous, in death. 'O death, where is thy victory? O death, where is thy sting?' It was Easter Sunday—Christ had conquered death. With Him, we are more than conquerors. That is what the serene expression on Father de Chardin's face silently said.

"Near Father de Chardin's body, on the floor, was a foot-wide, shallow bowl of water that was tinged with blood. Apparently, in falling, Father had hit his head on the floor, and the two ladies had tenderly wiped away the blood from the bruise on his head. The blood and water, intermingled, remind one in retrospect of divinity and humanity, of the blood and water from the dead Christ's own side, of the red richness of grace and the pale weakness of human nature. All of these were Father de Chardin's lifelong concern, his very life; it is fitting that a little bowl filled with blood and water, stark symbols, should have been present at his death.

"I anointed him, with the short form first, having first given conditional absolution. Then I supplied the longer form, anointing the five senses, remembering to anoint the hands on the back, since the palms had been anointed at his Ordination with the holy oils of the Priesthood, marking golden stigmata on his hands that make him forever a priest according to the order of Melchisedech, the mysterious, shadowy, sublime High Priest who emerges so briefly in the Old Testament. Then I read the prescribed ritual prayers over him. He was a fellow Jesuit; I never knew him; yet we were united by common bonds.

"Having ministered to Father de Chardin, I extended the words of sympathy and consolation to his friends. The coroner had been notified; he had three other deaths to certify, before he was able to come. We lit a candle and placed it on the floor next to Father's body, in a chiaroscuro of light and darkness, the warmth of the flame next to the marble cold of his body. This, too, was fitting. Father de Chardin had brought the light of his intellect and the warmth of his life to humanity. His brilliant mind had illuminated the dark mysteries of a cosmos; his human kindness had warmed all who met him. The Jesuits who had known him in life, and had lived with him, said that he was a saint.

"I returned to the rectory, and noted his death in the deathbook. Although he was a world-famous anthropologist and I knew how to spell his name as well as I can spell my own, I think I may have inadvertently, subconsciously, written: 'Father de Jardin, S.J.' Perhaps I wrote 'jardin,' the French word for 'garden,' because it was a flowering Easter Sunday, and because the impact on me, in giving him the Last Rites, was rather one of glad joy for him than of sadness." (In fact, the name is correctly recorded in the death register. It may be that Father Geraghty incorrectly spelled the name for the person who kept the register—all the entries at the time being in the one printed hand—who then caught the mistake in making the entry.)

Teilhard's death had no shattering impact on the Catholic community. By and large, the diocesan press passed it by for weightier stuff, like the theatrical debut at Loras College of Ronald Ameche, Don's boy, in *Finian's Rainbow*. *Commonweal* took no notice. Nor did Donald McDonald in the syndicated column that was the liberal Catholic press's touchstone of respectability. *America* handled the death in one cautiously worded paragraph in a column of notices.

The *New York Times* caught up with Teilhard's death in its Tuesday editions, printing a nine-paragraph obituary focusing on Teilhard's codiscovery of Peking Man and his belief in evolution. The *Times* reached back to the controversial 1937 press interview in Philadelphia, in which Teilhard held that man had evolved from lower orders of the animal kingdom, and quoted Teilhard's conviction that such a belief is not irreconcilable with religion. "I find absolutely no barriers and no hurdles between my beliefs as a scientist and as a priest," the *Times'* obit continued. "The two are parallel. As a scientist I must admit the evidence that man was born from the animal kingdom. But he was not an animal. The great, the tremendous, the significant fact about man is the coming of thought with and through him."

The obituary appeared on the day of Teilhard's funeral in St.

Ignatius Church. It did nothing for the house. Only a handful of people were present: a few close friends; the French ambassador, M. Hoppenot; Dr. Fejos from Wenner-Gren; and "about eight or ten Jesuits" from the St. Ignatius community. Most were said to have been away due to the Easter holidays. Father de Breuvery celebrated the Requiem—a low Mass, with no singing, no *In Paradisium*. Private Masses continued, assembly-line fashion, at side altars, with people coming and going. Outside it was a dismal, rainy day. The only flowers, says Cuénot, were a floral cross sent by Malvina Hoffman, the sculptress, Rodin's pupil, the dear friend who did the bust of Teilhard for the Paris Museum of Modern Art.

Father Leroy and the Father Minister of the St. Ignatius community accompanied the body to its burial place: the cemetery at the Jesuit novitiate of St. Andrew-on-Hudson, seventy-five miles north of the city. The fates followed. First the ground was too hard to be opened up, so the coffin had to be placed in a temporary vault to await the spring thaw. When the final interment took place, neither friend nor minister was present, only the gravediggers.

Then it was discovered that the headstone had been incorrectly carved. It read: "P. Pierre Teilhard, S.J." The embarrassment was corrected, and Teilhard got his full name and exact Latinization: "P. Petrus Teilhard de Chardin, S.J." But not before word got around.

Bedevilment continued. In 1962, Rome slapped a *monitum*, or warning, on Teilhard's philosophical and theological writings—an edict more honored now in the breach than in the observance, but nevertheless one that has never been formally withdrawn. Finally, a radically evolved world of religion left the departed Teilhard further isolated in the church he had hung with. St. Andrew's was closed down, and the buildings sold to the Culinary Institute of America. The cemetery remains, but the odors that waft over it are not those of sanctity but of food. Old St. Andrew's is now a cooking school and *très cher* restaurant.

If You Travel . . .

. . .tracking the spirit of Teilhard de Chardin, plan on visiting the churches of St. Vincent Ferrer (Lexington at Sixty-ninth Street) and Ignatius Loyola (Park Avenue at Eighty-fourth Street) in New York

City. There are no Teilhard memorials in either church, but many will find it uplifting to be in the same buildings where he worshipped. The Wenner-Gren Foundation for Anthropological Research, also without memorial, is at 14 East Seventy-first Street—for those who wish to stare at the building where he worked.

Teilhard de Chardin is buried in the small, private Jesuit cemetery above Poughkeepsie, seventy-five miles north of New York City. The cemetery is located directly behind the Culinary Institute of America, formerly the Jesuit novitiate, St. Andrew-on-Hudson. The Institute is not hard to find; next door is the Hyde Park home of President Franklin Delano Roosevelt. Hyde Park straddles U.S. Route 9 on the eastern side of the Hudson River. It can be reached via the New York Throughway (Interstate 87) or the Taconic Parkway.

Chapter
Seventeen

When You're in the Vicinity of . . .

MIDDLETOWN, Rhode Island

George Berkeley

On Berkeley Avenue in this pleasant Rhode Island community near Newport is Whitehall, a house known as the "shrine of America's cultural beginning." Whitehall was the home for three years of George Berkeley (1685–1753), noted Anglo-Irish philosopher and clergyman. Berkeley, a native of Kilkenny and a graduate of Trinity College, Dublin, came to Rhode Island in 1728 en route to the Bermudas, where, with the help of a promised British government grant, he planned to found a college "for the Christian civilization of America." The promise of the grant was withdrawn, however, towards the end of 1731. Berkeley returned to England, where he wrote more philosophical tracts, took a bishopric across the Irish Sea at Cloyne, then settled finally at Oxford, where he died and is buried.

As writer and clergyman, George Berkeley sought to counteract the ostensibly waning influence of religion by seeking a remedy against skepticism, materialism, and atheism. Out of such works as *Essay towards a New Theory of Vision* (1709), *Treatise Concerning the Principles of Human Knowledge* (1710), and *Dialogues between Hylas and Philonous* (1713) evolved Berkeley's subjectivist principle, *esse est percipi*, which Samuel Johnson sought to refute with his famous kick of the foot against a stone. Other Berkeley books were *Essay towards Preventing the Ruin of Great Britain* and *Alciphron, or the Minute Philosopher*. The latter book Berkeley wrote in Rhode Island and published in London upon his return there. Historically, George Berkeley is remembered as one of the noted Christian humanists of the eighteenth century and as a pioneer in the effort to harmonize the work of science, philosophy, and theology.

Whitehall is maintained by Colonial Dames in Rhode Island. It is

257

open daily, July through Labor Day, from 10:00 A.M. to 5:00 P.M. There is a small admission charge, with a discount for children. From New York, Middletown is reached via the New England Throughway/Connecticut Turnpike to Exit 76 at New London, where drivers should connect with Interstate 95 to Hope Valley, Rhode Island. There drivers should proceed on State Route 138 east to Middletown.

* * *

While in Rhode Island, persons interested in literary visiting places might enjoy calling at the Providence Athenaeum at 251 Benefit Street in Providence. The Athenaeum is one of America's oldest library companies, and it was here that Edgar Allan Poe courted Sarah Helen (Power) Whitman, after the death of Virginia Clemm in 1847. Poe and Mrs. Whitman, a widow, were engaged for a time in 1848, and the second of his two poems entitled "To Helen" was about her. Mrs. Whitman was herself a poet, and she, in turn, wrote several poems about Poe and defended him in *Edgar Poe and His Critics* (1860). Her collected poems, *Hours of Life*, appeared in 1853, with an enlarged edition rolling from the presses in 1879, the year after her death.

Providence Athenaeum is open weekdays from 8:30 A.M. to 5:30 P.M., and Saturdays from 9:30 A.M. to 5:30 P.M. From Middletown, drivers should follow State Route 114 to Providence. The distance is approximately twenty-five miles.

SARANAC LAKE, New York

Robert Louis Stevenson

In the spring of 1887, Robert Louis Stevenson's father died in Edinburgh. The ties binding him to Great Britain now severed, himself in especially poor health in his continuing struggle against tuberculosis, Stevenson sailed on August 17 for New York with his

American wife, his stepson, and his mother. He rested at Newport, Rhode Island, then went for the winter to Saranac Lake, New York, a noted tuberculosis-treatment center, there to be under the care of a physician.

Stevenson's fame had preceded him. *Treasure Island*, the exciting romantic thriller featuring Jim Hawkins, Captain Billy Bones, and Long John Silver (remember Long John's parrot, Captain Flint?), had appeared in 1883 and had fixed Stevenson's fame as a novelist. *Kidnapped* was published just the year before he came to Saranac Lake, and in Saranac Lake, as virtually everywhere else that English was read, young and old followed the adventures of David Balfour in overcoming his wicked Uncle Ebenezer and winning his rightful inheritance from his father.

In Saranac Lake, Robert Louis Stevenson (1850–1894) settled in a charming old farmhouse that is preserved yet as a memorial to the man who began as a writer of travel sketches, put his hand to poetry, and developed into one of the most popular novelists of his time, and time thereafter. The Stevenson Cottage is maintained by the Robert Louis Stevenson Society of America. It is claimed that the cottage houses the largest collection of Stevenson mementos in the United States. They include Stevenson's desk, smoking jacket, the ice skates that he used on Moody Pond, his yachting cap, original letters, photographs—even a lock of his hair. The Stevenson furniture is in the rooms yet, and the mantlepiece shows the burns of the writer's cigarettes.

Despite ill health, Stevenson was remarkably productive in Saranac Lake. Here, in the area he called "The Little Switzerland in the Adirondacks," Stevenson wrote the greater part of *The Master of Ballantrae*, which, along with *The Strange Case of Dr. Jekyll and Mr. Hyde*, ranks as one of his most notable pieces on the nature of evil. He wrote as well for *Scribner's Magazine*, and here turned his attention to *The Wrong Box*, which he was to finish in Honolulu, and *A Christmas Sermon*.

Stevenson actually did not stay long in Saranac Lake. In April of 1888, he went to the New Jersey shore for several weeks, then in June started for San Francisco and the Pacific. His wandering took him to the Marquesas, Tahiti, Hawaii (where he paid his famous visit to Father Damien and the leper colony at Molokai), the Gilbert Islands, then Samoa. He landed there on Christmas Day, 1889, and left six weeks or so later for Sydney and a long cruise on the trading steamer *Janet Nicholl*, before returning to Samoa for the last four years of his life. He died in December of 1894 and was laid to rest at the summit of the peak Vaca, the Pacific waves crashing at his feet.

The Stevenson Cottage in Saranac Lake is open from July 1 to September 15, Mondays excluded. Visiting hours are from 9:30 A.M. to noon, and from 1:00 to 4:30 P.M. There is a modest admission charge with a discount for children.

Saranac Lake is in upper New York State, some 310 miles from New York City. Drivers should connect with Interstate 87 going north and stay on it to State Route 73. One would then proceed on Route 73 to Route 86 into Saranac Lake.

BRATTLEBORO, Vermont

Rudyard Kipling

One usually does not think of Rudyard Kipling in terms of New England. His stories and ballads smack so much of Union Jack and Empire that his name is synonymous with old England: the Imperial England of Gunga Din, Mandalay, and *Plain Tales from the Hills*, which, of course, was the India of Kipling's experience . . . faraway, romantic, Dominion. Yet Kipling had his Vermont period. He had married Caroline Starr Balestier in January of 1892, and the following month they had sailed for the United States and a visit with Mrs. Kipling's family in Brattleboro. Just as quickly the Kiplings decided they should settle in Brattleboro. Family land was set aside for them, then off the newlyweds went on a trip across the American continent—United States and Canada—to Japan. In the spring, they were back in Brattleboro. They moved into Bliss Cottage, a small house on the Balestier estate, and proceeded about the building of Naulakha, an imposing home of weathered shingles and stone that Kipling was to describe as a ship: the propeller, or furnace and kitchen, at the stern; his study, opening upon a roomy piazza looking to the south and east, at the bow. The house was named in memory of Carrie's brother, Wolcott, with whom Kipling had earlier collaborated on a book of that title (although the *k* and the *h* got reversed by Wolcott in the writing, so that the title reads *Naulahka*). Wolcott Balestier had died of typhoid shortly before the marriage.

Rudyard Kipling (1865–1936) lived at Naulakha until August 28, 1896. In its library he wrote *The Jungle Book* (1894) and *The Second Jungle Book* (1895), stories collected as *The Day's Work* (1898), most of the poems included in *The Seven Seas* (1896), and *Captains Courageous* (1897). *Captains Courageous*, a yarn of deep-sea fishery, was born of a visit to Gloucester and Kipling's admiration for the courage and self-sacrifice of the fisherman. Kipling's father visited at Naulakha and inscribed on the mantle the words, "For the Night Cometh When No Man Works."

The years in Brattleboro ended disastrously for Kipling. England and the United States locked in dispute in 1895–96 over a frontier question in South America, and the tension between the two countries, so great as to make war a possibility, caused Kipling to decide an apparently growing ambivalence about nationality. During the same period, a family quarrel erupted with Beatty Balestier, Mrs. Kipling's brother, over rights to the land about Naulakha. There was an especially bad scene in which Beatty Balestier threatened Kipling's life. The threat may or may not have been intended literally. In any case, Kipling went to the police, and the police arrested Beatty Balestier. There was enormous publicity, all of which Kipling found excruciatingly embarrassing. He decided to leave. Before the trial could take place, he and his wife had packed their children and their things, and moved to England.

Naulakha is much discussed in books about Kipling. Likewise, it is pictured on postcards that can be purchased in the Brattleboro area. Naulakha, however, is not open to the public. It is a private home at 19 Terrace Street. The house can be seen at a distance from the public road. The owner hopes to open the house at some future date to visitors and scholars. (In correspondence, the owner used the Naula*hk*a spelling.)

The Brattleboro area Chamber of Commerce—180 Main Street, Brattleboro, Vermont, 05301—has a three-paragraph flyer about the house, available to those who inquire.

Brattleboro is ten miles north of the Massachusetts state line on Interstate 91.

Bibliography

Following is a selective list of books, pamphlets, reference volumes, and magazine articles dealing with those literary figures who are the subject of separate chapter treatment in this book. Titles of the principal works of these authors will be found in the respective essays. For purposes of knowing a writer, his or her books are, of course, indispensable. The books of the writers treated in this volume are generally available in public libraries. This bibliography should be regarded as an auxiliary reference tool to the books of the authors themselves.

THOMAS PAINE

Aldridge, Alfred Owen. *Man of Reason: The Life of Thomas Paine*. Philadelphia and New York: Lippincott, 1959.

Best, Mary Agnes. *Thomas Paine, Prophet and Martyr of Democracy*. New York: Harcourt, Brace and Company, 1927.

Berthold, S. M. *Thomas Paine: America's First Liberal*. Boston: Meador, 1938.

Burt, Struthers. In *There Were Giants in the Land*. New York: Farrar & Rinehart, 1942.

Conway, Moncure Daniel. *The Life of Thomas Paine*. New York, 1892. Reissued in 1969 by Benjamin Blom, Inc., New York.

Edwards, Samuel. *Rebel! A Biography of Thomas Paine*. New York–Washington: Praeger, 1974.

Fast, Howard, ed. *The Selected Work of Tom Paine*. New York: Duell, Sloan and Pearce, 1945.

Gurko, Leo. *Tom Paine, Freedom's Apostle*. New York: Crowell, 1957.

Hawke, David Freeman. *Paine*. New York: Harper & Row, 1974.

Pearson, Hesketh. *Thomas Paine, Friend of Mankind*. New York: Harper & Brothers, 1937.

Persons, Frederick T. "Paine, Thomas." In *Dictionary of American Biography*, vol. 14. New York: Scribner's, 1933.

Seager, Allan. *They Worked for a Better World*. New York: Macmillan, 1939.

Smith, Frank. *Thomas Paine, Liberator*. New York: Stokes, 1938.

Van der Weyde, William M. "Life of Thomas Paine." In *The Life and Works of Thomas Paine*. Patriots' Edition, vol. 1. New Rochelle, N. Y.: Thomas Paine National Historical Association, 1925.

263

Williamson, Audrey. *Thomas Paine: His Life, Work and Times*. New York: St. Martin's, 1973.

Woodward, W. E. *Thomas Paine: America's Godfather*. New York: Dutton, 1945.

JAMES FENIMORE COOPER

Boynton, Henry Walcott. *James Fenimore Cooper*. New York: Century, 1931.

Brownell, William Crary. "Cooper, James Fenimore." In *American Prose Masters*. Reprint edition. Edited by Howard Mumford Jones. Cambridge, Mass.: Harvard University Press, Belknap Press, 1967.

Cooper, Susan Fenimore. *Papers and Pictures from the Writings of James Fenimore Cooper*. New York: Townsend, 1861.

Clymer, W. B. Shubrick. *James Fenimore Cooper*. Boston: Small, Maynard, 1900.

Cunningham, Mary E., ed. *James Fenimore Cooper: A Re-Appraisal*. Cooperstown, N. Y.: New York State Historical Association, 1954.

Fulcher, William Gershom. *Mamaroneck Through the Years*. New York: The Larchmont Times, 1936.

Gouwens, Teunis E., ed. *Mamaroneck 1661–1961: A Panorama of Her First Three Centuries*. New York: Mamaroneck Tercentenary Committee, 1961.

Grossman, James. *James Fenimore Cooper*. The American Men of Letters Series. New York: Sloane, 1949.

Lounsbury, Thomas R. *James Fenimore Cooper*. Boston: Houghton Mifflin, 1882.

McWilliams, John P., Jr. *Political Justice in the Republic; James Fenimore Cooper's America*. Berkeley and Los Angeles: University of California Press, 1972.

Phillips, Mary E. *James Fenimore Cooper*. New York: Lane, 1913.

Ross, John F. *The Social Criticism of Fenimore Cooper*. Berkeley and Los Angeles: University of California Press, 1933.

Spiller, Robert E. *Fenimore Cooper, Critic of his Times*. New York: Minton, Balch, 1931.

Tuttleton, James W. *The Novel of Manners in America*. Chapel Hill, N. C.: University of North Carolina Press, 1972.

Waples, Dorothy. *The Whig Myth of Fenimore Cooper*. New Haven, Conn.: Yale University Press, 1938.

WASHINGTON IRVING

Aderman, Ralph M., ed. *Washington Irving Reconsidered—A Symposium*. Hartford, Conn.: Transcendental Books, 1969.

Boyle, Robert H. *The Hudson River, A Natural and Unnatural Beauty*. New York: Norton, 1969.

Boynton, Henry Walcott. In *American Writers on American Literature*. John Macy, ed. New York: Liveright, 1931.

Brooks, Van Wyck. *The World of Washington Irving*. New York: Dutton, 1944.

Butler, Joseph T. *Washington Irving's Sunnyside*. Tarrytown, N. Y.: Sleepy Hollow Restorations, 1974.

Hansen, Harry. *North of Manhattan, Persons and Places of Old Westchester*. New York: Hastings House, 1950.

Hellman, G. S. *Washington Irving, Esquire, Ambassador at Large from the New World to the Old*. New York: Knopf, 1925.

Irving, Pierre M. *The Life and Letters of Washington Irving, by his Nephew*. 4 vols. New York: Putnam, 1862–64. People's Edition, revised and condensed, 3 vols., New York: Putnam, 1869.

Myers, Andrew B., ed. *Washington Irving: A Tribute*. Tarrytown, N. Y.: Sleepy Hollow Restorations, 1972.

_____, ed. *The Worlds of Washington Irving, 1783–1859: An Anthology Exhibition from the Collections of The New York Public Library*. Tarrytown, N. Y.: Sleepy Hollow Restorations, 1974.

_____. *The Knickerbocker Tradition: Washington Irving's New York*. Tarrytown, N. Y.: Sleepy Hollow Restorations, 1974.

Putnam, G. P. *Studies of Irving*. New York: Putnam, 1880.

Spiller, Robert E. et al., eds. *Literary History of the United States*. 3 vols. New York: Macmillan, 1948.

Wagenknecht, Edward. *Washington Irving, Moderation Displayed*. New York: Oxford University Press, 1962.

Warner, Charles Dudley. *Washington Irving*. Boston: Houghton Mifflin, Riverside Popular Biographies, 1909.

Williams, Stanley T. *The Life of Washington Irving*. 2 vols. New York: Oxford University Press, 1935.

_____. "Irving, Washington." In *Dictionary of American Biography*, vol. 9. New York: Scribner's, 1933.

HORACE GREELEY

Cornell, William M. *Life & Public Career of the Hon. Horace Greeley*. Boston: Lee & Shepherd, 1872.

Fahrney, Ralph Ray. *Horace Greeley and The Tribune in the Civil War*. Cedar Rapids, Iowa: Torch Press, 1936.

Greeley, Horace. *Recollections of a Busy Life*. New York: J. B. Ford & Co., 1868.

Hale, William Harlan. *Horace Greeley, Voice of the People*. New York: Harper & Brothers, 1950.

Horner, Harlan Hoyt. *Lincoln and Greeley*. Champaign-Urbana, Ill.: University of Illinois Press, 1953.

Ingersoll, L. D. *The Life and Times of Horace Greeley*. Chicago: Union Publishing Co., 1873.

Isely, Jeter A. *Horace Greeley and the Republican Party*. Princeton, N. J.: Princeton University Press, 1947.

Nevins, Allan. "Greeley, Horace." In *Dictionary of American Biography*, vol. 7. New York: Scribner's, 1933.

Parton, James. *The Life of Horace Greeley, Editor of the New York Tribune*. New York: Mason Brothers, 1855.

Proceedings at the Unveiling of a Memorial to Horace Greeley, Chappaqua, N. Y. Albany, N. Y.: University of the State of New York, Division of Archives and History, 1915.

Seitz, Don C. *Horace Greeley, Founder of the New York Tribune*. Indianapolis, Indiana: Bobbs-Merrill, 1926.

Shapiro, Fred C. "The Life and Death of a Great Newspaper." *American Heritage*, October 1967.

Stoddard, Henry Luther. *Horace Greeley: Printer, Editor, Crusader*. New York: Putnam, 1946.

Van Deusen, Glyndon G. *Horace Greeley, Nineteenth-Century Crusader*. Philadelphia: University of Pennsylvania Press, 1953.

WALT WHITMAN

Allen, Gay Wilson. *The Solitary Singer, A Critical Biography*. New York: Macmillan, 1955.

_____. *Walt Whitman Handbook*. Chicago, Ill.: Packard, 1946.

Arvin, Newton. *Whitman*. New York: Macmillan, 1938.

Brooks, Van Wyck. *The Times of Melville and Whitman*. New York: Dutton, 1947.

Burroughs, John. *Notes on Walt Whitman as Poet and Person*. New York: American News Company, 1867; revised edition, 1871.

_____. *Whitman: A Study*. Boston and New York: Houghton Mifflin, 1896 and 1904.

Canby, Henry Seidel. *Walt Whitman, An American*. Boston and New York: Houghton Mifflin, Literary Classics, 1943.

Chase, Richard. *Walt Whitman Reconsidered*. New York: Sloane, 1955.

Fausset, Hugh L'Anson. *Walt Whitman: Poet of Democracy*. New Haven, Conn.: Yale University Press, 1942.

Kennedy, William Sloane. *Reminiscences of Walt Whitman: With Extracts from His Letters and Remarks on His Writings*. Paisley and London: Alexander Gardner, 1896.

————. *The Fight of a Book for the World*. West Yarmouth, Mass.: Stonecroft Press, 1926.

Perry, Bliss. *Walt Whitman, His Life and Work*. New York: Houghton Mifflin, 1906.

Spiller, Robert E., et al., eds. *Literary History of the United States*. 4th ed. revised. New York: Macmillan, 1974.

Traubel, Horace L., Richard Maurice Bucke, Thomas B. Harned, eds. *In Re Walt Whitman*. Published by the editors through David McKay, Philadelphia, 1893. (The editors were Whitman's literary executors.)

Van Doren, Mark. "Whitman, Walt." In *Dictionary of American Biography*, vol. 20. New York: Scribner's, 1936.

Winwar, Francis. *American Giant: Walt Whitman and his Times*, New York: Harper & Brothers, 1941.

BRONSON ALCOTT and FRUITLANDS

Alcott, Louisa M. "Transcendental Wild Oats." In *Silver Pitchers: and Independence, a Centennial Love Story*. Boston: Roberts Bros., 1876.

Barbour, Brian M., ed. *American Transcendentalism: An Anthology of Criticism*. Notre Dame, Indiana: University of Notre Dame Press, 1973.

Boller, Paul F., Jr. *American Transcendentalism 1830–1860, An Intellectual Inquiry*. New York: Putnam, 1974.

Cameron, Kenneth Walter. *Transcendental Climate*. Hartford, Conn.: Transcendental Books, 1963.

————. *The Transcendentalists and Minerva*. Hartford, Conn.: Transcendental Books, 1958.

Frothingham, Octavius Brooks. *Transcendentalism in New England: A History*. New York: Putnam, 1880.

Furnas, J. C. *The Americans, A Social History of the United States, 1587–1914*. New York: Putnam, 1969.

Gittleman, Edwin, ed. *The Minor and Later Transcendentalists: A Symposium*. Hartford, Conn.: Transcendental Books, 1969.

Goddard, Harold Clarke. *Studies in New England Transcendentalism*. New York: Columbia University Press, 1908.

Miller, Perry, ed. *The Transcendentalists: An Anthology, Their Articles, Essays, Poems and Addresses*. Cambridge, Mass.: Harvard University Press, 1950.

Sanborn, Franklin B., and Harris, William T. A. *Bronson Alcott: His Life and Philosophy*. New York: Bible and Tannen, 1965 (first printed 1893).

Sears, Clara Endicott. *Bronson Alcott's Fruitlands*. Boston and New York: Houghton Mifflin, 1915.

Shepard, Odell. *Pedlar's Progress: The Life of Bronson Alcott*. Boston: Little,

Brown & Co., 1937.
_____, ed. *The Journals of Bronson Alcott*. Boston: Little, Brown & Co., 1938.
Swift, Lindsay. *Brook Farm, Its Members, Scholars, and Visitors*. New York: Macmillan, 1900.

RALPH WALDO EMERSON

Brooks, Van Wyck. *The Life of Emerson*. New York: Dutton, 1932.
_____. *Emerson and Others*. New York: Dutton, 1927.
_____. *The Flowering of New England, 1815–1865*. New York: Dutton, 1936.
_____. *New England: Indian Summer, 1865–1915*. New York: Dutton, 1940.
Brownell, William Crary. *American Prose Masters*. Reprint edition. Edited by Howard Mumford Jones. Cambridge, Mass.: Harvard University Press, Belknap Press, 1967.
Cabot, James Elliot. *A Memoir of Ralph Waldo Emerson*. 2 vols. Boston: Houghton Mifflin, 1887.
Derleth, August. *Emerson, Our Contemporary*. New York: Crowell-Collier Press, 1970.
Jones, Howard Mumford. *Emerson Once More*. Boston: Beacon Press, 1953.
Mason, Gabriel Richard. "Ralph Waldo Emerson." In Mason, Gabriel Richard, ed., *Great American Liberals*. Boston: Starr King Press, 1956.
Miles, Josephine. *Ralph Waldo Emerson*. Minneapolis, Minn.: University of Minnesota Press, 1964.
Perry, Bliss. *Emerson Today*. Princeton, N. J.: Princeton University Press, 1931.
Rusk, Ralph L. *The Life of Ralph Waldo Emerson*. New York: Scribner's, 1949. Reprint. New York: Columbia University Press, 1957.
Russell, Phillips. *Emerson, The Wisest American*. New York: Brentano's, 1929.
Sanborn, Franklin B. *Ralph Waldo Emerson*. Boston: Small, Maynard & Co., 1901.
Van Doren, Mark. "Emerson, Ralph Waldo." In *Dictionary of American Biography*, vol. 6. New York: Scribner's, 1933.
Wagenknecht, Edward. *Ralph Waldo Emerson: Portrait of a Balanced Soul*. New York: Oxford University Press, 1974.
Waggoner, Hyatt H. *Emerson as Poet*. Princeton, N. J.: Princeton University Press, 1974.
Woodberry, George Edward. *Ralph Waldo Emerson*. New York: Macmillan, 1926.

HENRY WADSWORTH LONGFELLOW

Arvin, Newton. *Longfellow: His Life and Work*. Boston: Little, Brown & Co., 1963.

Bronson, W. C. "Longfellow, Henry Wadsworth." In *Dictionary of American Biography*, vol. 11. New York: Scribners, 1933.

Brooks, Van Wyck. *The Flowering of New England, 1815–1865*. New York: Dutton, 1936.

———. *New England: Indian Summer, 1865–1915*. New York: Dutton, 1940.

Davidson, Thomas. "Longfellow, Henry Wadsworth." In *Encyclopaedia Britannica*, 11th ed., vol. 16. New York: 1911.

Commager, Henry Steele. "The Search for a Usable Past." *American Heritage*, February 1965.

Gorman, Herbert S. *A Victorian American, Henry Wadsworth Longfellow*. New York: Doran, 1926.

Hatfield, James Taft. *New Light on Longfellow*. Boston and New York: Houghton Mifflin, 1933.

Higginson, Thomas Wentworth. *Henry Wadsworth Longfellow*. Boston and New York: Houghton Mifflin, 1902.

Howells, William Dean. *Literary Friends and Acquaintances*. New York: Harper & Brothers, 1900.

Longfellow, Ernest A. *Random Memories*. Boston and New York: Houghton Mifflin, 1922.

Longfellow, Samuel. *The Life of Henry Wadsworth Longfellow*. 2 vols. Boston and New York: Houghton Mifflin, 1886.

Massachusetts, A Guide to Its Places and People. American Guide Series, a Federal Writers' Project of the Works Progress Administration for the State of Massachusetts. Boston: Houghton Mifflin, 1937.

Russell, Foster W. *Mount Auburn Biographies*. Cambridge, Mass.: The Proprietors of the Cemetery of Mount Auburn, 1953.

Thompson, Lawrence Roger. *Young Longfellow*. New York: Macmillan, 1938.

Van Schaick, John, Jr. *The Characters in Tales of a Wayside Inn*. Boston: Universalist Publishing House, 1939.

Wagenknecht, Edward. *Longfellow: A Full-Length Portrait*. New York: Longmans, Green & Co., 1955.

———, ed. *Mrs. Longfellow: Selected Letters and Journals of Fanny Appleton Longfellow*. New York: Longmans, Green & Co., 1956.

NATHANIEL HAWTHORNE

Brooks, Van Wyck. *The Flowering of New England, 1815–1865*. New York: Dutton, 1936.

———. *New England: Indian Summer, 1865–1915*. New York: Dutton, 1940.

Brownell, William Crary. *American Prose Masters*. Reprint Edition. Edited by Howard Mumford Jones. Cambridge, Mass.: Harvard University Press, Belknap Press, 1967.

Cantwell, Robert. *Nathaniel Hawthorne: The American Years*. New York: Rinehart, 1948.

Cohen, B. Bernard, ed. *The Recognition of Nathaniel Hawthorne*. Ann Arbor, Mich.: University of Michigan Press, 1969.

Hawthorne, Julian. *Nathaniel Hawthorne and His Wife*. 2 vols. Boston: Houghton Mifflin, 1884.

Howells, William Dean. *Literary Friends and Acquaintances*. New York: Harper & Brothers, 1900.

Lathrop, George P. *A Study of Hawthorne*. Boston: Houghton Mifflin, 1876.

Lathrop, Rose Hawthorne. *Memories of Hawthorne*. Boston: James R. Osgood & Co., 1885.

Mather, Edward. *Nathaniel Hawthorne, A Modest Man*. New York: Thomas Y. Crowell, 1940.

Massachusetts, A Guide to Its Places and People. American Guide Series, a Federal Writers' Project of the Works Progress Administration for the State of Massachusetts. Boston: Houghton Mifflin, 1937.

Morris, Lloyd. *The Rebellious Puritan: Portrait of Mr. Hawthorne*. New York: Harcourt, Brace & Co., 1927.

Stearns, F. P. *The Life and Genius of Nathaniel Hawthorne*. New York: Longmans, Green & Co., 1906.

Stewart, Randall. *Nathaniel Hawthorne, A Biography*. New Haven, Conn.: Yale University Press, 1948. Reissued: Hamden, Conn.: Archon Books, 1970.

Tharp, Louise Hall. *The Peabody Sisters of Salem*. Boston: Little, Brown & Co., 1950.

Ticknor, Caroline. *Hawthorne and His Publisher*. Boston: Houghton Mifflin, 1913.

Van Doren, Mark. *Nathaniel Hawthorne*. New York: Sloane, 1949.

_____. "Hawthorne, Nathaniel." In *Dictionary of American Biography*, vol. 8. New York: Scribner's, 1933.

Wagenknecht, Edward. *Nathaniel Hawthorne, Man and Writer*. New York: Oxford University Press, 1961.

HERMAN MELVILLE

Berthoff, Warner. *The Example of Melville*. Princeton, N. J.: Princeton University Press, 1962.

Brooks, Van Wyck. *The Times of Melville and Whitman*. New York: Dutton, 1947.

_____. "Melville, Herman." In *Dictionary of American Biography*, vol. 12. New York: Scribner's, 1933.

Gale, Robert L. *Plots and Characters in the Fiction and Narrative Poetry of*

Herman Melville. Hamden, Conn.: Archon/Shoe String Press, 1969; Cambridge, Mass.: MIT Press, 1972.

Hillman, Tyrus. *Melville and the Whale.* Stonington, Conn.: Stonington Publishing Co., 1950 (pamphlet).

Howard, Leon. *Herman Melville: A Biography.* Berkeley and Los Angeles: University of California Press, 1951.

Levin, Harry. *The Power of Blackness: Hawthorne, Poe, Melville.* New York: Knopf, 1958.

Leyda, Jay, ed. *The Melville Log: A Documentary Life of Herman Melville, 1819–1891.* 2 vols. New York: Harcourt, Brace, 1951.

Mason, Ronald. *The Spirit Above the Dust.* London: J. Lehmann, 1951; second edition; Mamaroneck, N. Y.: Paul P. Appel, 1972.

Mansfield, Luther Stearns. "Glimpses of Herman Melville's Life in Pittsfield, 1850–1851—Some Unpublished Letters of Evert A. Duyckinck." In *American Literature*, vol. 9, pp. 26–48. Durham: 1938.

Miller, Edwin Haviland. *Melville.* New York: Braziller, A Venture Book, 1975.

Miller, James E., Jr. *A Reader's Guide to Herman Melville.* New York: Farrar, Straus and Giroux, 1962.

Parker, Hershel, ed. *The Recognition of Herman Melville: Selected Criticism Since 1846.* Ann Arbor, Mich.: University of Michigan Press, 1967.

Rosenberry, Edward H. *Melville and the Comic Spirit.* Cambridge, Mass.: Harvard University Press, 1955.

Sedgwick, William Ellery. *Herman Melville: The Tragedy of Mind.* Cambridge, 1944; New York: Russell & Russell, 1962.

Spiller, Robert E., et al., eds. *Literary History of the United States.* 4th ed. revised. New York: Macmillan, 1974.

Weaver, Raymond M. *Herman Melville, Mariner and Mystic.* New York: Doran, 1921.

EMILY DICKINSON

Bianchi, Martha Dickinson. *The Life and Letters of Emily Dickinson.* Boston and New York: Houghton Mifflin, 1924.

———. *Emily Dickinson, Face to Face: Unpublished Letters With Notes and Reminiscences.* Boston: Houghton Mifflin, 1932.

Bingham, Millicent Todd. *Ancestors' Brocades: The Literary Début of Emily Dickinson.* New York: Harper & Brothers, 1945.

———. *Emily Dickinson's Home: Letters of Edward Dickinson and His Family.* New York: Harper & Brothers, 1955.

———. *Emily Dickinson—A Revelation.* New York: Harper & Brothers, 1954.

Brooks, Van Wyck. *New England: Indian Summer 1865–1915.* New York:

Dutton, 1940.

Chase, Richard Volney. *Emily Dickinson, 1830–1886*. New York: Sloane, 1951.

Jenkins, MacGregor. *Emily Dickinson, Friend and Neighbor*. Boston: Little, Brown & Co., 1930.

Johnson, Thomas H. *Emily Dickinson: An Interpretative Biography*. Cambridge, Mass.: Harvard University Press, Belknap Press, 1955.

Leyda, Jay. *The Years and Hours of Emily Dickinson*. 2 vols. New Haven, Conn.: Yale University Press, 1960.

Longsworth, Polly. *Emily Dickinson: Her Letter to the World*. New York: Crowell, 1965.

Miller, Ruth. *The Poetry of Emily Dickinson*. Middletown, Conn.: Wesleyan University Press, 1968.

Mudge, Jean McClure. *Emily Dickinson and the Image of Home*. Amherst, Mass.: University of Massachusetts Press, 1975.

Sewell, Richard B. *The Life of Emily Dickinson*. 2 vols. New York: Farrar, Straus and Giroux, 1974.

Spiller, Robert E., et al., eds. *Literary History of the United States*. 4th ed. revised. New York: Macmillan, 1974.

Whicher, George F. "Dickinson, Emily." In *Dictionary of American Biography*, vol. 5. New York: Scribner's, 1930.

————. *This Was a Poet*. New York: Scribner's, 1938.

MARK TWAIN

Aldrich, Mrs. Thomas Bailey. *Crowding Memories*. Boston and New York: Houghton Mifflin, 1920.

Allen, Jerry. *The Adventures of Mark Twain*. Boston: Little, Brown & Co., 1954 (fictionalized biography).

Andrews, Kenneth R. *Nook Farm: Mark Twain's Hartford Circle*. Cambridge, Mass.: Harvard University Press, 1950.

Clemens, Clara (Gabrilowitsch). *My Father, Mark Twain*. New York: Harper & Brothers, 1931.

DeVoto, Bernard. *Mark Twain's America*. Boston: Little, Brown & Co., 1932.

Ferguson, (John) DeLancey. *Mark Twain: Man and Legend*. Indianapolis, Ind., and New York: Bobbs-Merrill, 1943.

Hill, Hamlin. *Mark Twain, God's Fool*. New York: Harper & Row, 1973.

Howells, William Dean. *My Mark Twain*. New York: Harper & Brothers, 1910.

Lawton, Mary. *A Lifetime with Mark Twain: The Memories of Katy Leary, for Thirty Years His Faithful and Devoted Servant*. New York: Harcourt, Brace, 1925.

Leacock, Stephen Butler. *Mark Twain*. London: P. Davies Ltd., 1932.

Meltzer, Milton. *Mark Twain Himself*. New York: Crowell, 1960 (a pictorial biography).

Paine, Albert Bigelow. *Mark Twain, A Biography: The Personal and Literary Life of Samuel Langhorne Clemens*. 3 vols. New York: Harper & Brothers, 1912.

———. *A Short Life of Mark Twain*. New York: Garden City Publishing Co., 1925.

Salsbury, Edith Colgate, ed. *Susy and Mark Twain: Family Dialogues*. New York: Harper & Row, 1965.

Spiller, Robert E., et al., eds. *Literary History of the United States*. 4th ed. revised. New York: Macmillan, 1974.

Twain, Mark. *Mark Twain's Autobiography*. New York: Harper & Brothers, 1924.

Van Doren, Carl. "Clemens, Samuel Langhorne." In *Dictionary of American Biography*, vol. 4. New York: Scribner's, 1930.

Wecter, Dixon. *Sam Clemens of Hannibal*. Boston: Houghton Mifflin, 1952.

HARRIET BEECHER STOWE

Adams, John R. *Harriet Beecher Stowe*. New York: Twayne, 1963.

Anthony, Katharine. "Stowe, Harriet Elizabeth Beecher." In *Dictionary of American Biography*, vol. 18. New York: Scribner's, 1936.

Bradford, Gamaliel. *Portraits of American Women*. Boston: Houghton Mifflin, 1919.

Brooks, Van Wyck. *The Flowering of New England, 1815–1865*. New York: Dutton, 1936.

———. *New England: Indian Summer, 1865–1915*. New York: Dutton, 1940.

Crozier, Alice C. *The Novels of Harriet Beecher Stowe*. New York: Oxford University Press, 1969.

Fields, Annie A., ed. *The Life and Letters of Harriet Beecher Stowe*. Cambridge, Mass.: Riverside Press, 1897.

Furnas, Joseph Chamberlain. *Goodbye to Uncle Tom*. New York: Sloane, 1956.

Gilbertson, Catherine. *Harriet Beecher Stowe*. New York: Appleton-Century, 1937.

Johnston, Johanna. *Runaway to Heaven—The Story of Harriet Beecher Stowe and Her Era*. New York: Doubleday, 1963.

McCray, Florine Thayer. *The Life-Work of the Author of Uncle Tom's Cabin*. New York: Funk & Wagnalls, 1889.

Stowe, Charles E. *The Life of Harriet Beecher Stowe: Compiled from Her Journals and Letters*. Boston: Houghton Mifflin, 1889. Reprinted, Detroit, Mich.: 1967.

————, and Stowe, Lyman Beecher. *Harriet Beecher Stowe: The Story of Her Life*. Boston: Houghton Mifflin, 1911.

Stowe, Lyman Beecher. *Saints, Sinners and Beechers*. Indianapolis, Ind.: Bobbs-Merrill, 1934.

Wagenknecht, Edward. *Harriet Beecher Stowe: The Known and the Unknown*. New York: Oxford University Press, 1965.

Weaver, Raymond. Introduction to *Uncle Tom's Cabin*, by Harriet Beecher Stowe. Limited Editions Club, 1938; subsequently carried in the Modern Library Edition.

Wilson, Edmund. *Patriotic Gore: Studies in the Literature of the American Civil War*. New York: Oxford University Press, 1962.

Wilson, Forrest. *Crusader in Crinoline: The Life of Harriet Beecher Stowe*. Philadelphia: Lippincott, 1941.

TEILHARD DE CHARDIN

Braybrooke, Neville. *Teilhard de Chardin: Pilgrim of the Future*. New York: Seabury, 1964.

Cargas, Harry J., ed. *The Continuous Flame; Teilhard in the Great Traditions*. A compilation. St. Louis: B. Herder, 1969.

Cristiani, Leon [Nicolas Corte]. *Teilhard de Chardin, His Life and His Spirit*. Translated by Martin Jarrett-Kerr. New York: Macmillan, 1960.

Cuénot, Claude. *Teilhard de Chardin; A Biographical Study*. Translated by Vincent Colimore. Edited by René Hague. Baltimore, Md.: Helicon, 1965.

Grenet, Paul. *Teilhard de Chardin, The Man and His Theories*. London: Souvenir Press, 1965.

Lubac, Henry de. *The Religion of Teilhard de Chardin*. New York: Desclee, 1967.

————. *The Man and His Meaning*. New York: Hawthorn, 1966.

Lukas, Mary and Lukas, Ellen. *Teilhard, The Man, The Priest, The Scientist*. New York: Doubleday, 1977.

Rabut, Olivier. *Teilhard de Chardin; A Critical Study*. New York: Sheed and Ward, 1961.

Raven, Charles Earle. *Teilhard de Chardin: Scientist and Seer*. New York: Harper & Row, 1962.

Speaight, Robert. *Teilhard de Chardin: A Biography*. London: Collins, 1967.

Index